ShipCraft Special

FLOWER CLASS CORVETTES

Seaforth PUBLISHING

HMCSs *Wetaskiwin*, *Agassiz*, *Trail* and *Chilliwack* as completed, early 1941, modified for Oropesa (wire) minesweeping.

ShipCraft Special

Flower Class Corvettes

Text by John Lambert and Les Brown

Colour profiles by Bob Pearson

All drawings by John Lambert

CONTENTS

Title page: The newly completed HMCS *Dawson* late in 1941. The fit is not very different from the first Canadian-built ships, which were generally slower to receive improvements (although the mainmast of the early ships has been omitted). *(Public Archives of Canada)*

First published in Great Britain in 2008 by Seaforth Publishing, an imprint of Pen & Sword Books Ltd, 47 Church Street, Barnsley, S Yorkshire S70 2AS

www.seaforthpublishing.com

This paperback edition first published 2010

Reprinted 2014, 2017, 2019, 2022

British Library Cataloguing in Publication Data

A CIP data record for this title is available from the British Library

ISBN: 978-1-84832-064-2 (PAPERBACK)

ISBN 978-1-78346-727-3 (KINDLE)

ISBN 978-1-78346-960-4 (EBOOK)

Typeset and designed by Stephen Dent

Printed and bound in the UK by Short Run Press Ltd, EX2 7LW

Design

In the late 1930s the Admiralty realised that in the event of war the Royal Navy would be woefully short of escort vessels, especially for the East Coast. In 1936 a whale-catcher/trawler design was discussed, but no firm orders followed. On 7 February 1939 the requirement was again considered and six options were put forward:

Converted trawlers of 620 tons, 11-12 knots, cost £3500 and four weeks for conversion.
Commercial trawlers built to Admiralty specifications, 510 tons, 12 knots, cost £57,500 and six months to build.
Whaler *Southern Pride* type, 700 tons, 16 knots, cost £75,000 and seven months to build.
Whaler built to Admiralty specifications, 700 tons, 16 knots, cost £90,000 and seven months to build.
1939 minesweeper design (A/S version of *Bangor* class), 500 tons, 17 knots, cost £135,000 and eight months to build.
Simplified *Guillemot* design (coastal sloops), 580 tons, 20/21 knots, cost £160,000 and eight months to build.

On 8 February another meeting was convened between the DNC (Director of Naval Construction) and Mr Reed, a representative of Smith's Dock, a specialist in trawler-size vessels and the builders of *Southern Pride*, where it was agreed that an improved design could be produced. By 27 February the Director of the Tactical Division had stated that the whale-catcher design seemed an attractive alternative – faster than trawlers, seaworthy and requiring a smaller crew than a patrol vessel.

By 13 April the Controller, Rear Admiral Bruce Fraser, had taken the decision to proceed with the Smith's Dock whale-catcher anti-submarine patrol vessel design. They were to have modern A/S equipment, a 4in gun, Type 12B radio and very fortunately (after some discussion of coal-firing) oil-fired cylindrical boilers with a standard steam reciprocating engine, similar to that fitted to *Southern Pride*. The proposals were agreed on 24 April 1939 and the sketch requirements were presented to Smith's Dock (the parent firm) just eight days later. The following details were agreed:

Type 123 Asdic (sonar). (This was the same as provided for new destroyers.)
The dome to be positioned on the centre line 35-40ft from the bow. (This necessitated

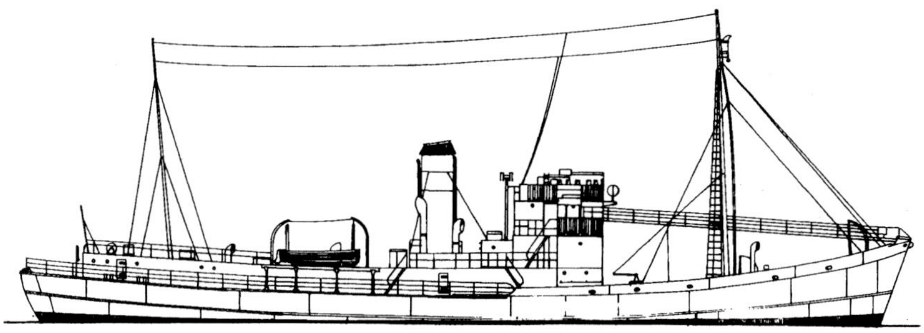

Above: The Smith's Dock whale-catcher *Southern Pride* was the starting point for the 'Flower' class design, although its relationship was more distant than often claimed.

Below: Although one of the third batch to be ordered, *Periwinkle* was one of the first of the 'Flowers' to complete, having been built by one of the largest yards, Harland & Wolff. Seen here at sea in the spring of 1940, she has an external degaussing cable and an air lookout position atop the compass platform. *(IWM A5521)*

Still with the builders on board, *Gardenia* is towed down the Clyde in May 1940. One of the first ordered, the ship shows the original two-masted arrangement to carry the aerials of a planned long-range radio installation (for a time it was intended to use them for blockading duties with the Northern Patrol, but the requirement was dropped before the ships entered service). She has two 0.303in Lewis guns aft. *(The Ballast Trust)*

interchanging the fuel and A/S compartments as shown in the original proposals.)

The main gun was to be a single 4in BL Mark IX Gun on a CPI mounting with 100 rounds. These were available from storage. 0.303in Lewis machine guns to be fitted on each side of the bridge. Two Mark II depth charge throwers and 25 depth charges.

The complement was estimated to be 2 officers and 27 men.

To be fitted with the standard trawler wireless outfit: Type 12B.

Power to be provided by a 15kW generator set. (More power could be provided later.)

Smith's Dock stated that manoeuvrability would be improved by the provision of a spade rudder and by the cutting away of the deadwood, instead of the rudder and sternpost shown on the original drawing.

It was agreed that the complete design be ready by 23 May but Smith's Dock requested a further three weeks to complete proposed modifications.

The new, untried Coastal Escort design was prepared just in time. As the major shipbuilders were fully committed, small commercial shipyards were employed. Following mercantile building practice and complying with the requirements of Lloyd's Register and of the British Corporation, the original design had an enclosed wooden compass platform and wheelhouse with opening windows. The compass platform was built high, for visibility over the 4in

'FLOWER' CLASS SPECIFICATION

Displacement	940 tons (standard), 1170 (full load)
Dimensions (ft–in)	Length (pp) 190–0; Length (oa) 205–0; Breadth 33–0; Draught (fwd) 7–9; Draught (aft) 14–10
Machinery	4-cyl triple expansion steam reciprocating engine.
Boilers	Two Scotch (cylindrical)
Shafts	One
Indicated Horse Power	2750
Maximum Speed	16 knots
Complement	47
Oil Fuel	200 tons
Endurance	4000 miles at 12 knots
Armament	1 – 4in BL gun on CPI mounting (100 rounds) , 2 twin Lewis 0.303in machine guns (later 1– 2pdr)
Depth Charges	25
DC Throwers	2 Mark II

Above: The newly completed *Camellia* in the summer of 1940 awaiting both a pendant number and close-range armament. *(Ulster Folk & Transport Museum)*

Below: Another of the first batch ordered, *Geranium* is shown as completed in June 1940. The DG coil is now fitted internally. The first group were allocated 'M' pendant numbers but the flag superior was soon changed to 'K', although the numbers remained the same. *(The Ballast Trust)*

Above: Another of the first batch to be ordered, *Candytuft* is shown as completed in October 1940. She was one of the ships transferred to the US Navy in 1942, being renamed USS *Tenacity*. *(The Ballast Trust)*

Below: The lines of the original short-forecastle design shown off by the hull of HMCS *Weyburn* just prior to her side launch at Burrard Dry Dock, North Vancouver on 26 July 1941. The wartime Canadian shipbuilding effort was an immense achievement, springing from a very small pre-war industrial base. *(Author's collection)*

Completed only a few months later than *Candytuft* by the same builders, *Carnation* shows some minor differences, notably steel splinter screens abreast the 4in gun and the beneath the 2pdr position aft. *(The Ballast Trust)*

gun, and many had an Air Lookout position built above the compass house.

Such was the urgent requirement for escort vessels that the first twenty-six ordered on 25 July 1939 (plus four French contracts) were rapidly followed by thirty ordered on 31 August and twenty more on 19 September. This was a big leap of faith in a new design, effectively still on the drawing board. More orders were placed for ten, eighteen, and two units before the end of that year, with more orders in 1940, 1941 and 1942 (see building lists). In total 269 corvettes were built for the Allies in British and Canadian yards (plus a few in France), but that did not mean that it produced an endless supply of identical ships. As they went to sea the design constantly evolved as a result of the hard lessons learned.

FIRST-OF-CLASS TRIALS

The first 'Flower' (launched on 24 January 1940) was HMS *Gladiolus* built by Smith's Dock at Middlesbrough. On Wednesday 20 March she proceeded downriver to adjust compasses and without DG (degaussing) coils in operation. The control board was not fitted and, carrying a temporary rig, she put to sea on builder's trials on 20 March. The compass had to be dropped by 8 inches and it was decided that a further adjustment trial be carried out prior to the acceptance trial, but it was established that the bullet-proof protection fitted for the helmsman in the wheelhouse and the conning tower on the compass platform had no effect on the compass. Gun trials of the 4in BL (Breech Loading) gun were then undertaken. There was no permanent set to the deck as a result of firing trials. The 2pdr gun had not been delivered, although the ready-use ammunition lockers were in place, but twin-mounted 0.303in Lewis guns had been fitted to the starboard side of the 2pdr packing ring. Anchor trials were carried out and power was worked up to 175 revolutions with turning trials. The next day she proceeded for Full Power Trials, which gave an indicated horsepower of 2825 and 85 revolutions before it was necessary to stop the ship due to a hot bearing. The ship was then six miles out and in water too deep to anchor, so signals were made for assistance to tow to a suitable anchorage whilst a spare bearing was fitted. A trawler duly arrived and a tow passed, but later the ship returned to Smith's Dock under her own steam. Due to intervening holidays and difficulties in obtaining overtime for yard staff it was not possible to repeat the trial until Tuesday 25 March. The steering gear trials, etc were then carried out as arranged. Practically complete in all aspects, except for minor fittings, including the A/S recorder, the ship was officially considered highly satisfactory. However, it was not possible to complete all the trials before the ship left the builders.

Further sea trials were carried out the following month when the ship went to Portsmouth for final fitting out. She sailed for Stokes Bay at 09.15 on 14 April at a

continued on p.14

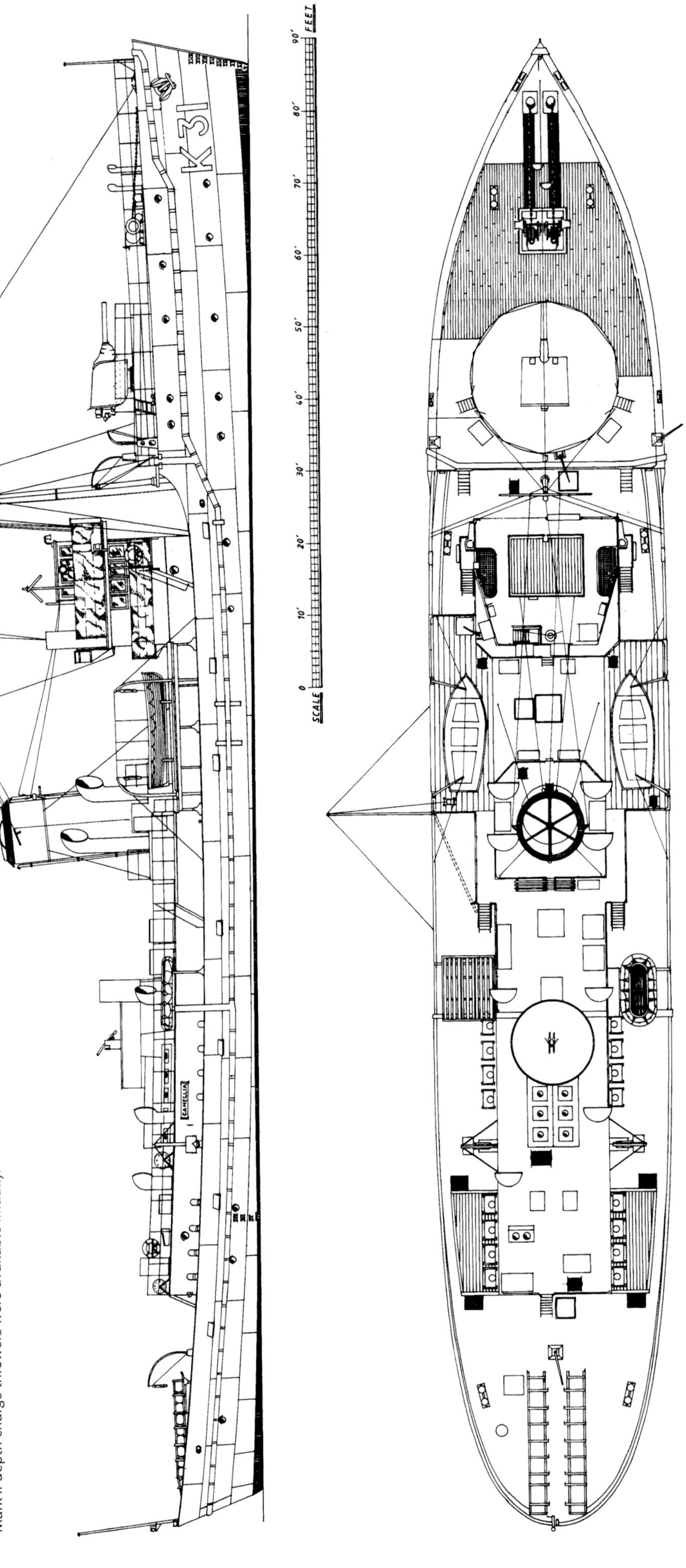

HMS *Camellia*, June 1940
One of a bulk order of twenty awarded to Harland & Wolff, Belfast, *Camellia* was among the first to complete, having taken just over seven months to build. She shows the external degaussing cable fitted as an emergency measure against the new threat of the magnetic mine; the DG coil was later fitted internally. She had to make do with a twin 0.303in Lewis machine gun mount in lieu of a 2pdr, and only two Mark II depth charge throwers were available initially.

HM Ships *Honeysuckle*, *Hydrangea* and *Jasmine*, as completed 1940
Typical of the early units and lacking many of the later features, this is the original short forecastle design from the second group, ordered on 31 August 1939. As completed *Hydrangea* carried a quad 0.5in Mark III mount and *Honeysuckle* a steam-powered Holman Projector Mark II instead of the 2pdr pom-pom.

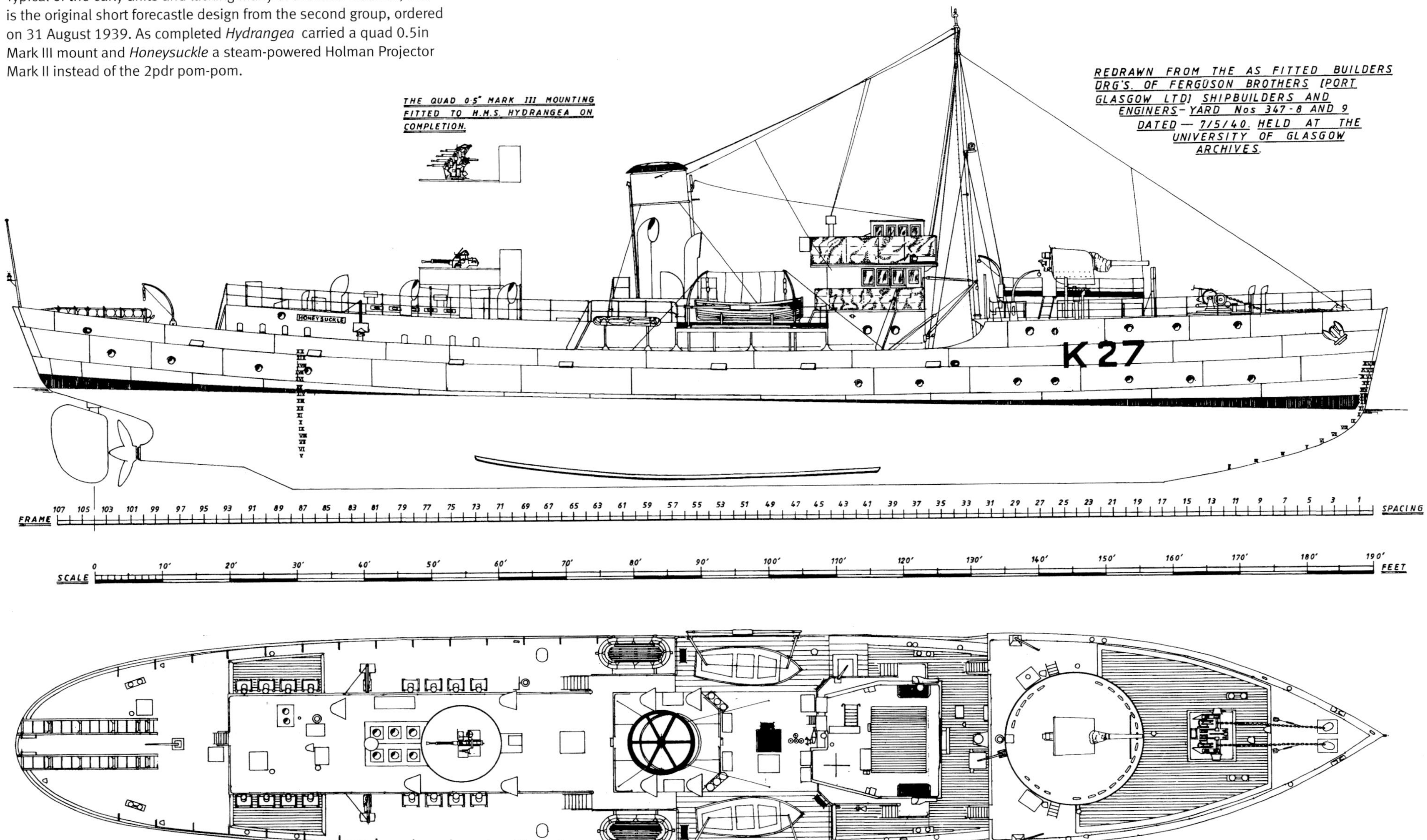

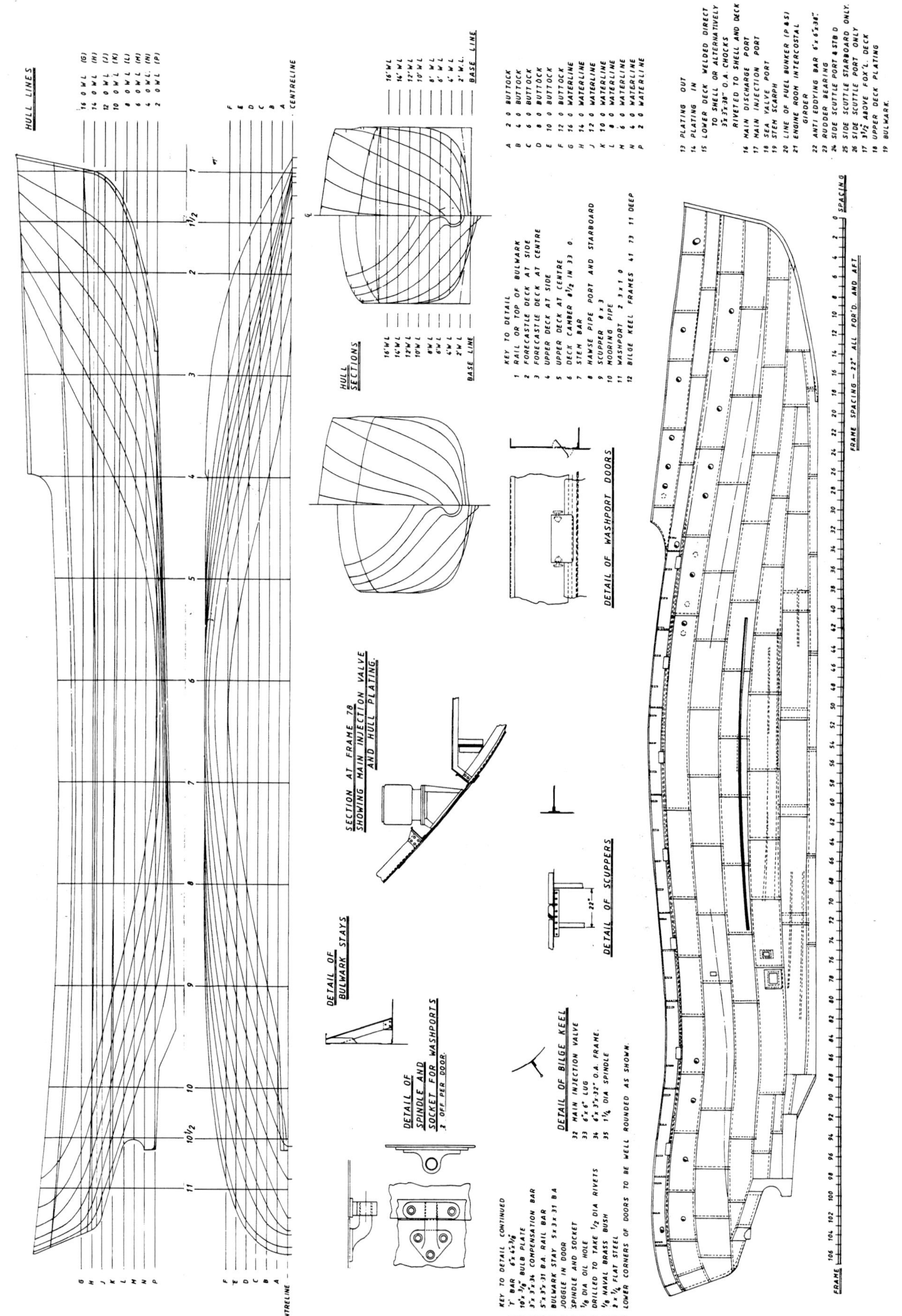

Hull lines, sections and shell expansion of the original short forecastle design Based on the plans of *Gladiolus*.

Framing plan for the original corvette hull form, but with extended forecastle

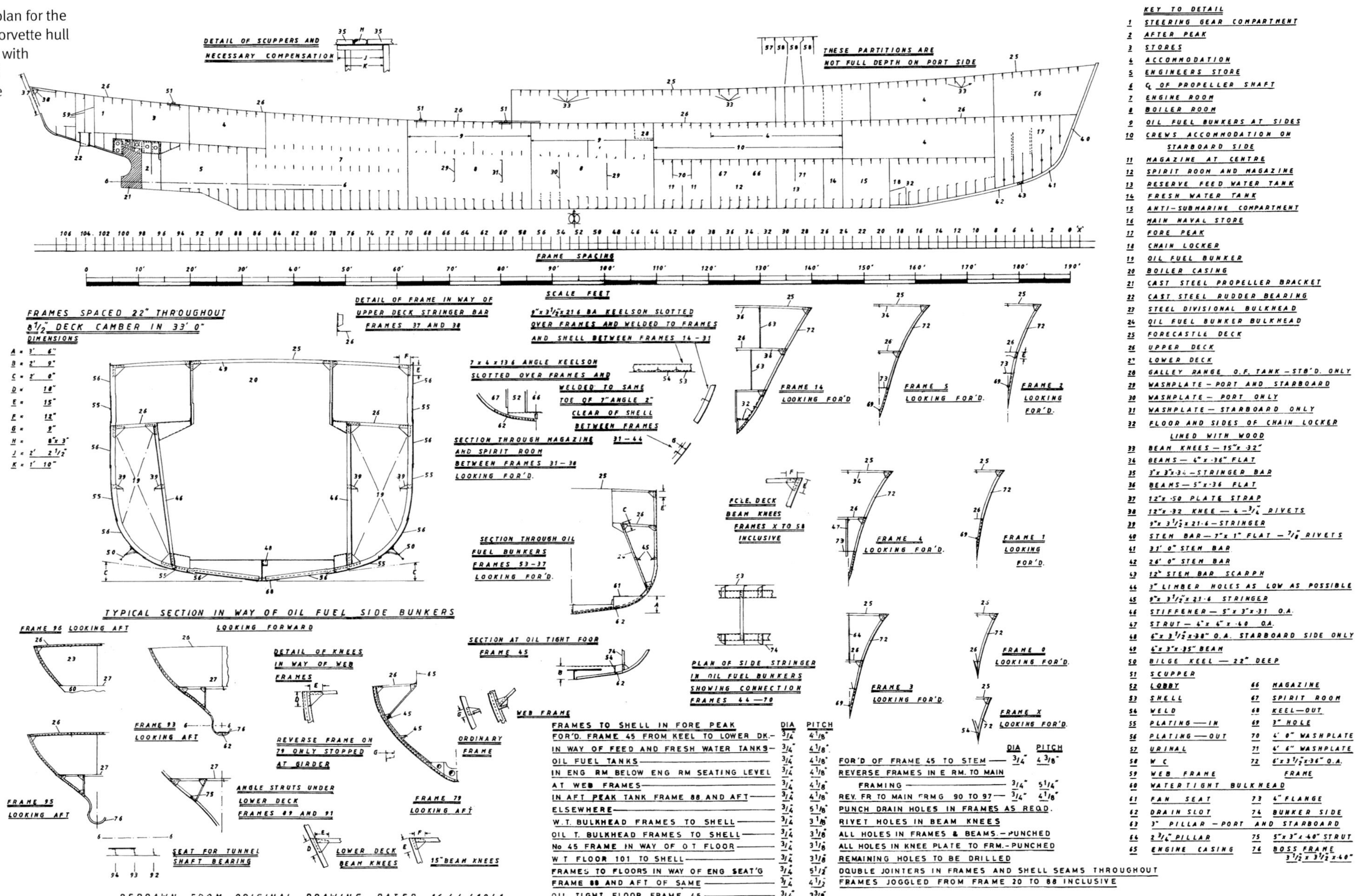

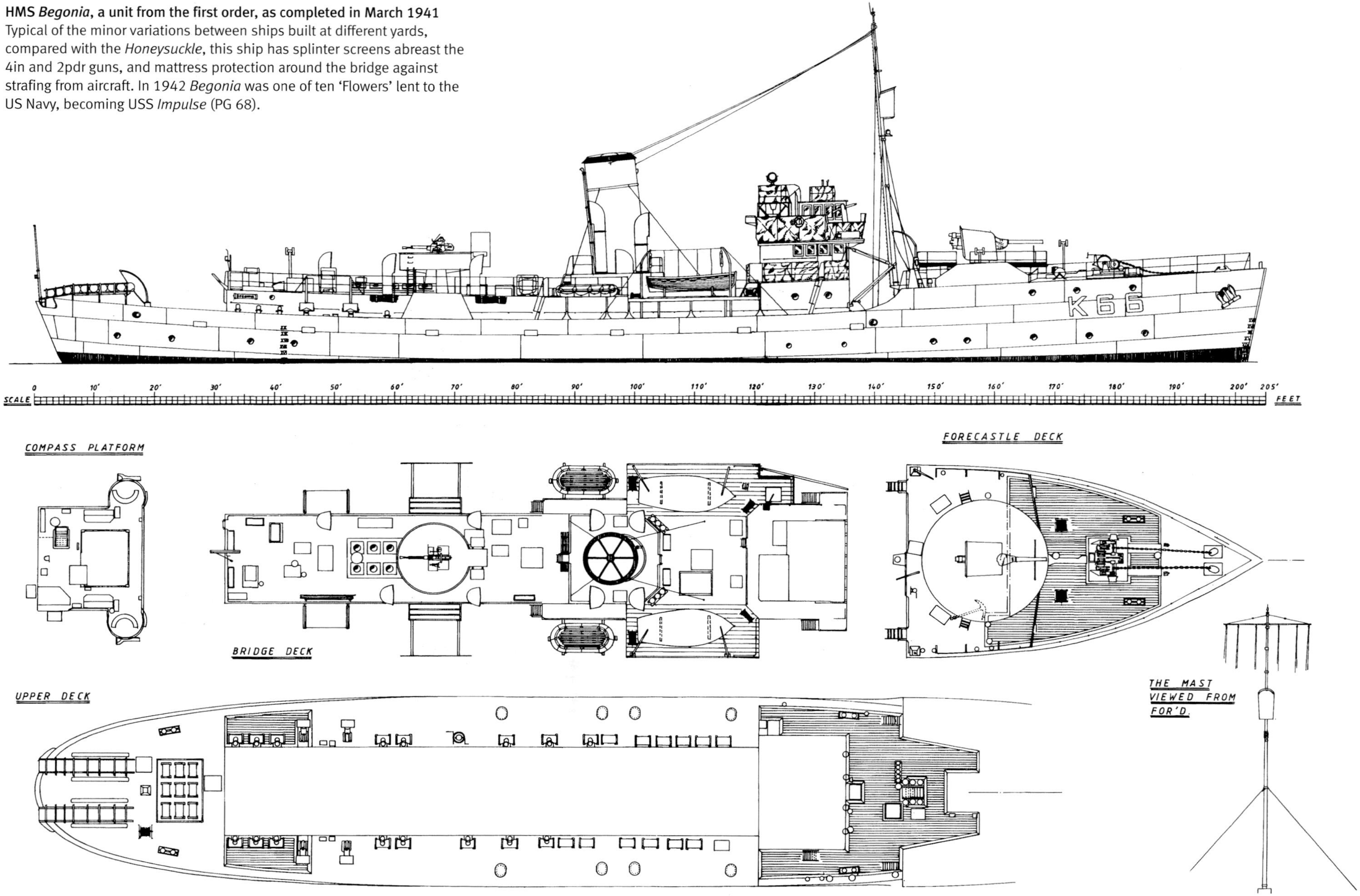

HMS *Begonia*, a unit from the first order, as completed in March 1941
Typical of the minor variations between ships built at different yards, compared with the *Honeysuckle*, this ship has splinter screens abreast the 4in and 2pdr guns, and mattress protection around the bridge against strafing from aircraft. In 1942 *Begonia* was one of ten 'Flowers' lent to the US Navy, becoming USS *Impulse* (PG 68).

HMCS *Wetaskiwin*, as completed in December 1940
Typical of the early Canadian-built 'Flowers', *Wetaskiwin* was the first corvette built on the West Coast to complete. Compared with the appearance of British-built ships, she has two masts, so the 2pdr is mounted further aft, and she is fitted for wire minesweeping, with Oropesa Mark II gear on the quarterdeck. Refitted in spring 1942 and again early in 1943, but she did not have the forecastle extended until the long refit at Galverston, Texas completed in March 1944.

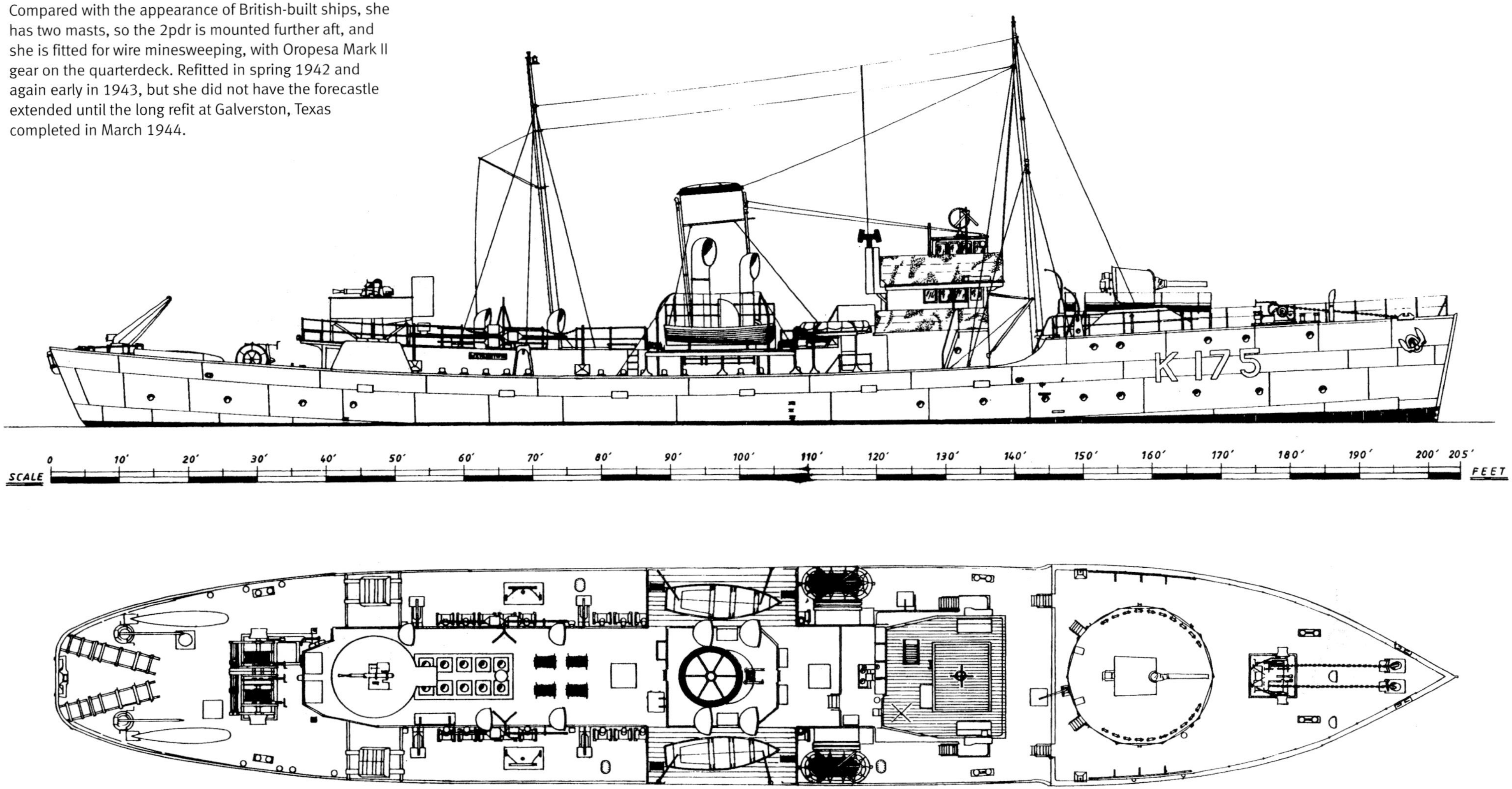

Opposite, top: HMCS *Moose Jaw* off Halifax, NS in June 1942 and newly commissioned. Nearly two years after the first British 'Flowers' went to sea, the ship still has a Lewis gun aft and few improvements, although she has the home-grown SW-1C Canadian radar at the masthead. *(Public Archives of Canada)*

displacement of 1125 tons with 200 tons of fuel oil, 28 tons of reserve feed water and 12 tons of fresh water. The 4-hour consumption trial commenced at 10.30 during which four runs were made over the Stokes Bay course. Measuring tanks had been placed aboard in order that fuel consumption could be checked with precision. Records were taken every 30 minutes. From this data it was estimated that with 230 tons of oil fuel (95 per cent capacity) endurance at 13.2 knots would be 4650 nautical miles, allowing for 15 per cent residual oil remaining in the tanks. Following these, circle trials were undertaken and these proved quite satisfactory.

The next day the vessel left at 09.10, loading being noted by her draught marks giving a displacement of 1118 tons. Progressive trials were carried out over four runs. There was then two hours trial at full speed, and four runs made on the measured mile. She had a maximum speed of 16.56 knots and these figures proved to be about standard for the rest of the class.

In general it was considered that the results obtained were entirely satisfactory. The propulsive coefficients based upon the estimated horsepower of the model tried by Haslar were found to be higher than those usually found with reciprocating engines. The vessel steered very easily, but at low speeds about 2 degrees of port helm was necessary to keep on course. It was probably due to the effect of wind and tide, and was unnecessary at higher speeds. No objectionable vibrations were noted at any speed and there was no 'singing' from the propeller. The machinery space temperatures were considered moderate in spite of the reliance on natural ventilation.

The new degaussing (DG) coil had already been fitted as a defence against magnetic mines, but she had only paired 0.303in Lewis guns aft as the single 2pdr (40mm) pom-pom (Mark VIII Gun on the Mark VIII Mounting) was not yet available. There seems to be no photograph of her at this early stage, although photographs of the ship after her first refit, with an extended forecastle, are available.

MODIFICATIONS

The learning curve with the corvette was a steep one. Originally intended for coastal work and not the North Atlantic, these rather basic warships were soon asked to fill other gaps besides ocean escort. In 1940 approval was given for twenty-four to be fitted for Oropesa wire minesweeping, with steam winches aft. A further eight (later sixteen) were to be fitted with 'LL sweeps', stowed on large reels for dealing with

At sea shortly after commissioning in March 1941, *Begonia* already shows signs of wear to her overall grey paint, the usual early-war scheme. The ship has the full authorised weapon fit, with 2pdr aft and twin Lewis guns on the bridge wings. *(IWM A5483)*

Below: Wearing a two-tone grey camouflage scheme (probably 507b and 507c) but otherwise much as completed, *Hibiscus* protects the flank of a convoy in this undated photo. *(Author)*

In this later view, *Hibiscus* sports exactly the same camouflage (although the funnel number has changed from 34 to 35) but now carries Type 271 radar, presumably fitted during a refit too short to warrant repainting. The ship was transferred to the US Navy in 1942 and renamed *Spry*. *(Ministry of Defence)*

magnetic mines. As previously mentioned, with the advent of magnetic mines early in 1940 degaussing cables were added for passive protection, early units having them outboard, but they were soon built into the hull. By April 1940 crew protection against air attack was found wanting, and splinter protection plates were added outboard of the 4in and 2pdr guns. An X-shaped bullet-proof conning tower was supplied for the compass platform.

One early modification was the extension of forecastle hull plating aft to the funnel to give greater internal volume and improve accommodation – necessary because crew numbers were increased, and as new equipment was added, increased again.

The introduction of Type 271 surface search radar in its distinctive lantern helped turn the tide against U-boats, which had taken to attacking on the surface and in the dark. Improved Asdic (sonar) and the addition of a 20mm Oerlikon in the bridge wings soon led to improved bridges. A total of six bridge variations were eventually built into the class.

The original depth charge outfit was 25,

MAJOR MODIFICATIONS

October 1939	Complement increased to 47 for ocean escort duties.
May 1940	Draught marks to be carried up to upper deck level.
June 1940	A number to be fitted with 'LL' minesweeping gear; 10 depth charges to be retained.
June 1940	An allocation of quad 0.5in Mark III mountings to improve AA defence.
July 1940	Side scuttles reduced by 50 per cent for economy in shipbuilding.
September 1940	Depth of bilge keels increased from 11in to 22in for greater stability.
October 1940	A crowsnest added to the foremast. A 20in searchlight added to the bridge.
November 1940	A proposal to improve the towing arrangements.
December 1940	Twenty-four units to be fitted for Oropesa (wire) minesweeping. A modified bridge fitted to the first ship. Eight units to be fitted for 'LL' (magnetic) minesweeping.
February 1941	'LL' fitted ships in home waters to have SA (acoustic sweep gear) also.
June 1941	Hedgehog ahead-throwing weapon to be fitted. The 2pdr to be moved aft, to fit a third 20mm Oerlikon.
August 1941	Fittings for Oiling at Sea to be added, to increase ship's range.
September 1941	New open bridges to take single 20mm Oerlikons in the bridge wings. Type 271 radar to be fitted on a priority basis.
January 1943	2in Rocket Flare projectors to be added to the 4in gun shield.
March 1943	Four extra single 20mm Oerlikons in sided gun sponsons to be fitted.
July 1943	The limited fitting of two 6pdr guns on bridge wings.
August 1943	Foxer gear to be fitted urgently.

Above: *Clarkia* was one of the first to complete, in April 1940, but in this photo taken on 4 October 1942 the forecastle has been extended, Type 271 added and the mast restepped abaft the bridge. However, there are as yet no Oerlikons in the bridge wings. *(Ministry of Defence)*

Below: *Jasmine* in the spring of 1941 shows some of the interim modifications applied to the early 'Flowers', most noticeably the extended forecastle, although the mast is still stepped before the bridge and there are no additions to the close-range armament. *(IWM A5519)*

Above: *Spiraea* in 1942, after a refit similar to *Nasturtium*'s. There are Oerlikons in the bridge wings, but she also has twin Lewis guns right aft on the casing. *(Author's collection)*

Below: *Starwort* in 1942 with most of the mid-war alterations, although the mast is still stepped forward of the bridge. She has Oerlikons in the bridge wings, but also retains twin Lewis guns right aft on the casing. *(IWM A8421)*

The refitted *Nasturtium* in June 1942 now has the lengthened forecastle, Type 271 and a modified bridge, but retains the mast forward and, surprisingly, the 'pro tem' 0.5in quad aft where the 2pdr should be. *(Ministry of Defence)*

with two rails and two Mark II throwers. In August 1940 it was increased to 50 charges and four throwers, though not in those units modified for minesweeping where weight was already critical. By 1943 the new improved Mark IV thrower was being fitted. Here only the depth charge was thrown, not the 'arbor' or DC carrier as with the earlier mounting. From June 1941 the ahead-throwing Hedgehog spigot-mortar was introduced, the mounting being fitted on the starboard side behind the 4in gun, which now had 2in rocket flare frames bolted to the splinter shield, with the flare ready-use locker being positioned on the port side.

A few units carried a single 6pdr QF Hotchkiss gun on non-recoil mounting in the bridge wings instead of Oerlikons to provide a greater punch when facing surfaced U-boats, whose pressure hulls had proved difficult to penetrate with the existing guns. In September 1943 Foxer gear was fitted, to be towed as a countermeasure to German acoustic torpedoes that homed on propeller noise.

After the USA officially entered the war, ten 'Flowers' with their crews were lent to the US Navy in the spring of 1942, and a further fifteen under construction in Canadian yards for the RN were made available to the US.

The many changes are too numerous to list in full detail, but major modifications authorised are summarised in the table on page16.

The 'Flowers' were the only class of mass-produced warships forced to undertake such a severe review of operational duties, so besides these detail modifications more substantial structural changes were required. To improve sea-keeping and provide more space the original short forecastle design was radically improved by adding plating aft, and later completing ships of these early orders appeared with the forecastle deck already extended aft to the funnel. From 1941 greater sheer and flare was built into the bow, enabling the ships to ride the waves more easily, *Samphire* being the first, in mid 1941. Some units sent to the Mediterranean in 1940 did not return home until later in the war and so did not receive these alterations. However, Mediterranean 'Flowers' carried an increased, but very varied AA armament depending on what weapons were available.

CANADIAN 'FLOWERS'

The numbers of corvettes built depended heavily on a truly remarkable shipbuilding effort in Canada, where a warship building programme was conjured from very limited pre-war experience and resources. Drawings were provided from the UK and the Canadian-built units closely followed the basic design and modifications.

continued on p.27

Emerging after refits in 1942 *Crocus* and *Wallflower* (K 44) appear generally similar, but *Wallflower* still has twin Lewis guns in the bridge wings whereas *Crocus* has Oerlikons. *(IWM A8818 – Wallflower; A13011)*

Above: *Penstemon* in 1944, with a close-range armament that includes six single 20mm Oerlikons – two in the bridge wings and two sided amidships and aft on sponsons carried out to the hull sides. Note the TBS ('Talk Between Ships') aerials on the masthead yard. *(IWM A15630)*

Below: HMCS *Alberni* in 1943, fitted for wire minesweeping. Although the forecastle is still short, the bridge has been extended, radar added and the mast restepped. The ship has the relatively luxurious close-range armament of seven 20mm Oerlikons. The censor has removed the pendant number, K 103. *(Public Archives of Canada)*

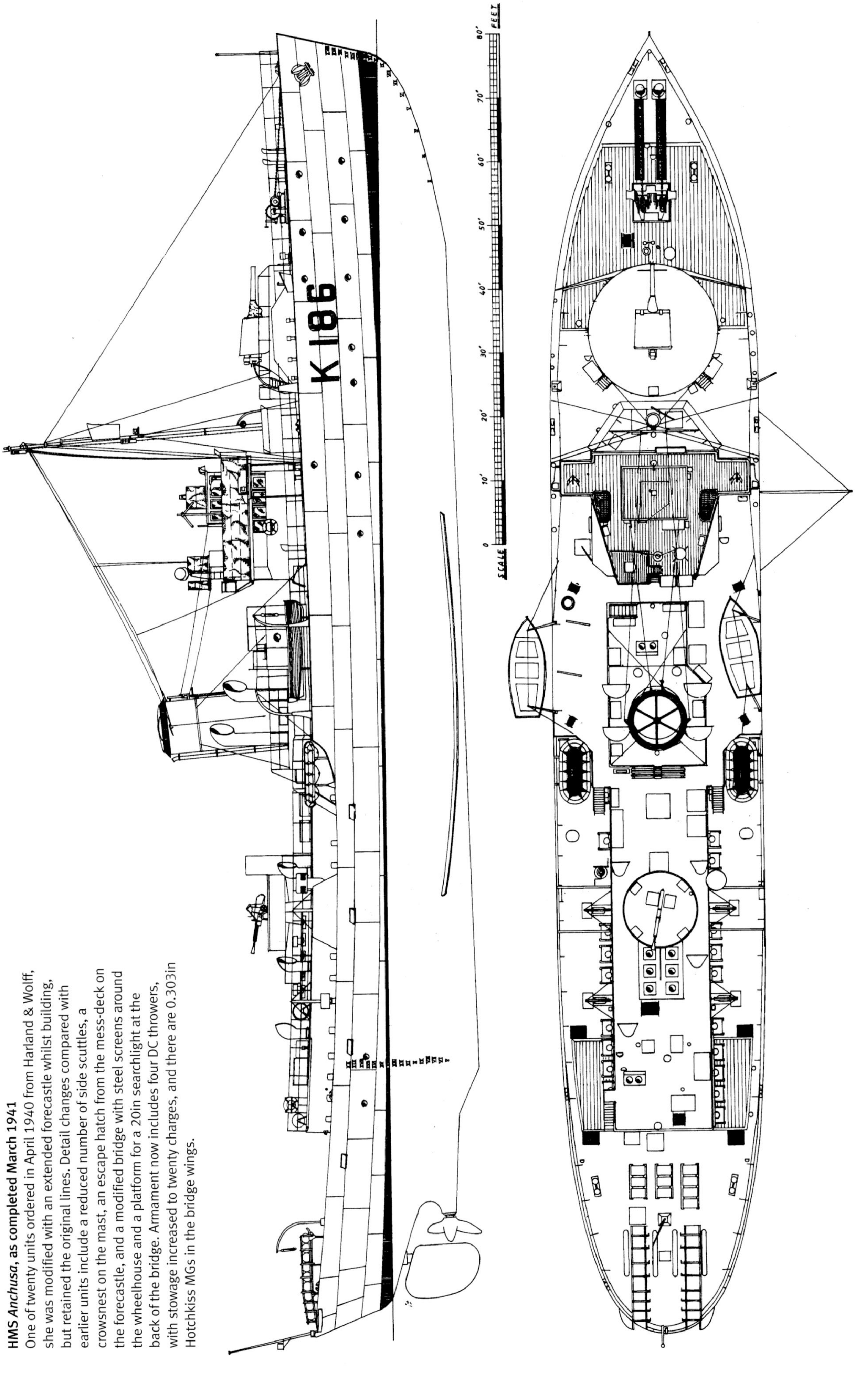

HMS *Anchusa*, as completed March 1941
One of twenty units ordered in April 1940 from Harland & Wolff, she was modified with an extended forecastle whilst building, but retained the original lines. Detail changes compared with earlier units include a reduced number of side scuttles, a crowsnest on the mast, an escape hatch from the mess-deck on the forecastle, and a modified bridge with steel screens around the wheelhouse and a platform for a 20in searchlight at the back of the bridge. Armament now includes four DC throwers, with stowage increased to twenty charges, and there are 0.303in Hotchkiss MGs in the bridge wings.

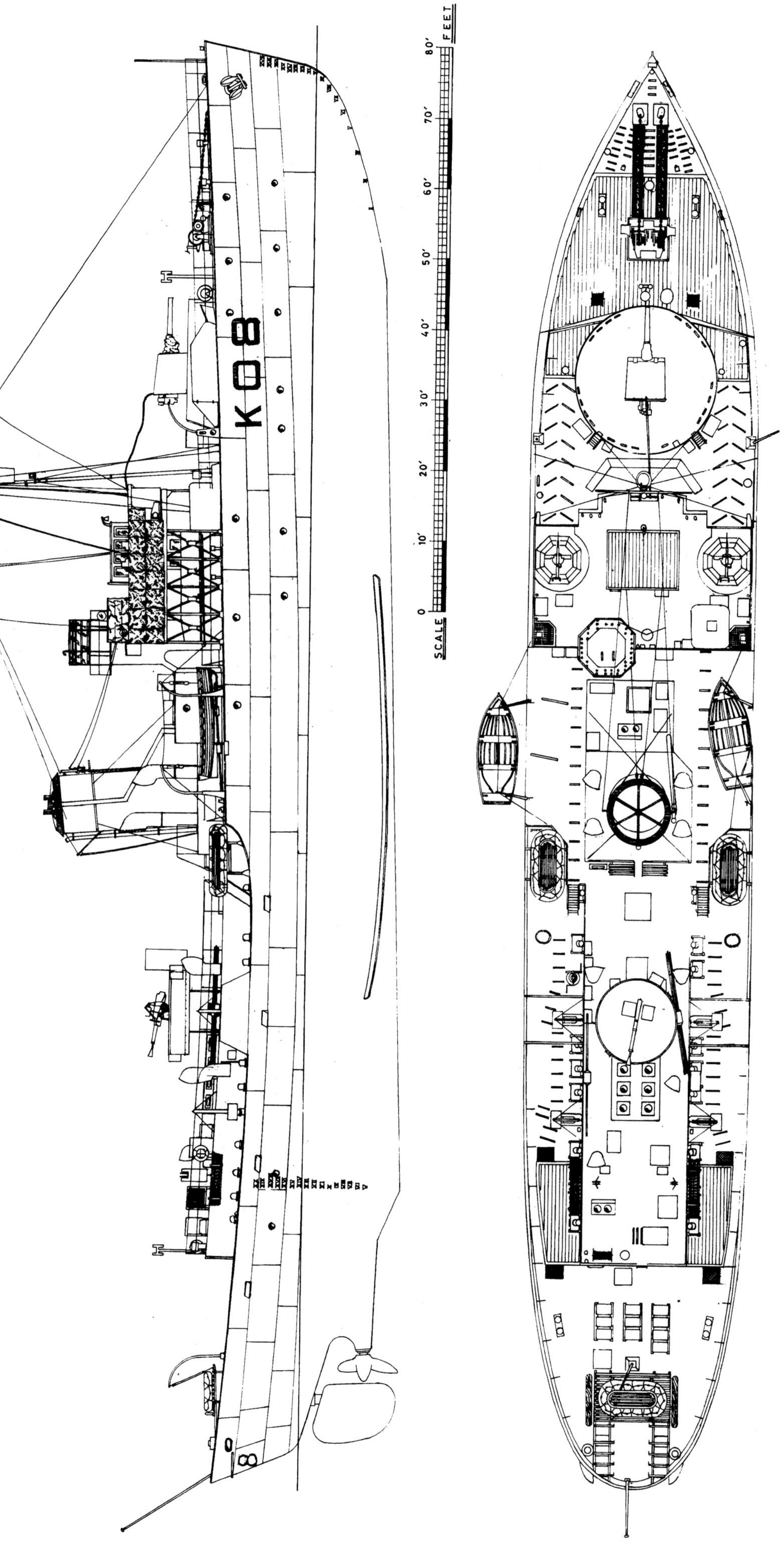

HMS *Spiraea*, as refitted, June 1942
The forecastle has been extended, the bridge wings added (to mount single 20mm Oerlikons, with the 0.303in Lewis guns relocated on the after casing), and the lantern and office of Type 271 radar positioned to port at the rear of the bridge.

HMS *Potentilla* as complete, February 1942

One of six units ordered on 3 August 1940, the design was something of a hybrid, incorporating many of the improvements that later formed the basis of the 'Modified Flower' class. Most noticeably, these included a hull form with greater sheer and flare (as well as enlarged bilge keels), and Admiralty water-tube boilers; the latter banished the prominent cowl ventilators of earlier ships, and the former required a higher 4in gun platform (and a taller bridge to see over it). Other visible difference were an upright funnel and foremast, with a smaller mainmast aft that displaced the 2pdr mount to the end of the engine room casing, as in Canadian ships. She had single Oerlikons in the bridge wings, but an unusual feature of this ship was a pair of twin 0.5in Colt water-cooled MGs just abaft the funnel, a weapon supplied in limited numbers from the USA.

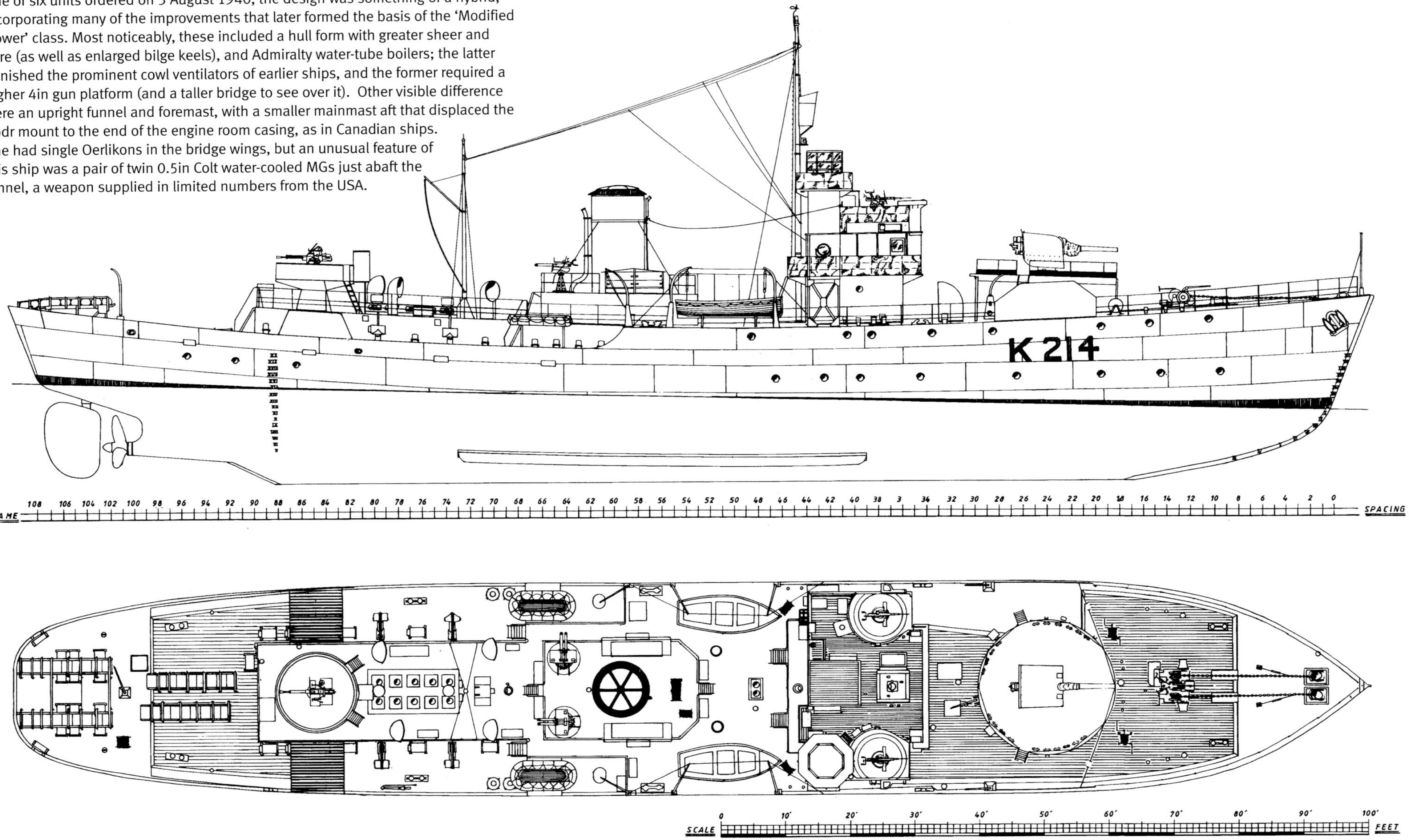

'Modified Flower' class corvettes HMS *Burnet*, HMCS *Forest Hill* (*ex-Ceanothus*) and HMS *Charlock* of late 1943/early 1944
The 'Modified Flowers' were a long way from the 1940 design and virtually small frigates. They carried four Mark IV DC throwers (repositioned right aft) and a Hedgehog ahead-throwing mortar to starboard of the bridge front. Close-range armament of these ships was seven single 20mm Oerlikons, although some (including *Charlock*) had a twin Mark V power mounting on the bandstand aft, for a total of eight 20mm. The 4in gunshield carried rocket flare launcher rails.

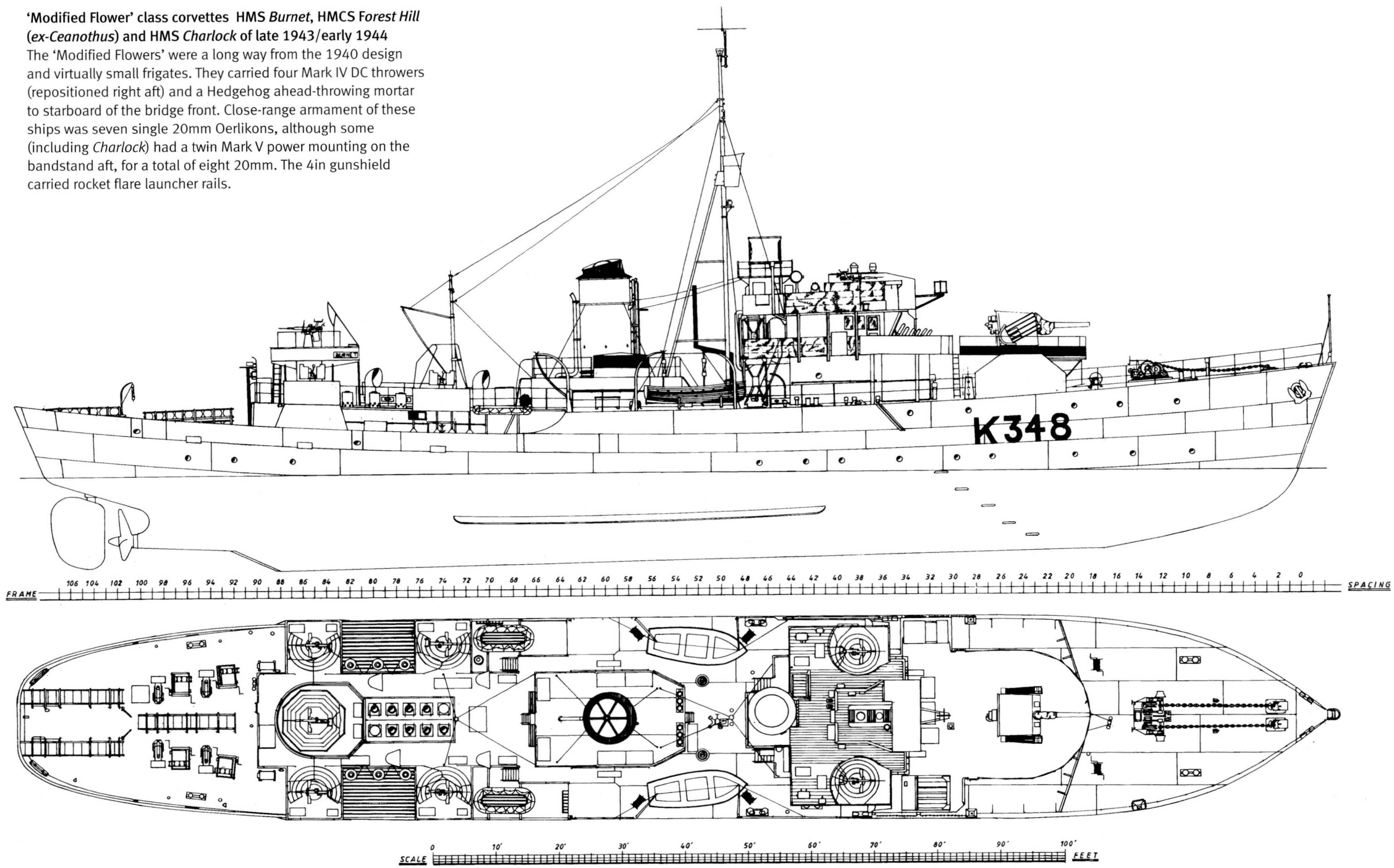

THE 'MODIFIED FLOWER' CLASS SPECIFICATION

Displacement	1015 tons (standard)
Dimensions (ft–in)	Length (pp) 193–0; Length (oa) 208–3; Breadth 33–3; Draught (fwd) 11–10; Draught (aft) 15–7
Machinery	4-cyl triple expansion steam reciprocating engine.
Boilers	Two Admiralty three-drum watertube
Shafts	One
Indicated Horse Power	2850
Maximum Speed	16 knots
Complement	109
Oil Fuel	300 tons
Endurance	7400 miles at 10 knots
Armament	1 – 4in BL gun on CPI mounting or
	1 – 4in Mark XIX gun on CP Mark XXIII mounting (some)
	1 – 2pdr or twin 20mm Oerlikon in power-operated Mark V mounting
	6 – 20mm single Oerlikons
	2 – 2in Rocket Flare projectors (on the 4in mounting)
Depth Charge rails	2
DC Throwers	4 Mark IV
Hedgehog	1
Minesweeping Gear	No
Radar	Type 271Q
M/F D/F	1
Foxer Gear	Yes

Below: The piecemeal improvements to the 'Flowers' were eventually consolidated into a single design known officially as the 'Modified Flower' class. The main features are displayed by *Arabis* in this 1944 photo taken shortly after commissioning: a hull form with more sheer and flare requiring the 4in gun mounting to be raised and in turn a higher bridge for visibility over it. Improved armament included the Hedgehog mortar on the platform to starboard between the bridge and the 4in gun, which has rocket flare launchers on the side. Aft, the single 2pdr was replaced by a twin power-operated 20mm Oerlikon, and there were a further six single 20mm. This ship was transferred to the Royal New Zealand Navy in 1944. *(IWM A22519)*

The late-war appearance of a Canadian-built 'Flower', HMCS *Chicoutimi* at Deep Brook, NS in September 1944. The short forecastle has been retained, but most of the standard modifications have been adopted. The ship has the truncated after superstructure of the minesweepers, but its form makes an interesting comparison with *Alberni*'s. An emblem painted on the side of the gunshield was not uncommon in Canadian corvettes. *(Public Archives of Canada)*

Seventy-nine original 'Flowers' were built in small yards, the first fifty-four being fitted for Oropesa wire minesweeping. The remaining twenty-five were not so equipped, but were strengthened for sweep gear in case it was a later requirement. Smith's Dock sent drawings over for units with increased sheer and flare in June 1941 and forty-two of these were constructed in Canadian yards. There are a number of visual differences seen in Canadian vessels, the most obvious being the 2pdr gun, which was usually positioned further aft, and two standard 27ft naval whalers carried by many as sea-boats. Fittingly, the only surviving 'Flower' is the restored museum ship HMCS *Sackville* at Halifax, Nova Scotia.

THE 'MODIFIED FLOWER' CLASS

With so many alterations and modifications, a point came when it was deemed sensible to combine everything in any new orders. Thus a separate design, the 'Modified Flower' class, came into being, but as was inevitable, there were ships building which had most but not all of the changes. Their main distinguishing features were the increased sheer and flare, a longer upper deck, a higher boxy bridge with a more 'frigate' appearance, and an upright mast and funnel (many having a funnel cap). With the introduction of forced-draft boilers, the prominent ventilator cowls of the earlier ships disappeared.

By April 1943, about the time that the 'Modified Flowers' were coming on stream, building switched to the slightly larger 'Castle' class. Some fifty-seven 'Modified Flowers' were projected for the RN to be constructed in British yards, but no job numbers, builders or names were allocated before they were cancelled. Only ten 'Modified Flowers' were built in the UK and all were transferred out of RN service: four to Canada, two to New Zealand and four to India.

By late 1944 the Battle of the Atlantic was won (but not over) and 'Flowers' were being replaced by larger and more efficient ocean escorts. The 'Herbaceous Borders' joined the ranks of obsolete warships, and after the war most were soon scrapped, but a number were sold to new navies regaining their pre-war status (Norway, Holland, Belgium, Greece, China, etc) while others were disarmed and converted for mercantile use.

ENGINEERING

It is very fortunate that early in the design stage it was decided that the new escort would burn furnace fuel oil rather than

This broadside view of the Canadian 'Modified Flower' *Beauharnois* demonstrates perfectly the most obvious identification features of the new design – the absence of cowl ventilators resulting from the adoption of forced-draft water-tube boilers. Furthermore, the mast and funnel were upright and many examples also had a funnel cowl. One of the attractions of the design in Canada was that it was small enough to be built on the Great Lakes, whose exit was limited by the Lachine Canal. *Beauharnois* is seen here shortly after commissioning off Quebec City, where she was built. *(Public Archives of Canada)*

coal, which was briefly considered (it was the norm in trawlers). Apart from the problems of coaling ship during their worldwide service, it would have made refuelling at sea all but impossible. Simple trawler-type engineering practice was used, although in fairness it was well thought out. A new engineering system had to be designed that was reliable and capable of being steamed by new hostilities-only ratings with little training, and with only a small number of senior rates to run, train and supervise. Usually the Engine Room Department was supervised by a Commissioned Engineer or senior Chief ERA.

The engineering spaces were divided into three separate watertight compartments: two boiler rooms forward, with the larger engine room containing the single steam engine aft. Each boiler room contained a standard Scotch Cylindrical single-ended boiler with a working pressure of 225psi, although each boiler was tested by hydraulic pressure to 388psi for safety. The boilers were 16ft 9in in diameter and 12ft 6in long, each having three oil-burning Deighton furnaces, and having a direct spring Mumford 'High lift' safety valve. Each boiler room was self contained, having its own machinery – exhaust steam feed heater, main feed pump, 42in Howden forced draft fan, a self contained oil fuel plant (Wallsend Howden System) and a transfer pump.

The engine room contained the single triple expansion steam engine with one HP (high pressure) and two LP (low pressure) cylinders. Cylinders measured 18½in x 31in x 38½in x 38½in x 30in stroke, producing 408 nominal horsepower, which gave about 16.5 knots at 185 maximum revolutions. The engine room also housed the condenser, to port of the main engine, a 15kW steam generator, evaporator, feed water distiller, distilling plant pump (for making fresh water for feed and domestic purposes), 14in circulating pump, Hotwell tank, feed water heater, monotype air pump, vertical air pump, general service pump, and vertical bilge pump. All were reciprocating type machinery.

The propeller shaft, supported by plumber blocks ran aft through the stern gland compartment, through the stern gland itself and out to drive the single 10ft 6in diameter three-bladed bronze propeller, which weighed 2 tons 17½cwt, and a propeller cone.

These features can be seen in greater detail in the accompanying drawings.

Compared with *Beauharnois* (opposite), these two views of *Camellia* as completed in June 1940 demonstrate how far this apparently austere design was 'stretched' in capability. *(The Ballast Trust)*

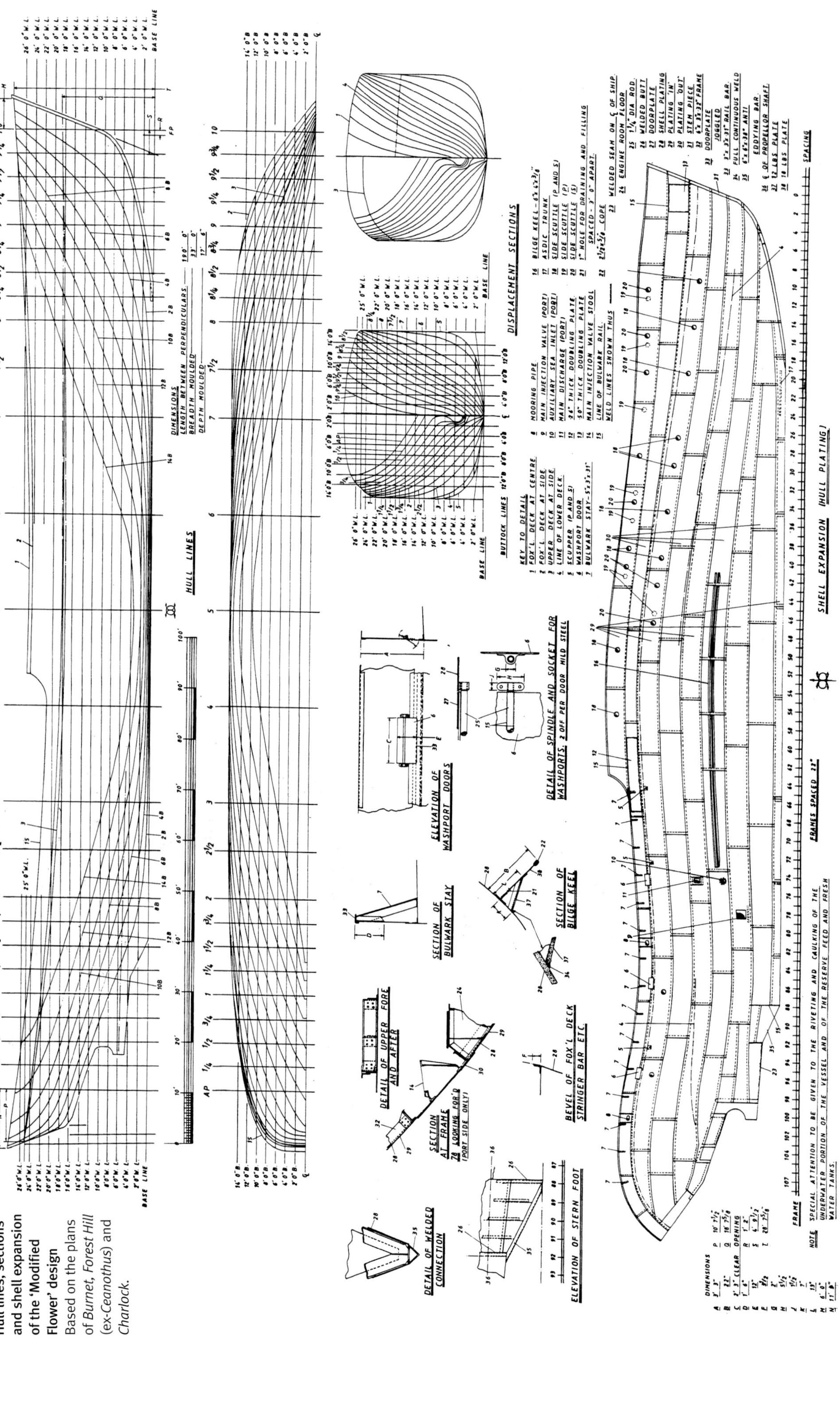

Hull lines, sections and shell expansion of the 'Modified Flower' design
Based on the plans of *Burnet*, *Forest Hill* (ex-*Ceanothus*) and *Charlock*.

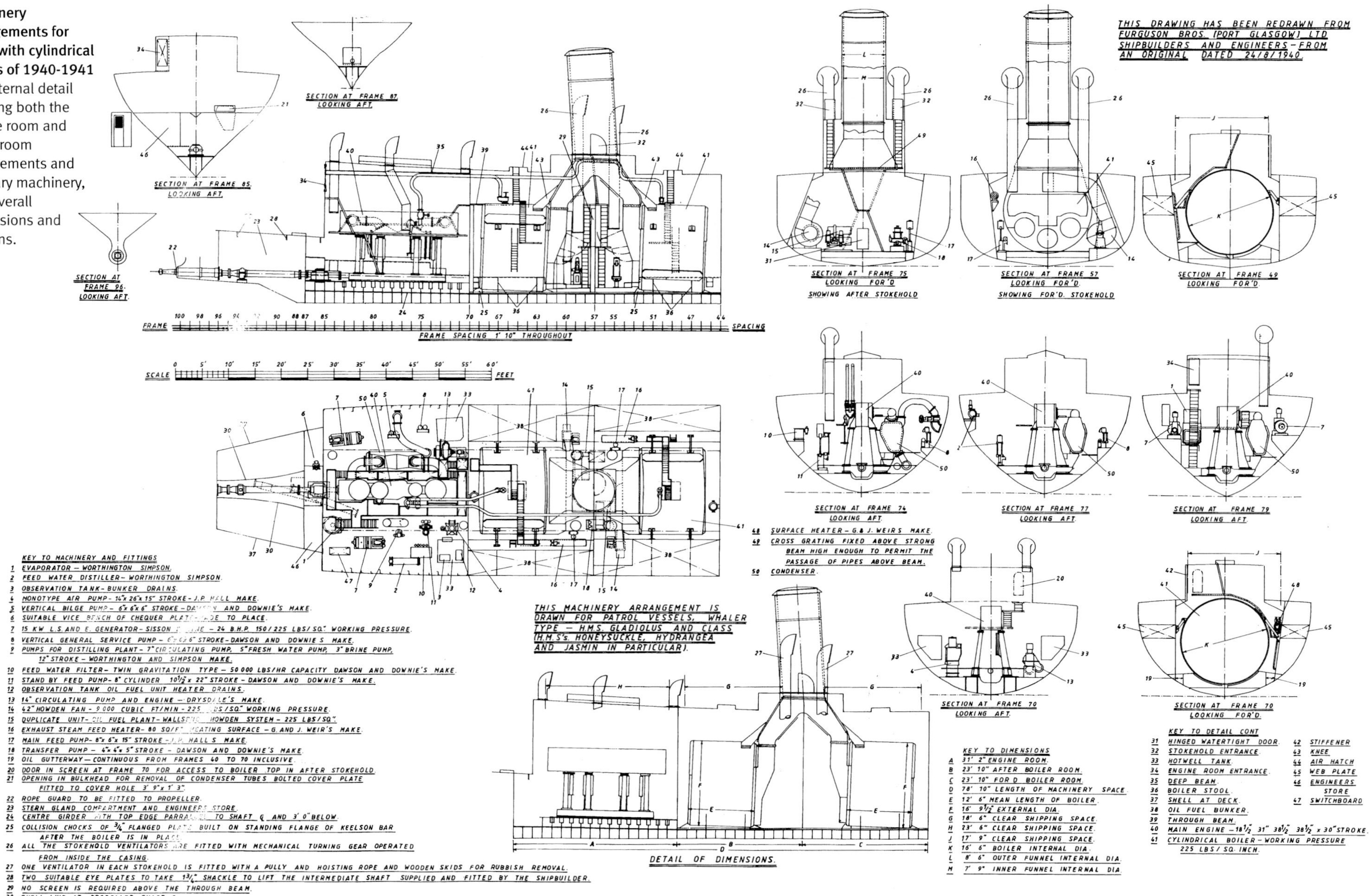

Machinery arrangements for ships with cylindrical boilers of 1940-1941 The internal detail showing both the engine room and boiler room arrangements and auxiliary machinery, with overall dimensions and sections.

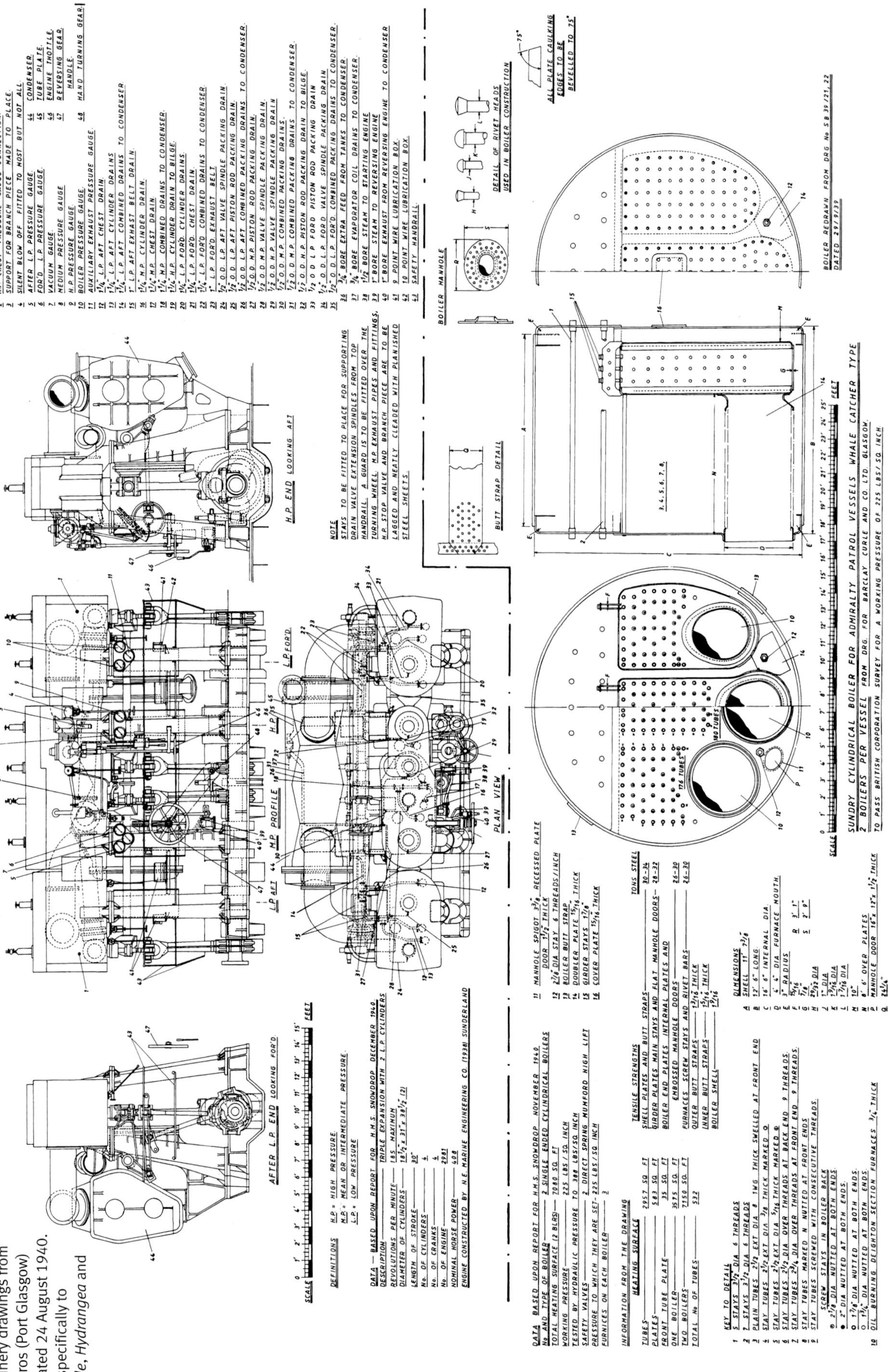

Detail of main engine and boilers
Both machinery drawings from Ferguson Bros (Port Glasgow) originals dated 24 August 1940. They refer specifically to *Honeysuckle*, *Hydrangea* and *Jasmine*.

Model Products

The 'Flower' class corvette is a popular subject for modelmakers but anybody who tries to produce an accurate model soon realises that no two vessels were identical, and many vessels changed their appearance during the course of their careers. The major differences, such as long and short forecastle, rounded and squared stern, relative positions of the mast and bridge, are obvious, but details of equipment carried and deck layout, such as minesweeping gear and boat/carley rafts, are more difficult to determine. Clear, dated photographs are essential to produce an accurate model.

Models of these vessels vary in scale from 1/3000 (less than one inch long) to 1/48 (over four feet long). Many manufacturers have produced models at 1/1200 or 1/1250 scales, invariably in white metal. These vary greatly in the level of detail portrayed, some representing specific vessels and some a generic 'Flower class corvette'. Some manufacturers, such as Navis/Neptun, produce complete painted models (overall grey with a few highlights of other colours), whilst others, such as Noble Miniatures Figurehead Ships, manufacture kits, in this specific case including a separate bridge, forward gun and mast. The availability of these models tends to be sporadic, but an interesting collection of models, highlighting the major class differences, can be built up.

In addition to the models described below, there are known to have been two other 1/700 scale models available at various times. One was a resin model by Jim Shirley of a long forecastle 'Flower' (JNL013) and the other was another resin kit, including some white metal parts, by Clipper Models of Japan. The latter included details for the Canadian vessels *Agassiz*, *Battleford* and *Snowberry*.

In 1978 there was also another 1/96 scale kit produced by the English company of John Piper (Accessories) Ltd. This was considered to be a very high quality kit, particularly for its time, and the white metal fittings were especially well regarded. Some of these fittings were later re-released by Aries Services, also from England, but no

'Flowers' in kit form from Noble Miniatures.

Short and long forecastle 'Flowers' from Navis/Neptun in 1/1250 scale.

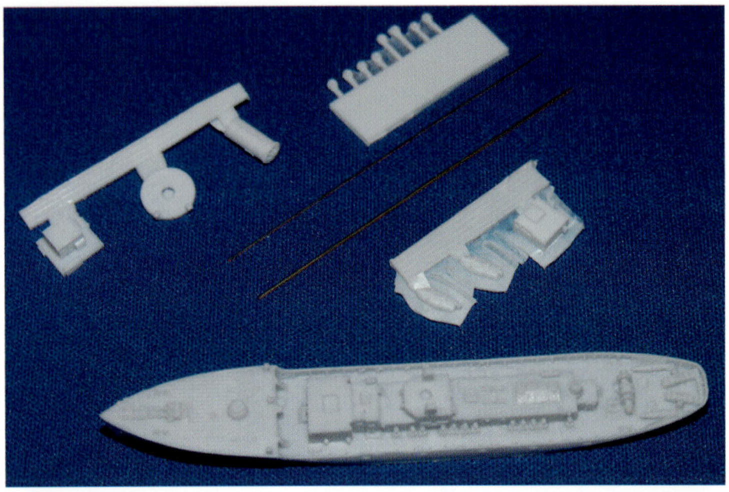

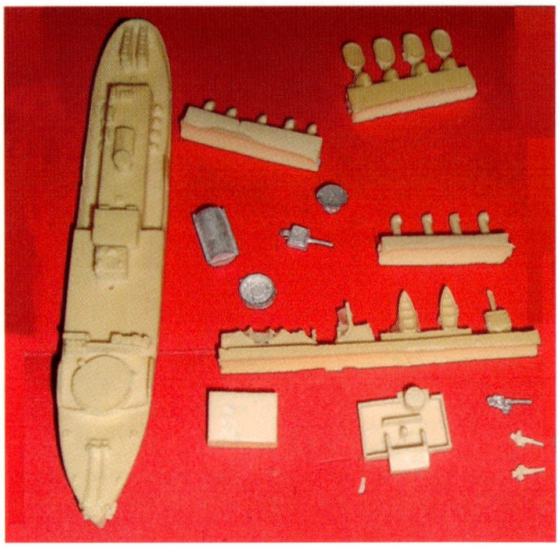

complete ship models. When these kits appear today, they are considered as very rare items and the accompanying price reflects this.

During 2008 five new models of 'Flower' class corvettes have been advertised for release. Two are in plastic at 1/400 scale and come from Mirage Hobby of Poland – a vessels from the 1939-1940 programme with a short forecastle and one from the later 'increased endurance programme'. Two are from Commander Series Models, Inc in the United States at 1/192 scale. They will be of two Canadian designs - one a vessel as-built from the 1939-40 programme and the other a vessel with increased endurance from the 1942-43 programme. The fifth model is a ready-to-run radio control model from Eastern Europe.

Top left: Resin and white metal kit from Clipper Models of Japan at 1/700 scale.

Top right: 1/700 resin kit from Jim Shirley.

Above: The 1/96 John Piper kit made up as HMS *Bluebell*.

HP MODELS 1/700 Scale

HP Models of Germany include twelve different models in their catalogue, ten British vessels, one Canadian and an American vessel (see table). The models are cast in resin and represent a waterline configuration, with ports but no plating details. Each kit comprises a major hull moulding plus a resin wafer including the superstructure and other details. There are two basic hull mouldings, a short and a long forecastle version. The long forecastle moulding also includes a prominent, curved

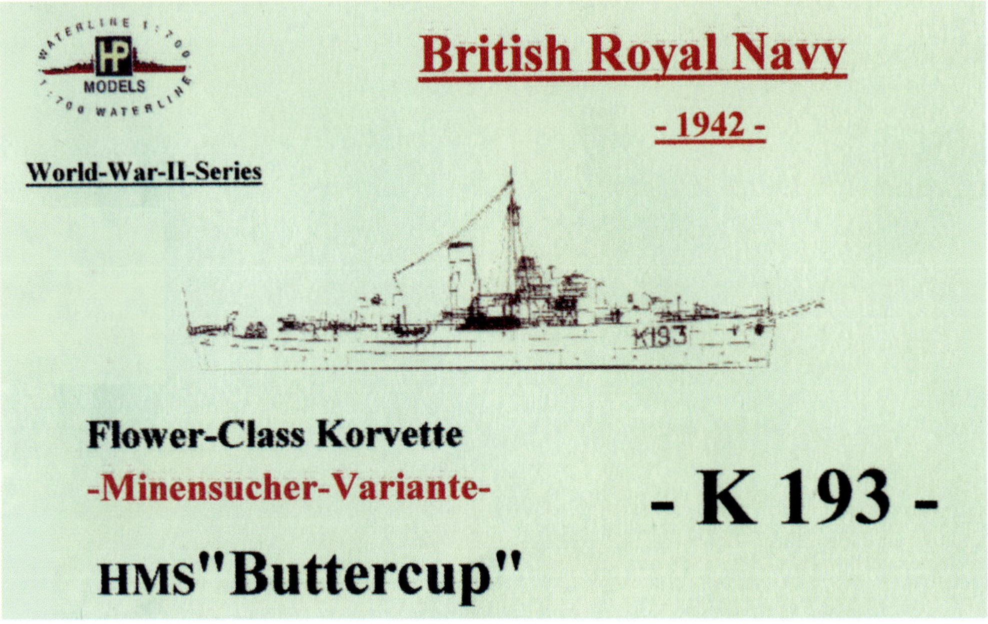

FLOWER CLASS CORVETTE KITS FROM HP MODELS

WW II-WL-GB-028	Flower-Class Corvette – K 47, *Polyanthus* (1942)
WW II-WL-GB-029	Flower-Class Corvette – K 48, *Anemone* (1942)
WW II-WL-GB-030	Flower-Class Corvette – K 49, *Crocus* (1942)
WW II-WL-GB-031	Flower-Class Corvette – K 80, *Bluebell* (1942)
WW II-WL-GB-032	Flower-Class Corvette – K 68, *Jonquil* (1940)
WW II-WL-GB-033	Flower-Class Corvette – K 185, *Alisma* (1943)
WW II-WL-GB-034	Flower-Class Corvette – K 166, *Snowberry* (1943)
WW II-WL-GB-035	Canadian Flower-Class Corvette – K 15, *Atholl* (1943)
WW II-WL-GB-036	Flower-Class Corvette as Minesweeper - K 193, *Buttercup*
WW II-WL-GB-048	Flower-Class Corvette – K 348, *Forest Hill* (1944)
WW II-WL-GB-049	Flower-Class Corvette – K 395, *Charlock* (1944)
WW II-WL-US-023	Flower-Class Corvette – PG 65, *Saucy* (1943)

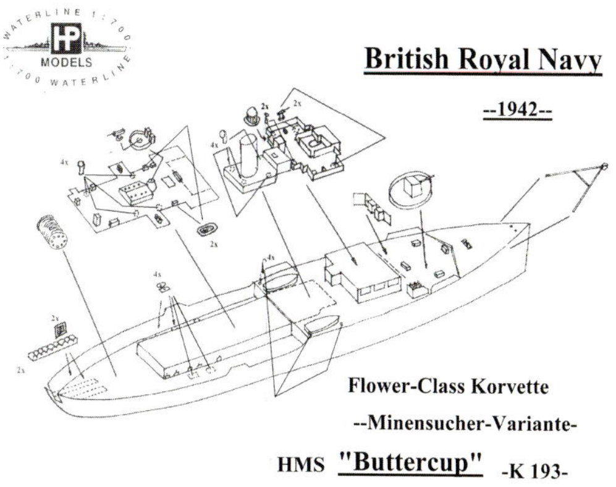

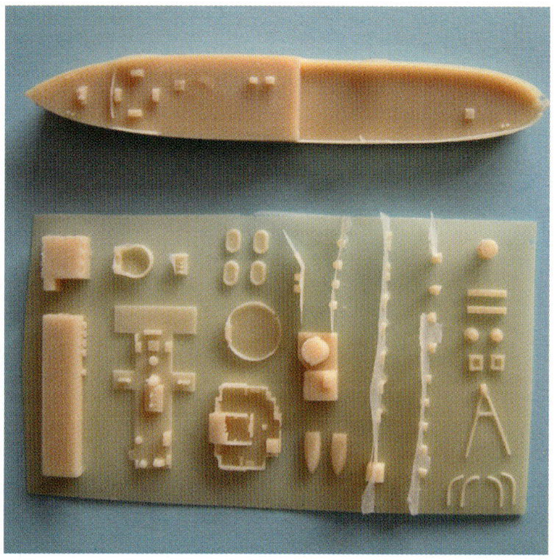

breakwater and a long superstructure section aft of the forecastle break. Care is required when removing the parts from the resin wafer, particularly some of the smaller parts, to ensure that too much material is not removed hence destroying some of the detail. Additional brass or plastic rod is required for masts but no dimensions for these are given.

The instructions comprise two sheets of A4 paper, one giving a plan and profile drawing (approximately two and a half to three times the actual size of the model) and the other an isometric assembly drawing. Some kits also include a third sheet giving a colour camouflage profile but there are no detailed painting instructions.

WHITE ENSIGN MODELS
HMS *BLUEBELL* and HMS *BUTTERCUP* 1/700 Scale

White Ensign Models of England offer models of just two different vessels; both are resin kits in a full hull configuration. The hull is split into two parts at the waterline, the major parts of the superstructure being moulded in position on the upper section. Once again, ports are included in the hull moulding but there is no plating detail. Other details are provided in resin, together with a small etched brass sheet. The mouldings are all very crisp and clean, particularly the major hull mouldings, with just small amounts of excess resin to be removed and cleaned up.

The comprehensive instructions occupy

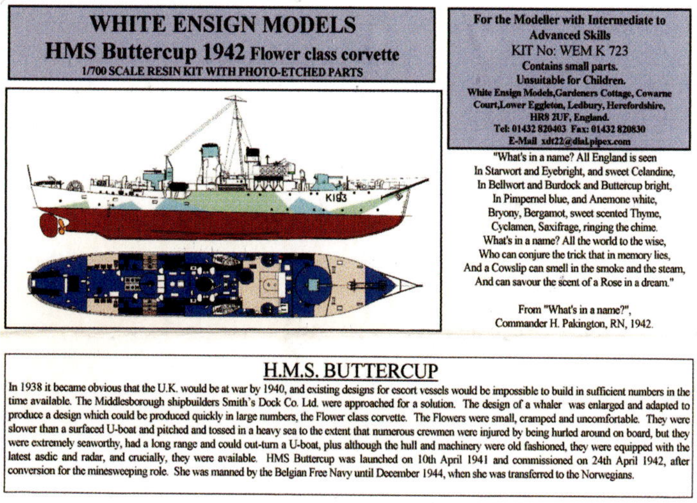
WHITE ENSIGN MODELS
HMS Buttercup 1942 Flower class corvette
1/700 SCALE RESIN KIT WITH PHOTO-ETCHED PARTS

For the Modeller with Intermediate to Advanced Skills
KIT No: WEM K 723
Contains small parts.
Unsuitable for Children.
White Ensign Models,Gardeners Cottage, Cowarne Court,Lower Eggleton, Ledbury, Herefordshire, HR8 2UF, England.
Tel: 01432 820403 Fax: 01432 820830
E-Mail xdt22@dial.pipex.com

"What's in a name? All England is seen
In Starwort and Eyebright, and sweet Celandine,
In Bellwort and Burdock and Buttercup bright,
In Pimpernel blue, and Anemone white,
Bryony, Bergamot, sweet scented Thyme,
Cyclamen, Saxifrage, ringing the chime.
What's in a name? All the world to the wise,
Who can conjure the trick that in memory lies,
And a Cowslip can smell in the smoke and the steam,
And can savour the scent of a Rose in a dream."

From "What's in a name?",
Commander H. Pakington, RN, 1942.

H.M.S. BUTTERCUP

In 1938 it became obvious that the U.K. would be at war by 1940, and existing designs for escort vessels would be impossible to build in sufficient numbers in the time available. The Middlesborough shipbuilders Smith's Dock Co. Ltd. were approached for a solution. The design of a whaler was enlarged and adapted to produce a design which could be produced quickly in large numbers, the Flower class corvette. The Flowers were small, cramped and uncomfortable. They were slower than a surfaced U-boat and pitched and tossed in a heavy sea to the extent that numerous crewmen were injured by being hurled around on board, but they were extremely seaworthy, had a long range and could out-turn a U-boat, plus although the hull and machinery were old fashioned, they were equipped with the latest asdic and radar, and crucially, they were available. HMS Buttercup was launched on 10th April 1941 and commissioned on 24th April 1942, after conversion for the minesweeping role. She was manned by the Belgian Free Navy until December 1944, when she was transferred to the Norwegians.

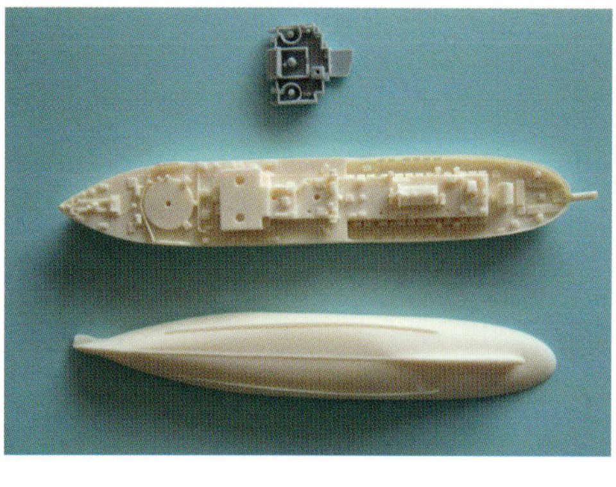

eight sheets of A4 paper, starting with some historical information on the original vessel and including a plan and profile drawing (approximately three times the actual size of the model) and an isometric assembly drawing. Dimensional drawings of the mast, to be made from the supplied brass and plastic rod, are included. There is also an A4 colour sheet giving details of the camouflage scheme carried by the vessel at the date portrayed by the model.

SKYTREX LIMITED **HMS *CROCUS*** 1/600 Scale

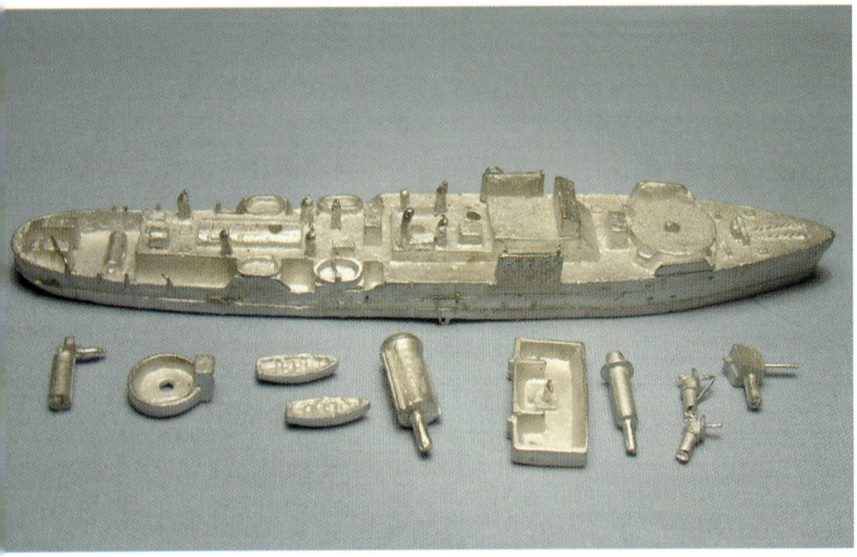

Skytrex Limited of England produces a white metal model which is intended primarily for wargamers. It comprises a waterline hull with separate castings for items such as the funnel, bridge, radar, guns and boats. The hull includes plating detail and ports but does require some cleaning up and the removal of a mould line, an operation which can easily obliterate the detail. The smaller parts are cleanly moulded and require little attention before they can be installed using the clearly defined spigots and location holes.

There are no instructions, just a few words giving details of the original vessel, and a small profile assembly line drawing. This drawing does not include any indication of either the mast size or arrangement, so details must be sought elsewhere, as must details of any colour scheme.

L'ARSENAL **FLOWER CLASS CORVETTE** 1/400 Scale

L'Arsenal of France includes two variants of the 'Flower' class corvette in their range. Although the box titles are generic, the instructions (in French but also available in English) do give details, including camouflage patterns, of specific ships (see table).

Each kit comprises a full hull resin moulding, including ports and hawseholes but no plating, with major areas of superstructure, a number of resin details plus two or three (depending on the kit) sheets of etched brass and a small sheet of decals. The two hull mouldings are for ships with the same length of forecastle but differing significantly in detail, particularly around the area of the bridge. All mouldings are crisp, the hull requiring just the mould line along the keel to be removed, but the smaller details do include some very significantly sized 'pours' or sprues. Although large, the sprue is easily removed with a sharp knife.

The etched brass includes one sheet of general guardwires and the others are of specific details, including the open areas of the bridge and bridge wings. The decals comprise pennant numbers for the different vessels and bridge windows.

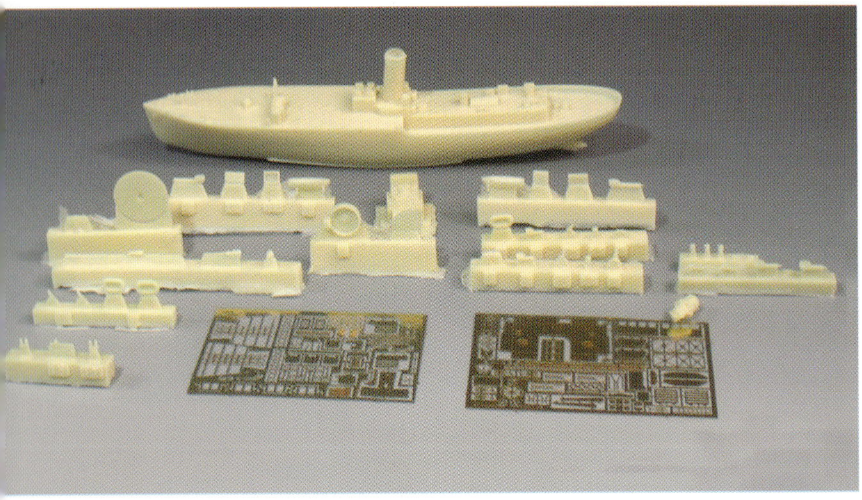

FLOWER CLASS CORVETTE VARIANTS FROM L'ARSENAL

KIT REFERENCE 400-03:

FNFL *Aconit* K 58

FNFL *Roselys* K 57

FNFL *Commandant Drogou* K 195

HMCS *Midland* K 220

HMC *Orillia* K 119

USS *Saucy* PG 65

HMS *Lobelia* K 05

HMS *Alisma* K 195

HMS *Wallflower* K 44

Commandant Detroyat K 183

KIT REFERENCE 400-04:

HMS *Campion*

FNFL *Mimosa*

FNFL *Alysse*

COMMANDER SERIES MODELS INC **FLOWER CLASS CORVETTE**

1/350 Scale

Commander Series Models Inc. (formerly known as Iron Shipwright) of the United States of America feature three different 'Flower' class corvettes in their range – HMCS *Sackville* (Canadian short forecastle 'Flower'), 'Flower' class corvette 1940/41 (Canadian long forecastle 'Flower') and 'Flower' class corvette 1943 [Late Canadian Improved Version]. The first kit was released under the name of Iron Shipwright some years ago but has now undergone an updating and improvement process.

Each kit includes a full hull moulding, with the major areas of superstructure and funnel, and there are two significantly different mouldings – short and long forecastle variants. The details, which have varying quantities of flash, are supplied in a plastic container and there is a sheet of etched brass and a length of brass rod.

Instructions are rather limited, being confined to just a single A4 sheet, and there are no colour or historic details of the vessel. Considerable additional research is required to produce an accurate model.

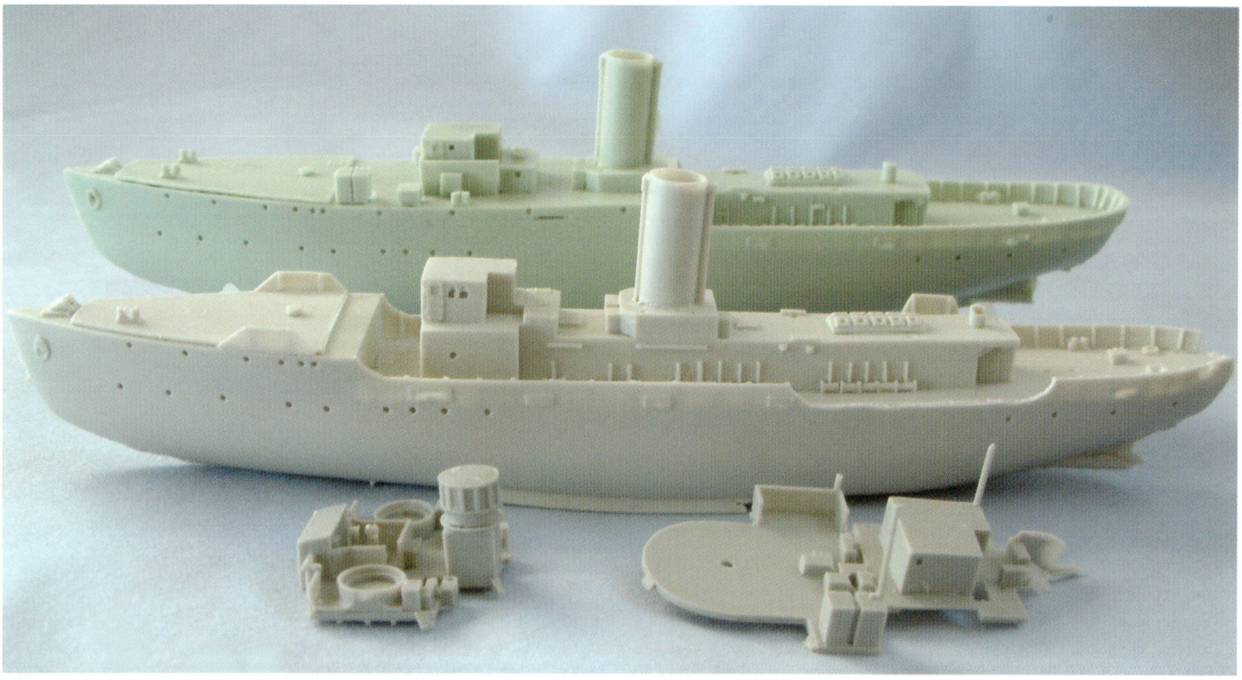

SKYTREX LIMITED **HMS *CROCUS***

1/350 Scale

As well as their 1/600 scale kit, Skytrex Limited offer a larger white metal model. This is not the same model scaled up but a significantly different and more detailed casting. It can be purchased as either a kit or a completed model, with or without a base. The main hull casting includes ports, anchors and plating detail, and is integral with the bridge, funnel, forward gun platform, carley floats, and depth charges, as well as other small details. The inclusion of carley floats does result in solid supports for them which should be removed and replaced for greater accuracy.

Separate details include the aft gun plat-

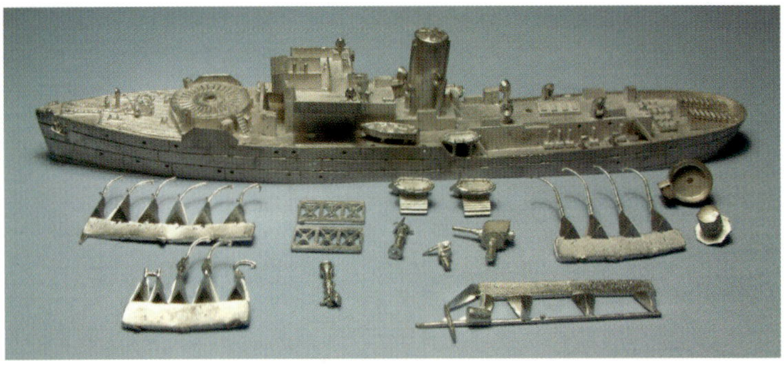

form and both gun mountings, davits, a second pair of carley floats (the supports of which are also cast solid), the radar lantern and mast. There are also some lattice supports for the bridge wings. Limitations in the casting process result in these being rather thick and so they should be thinned or replaced by etched brass for a more realistic appearance. There are no instructions, just a photograph of a completed model, but this should be sufficient to complete the model as supplied.

MODELIK **HMCS *AGASSIZ*** 1/200 and 1/100 Scales

Modelik of Poland offers two card models of the Canadian corvette HMCS *Agassiz*. The smaller scale version also includes the option of HMCS *Wetaskiwin*. These are well printed on good quality card, four A4 sheets at the smaller scale and twelve A4 sheets at the larger scale. Each book also includes some parts, such as the base and internal formers, on paper which require reinforcing with card before use.

The books include comprehensive, well illustrated instructions of sub-assemblies, clearly identifying the location of each of the card parts. General arrangement drawings, again with the location of parts clearly marked and identified, provide further assistance. The fact that the instructions are in Polish therefore does not cause major problems.

DEANS MARINE **HMS *COMPASS ROSE*** 1/96 Scale

Deans Marine of England produces a model which is intended primarily for radio control. Although carrying the name of the vessel made famous in Nicholas Monsarrat's book *The Cruel Sea*, the model is actually based on HMS *Campanula*. The

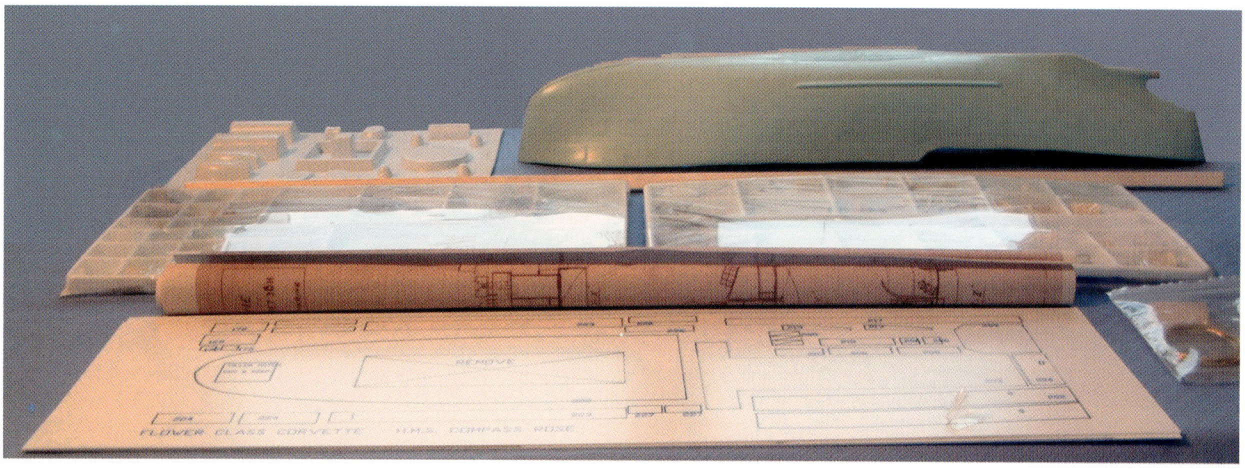

model performs well on the water and, being of relatively small size, is an ideal model for the beginner or those who do not have a lot of room.

The kit includes a grp (glass reinforced plastic) hull, complete with plating, pre-printed plastic card for the decks and main parts of the superstructure, two trays including resin, white metal and etched brass details, a shaft with a white metal propeller, some strips of wood and a full size drawing. The mouldings, no matter what the material, require a small amount of cleaning up before installation.

An A4 booklet of instructions provides clear directions for assembly of the model and includes photographs of a model being constructed to assist the modelmaker.

REVELL AG **HMCS *SNOWBERRY*** 1/72 Scale

The re-release by Revell AG of Germany of the original Matchbox kit was warmly welcomed by many modelmakers. When re-released the kit included details of two different vessels – HMCS *Snowberry* and USS *Saucy* – whilst the original release also included HMS *Bluebell*. The differences given between these two vessels, apart from colour scheme and pendant number, are only minor. There were more significant differences with HMS *Bluebell*.

The hull is moulded in four grey coloured sections, being split along the keel with the midships break following the

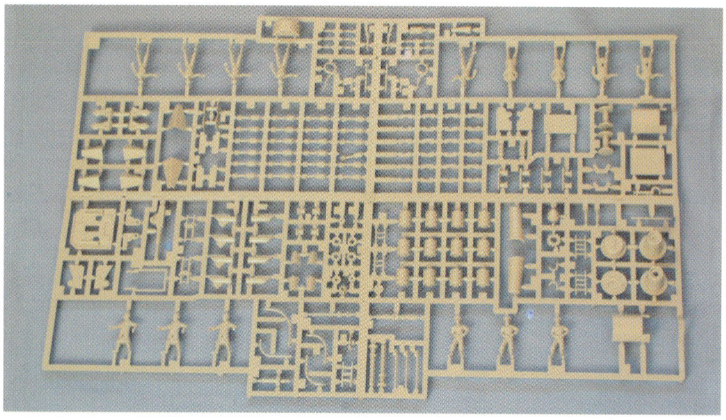

rather heavy plating. There are two main deck sections moulded in tan colour, as are the forecastle, bridge, and ship's boats. There are three grey plastic sprues containing the funnel, major parts of the superstructure, depth charges and propeller, and four light grey sprues containing the rudder, vents and other

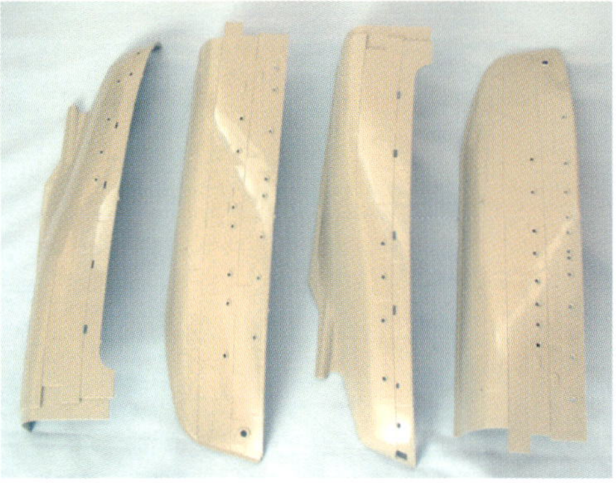

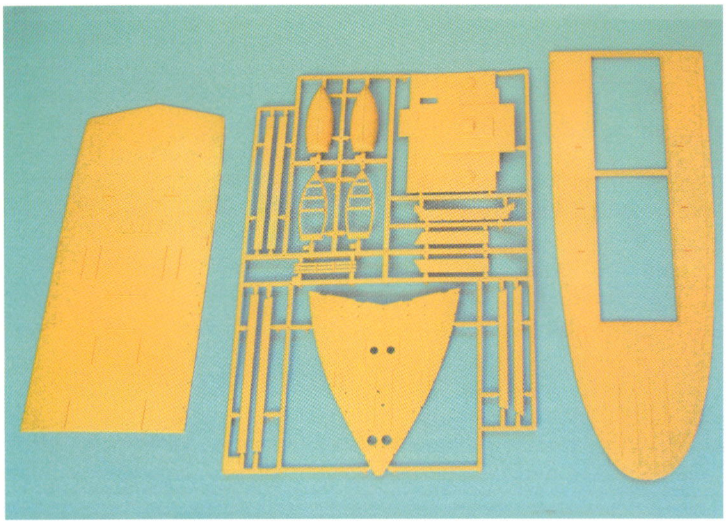

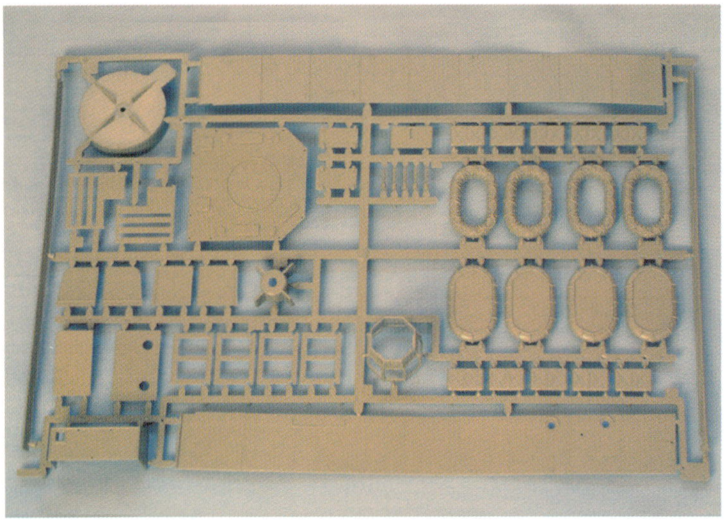

details, including fifteen crew members. A clear sprue contains the parts for the base, ships' nameplates, portlights and windows.

The mouldings are identical to when first released and so all the parts (except for the decals) required to produce HMS *Bluebell* are supplied. The differences between the vessels which are described in the kit are quite small – a searchlight platform forward of the amidships 2pdr pom-pom mounting on *Saucy*, different rigging, different vents on the forecastle and different location of the ensign staff amongst them. The drawings indicate that *Snowberry* had the 'square' 4in gun shield whilst *Saucy* had the 'rounded' one but this is not mentioned in the assembly diagram. This was also an omission on the original Matchbox instructions.

A short length of chain, two sets of cord, some lengths of plastic rod, a decal sheet and some paper flags complete the kit. The naval ensigns supplied are much smaller than those in the original kit, although the signal flags are of the same size, which were previously printed on material. The comprehensive instruction booklet runs to forty-eight A4 pages with shaded drawings included for the camouflage schemes. Originally there had been two instruction books, one in full colour giving brief histories of all three vessels as well as details of the colour schemes.

APS MODELS **HMS *BLUEBELL*** 1/72 Scale

APS Models of Australia actually produce two grp hulls – a round stern version that is a direct replacement for the four sections of the hull of the Revell kit, and a square stern version which will require some considerable modifications to the basic kit. The round stern version has the same basic faults as the Revell kit hull but the square stern version has been improved and corrected. APS also advertise a very limited number of weapons for use with the hull.

METCALF MOULDINGS **HMS *BRYONY*** 1/72 and 1/48 Scales

Metcalf Mouldings in England also produce a 1/72 grp hull to match the Revell kit, hence simplifying the task for anybody who wishes to produce a working model from the kit. Their main offering however is a larger 1/48 scale grp hull of the long forecastle vessel, HMS *Bryony*. This is supplied with a very detailed two-sheet plan set by the late David MacGregor which shows the vessel as in 1942 when fitted out for acoustic and magnetic minesweeping. The model hull has all plate lines, portholes, hawseholes and washports moulded in.

P S SHIPS **HMS *BLUEBELL*** 1/48 Scale

Another English company P S Ships, formerly known as Sirmar, also produce a 1/48 scale grp hull – this is of HMS *Bluebell*. The hull is moulded in white grp and is complete with plating detail. Hawseholes, scuttle plugs, and scuttle 'eyebrows' are provided separately, to enable a different scuttle configuration to be modelled. A drawing is supplied on two, full sized sheets.

Ten 'fittings packs' are available to assist in the construction of the model. The first contains the main items of gun armament; the second, depth charges and compasses; the third, the Hedgehog mortar and more depth charges, watertight doors and bollards; the fourth, fifth, sixth, seventh and eighth contain various fittings; the ninth some figures for the crew and the tenth, the running gear.

FLEETSCALE (WESTWARD MOULDINGS) **HMS *BRYONY*, HMCS *AGASSIZ*** 1/48 Scale

Fleetscale (Westward Mouldings) of England produce two 1/48 scale grp hulls of HMS *Bryony* and HMCS *Agassiz*, the latter with the 'square' stern. Both versions of the hull are supplied with detailed drawings.

In the case of HMS *Bryony*, Fleetscale also offer a set of fittings, including all the main gun and anti-submarine armament, bollards and fairleads, Carley floats, vents and stanchions. These fittings are actually manufactured by P S Ships. There is also a set of running gear, including the rudder, available.

Accessories

For the smaller scale models, a number of general purpose accessories, mainly in etched brass, such as guardrails, ladders and small calibre guns, are available from Gold Medal Models (USA), Tom's Modelworks (USA), Eduard (Czech Republic), L'Arsenal (France) and White Ensign Models (UK), but it is only this last company which has released a sheet specific to 'Flower' class corvettes. This is the same etched brass sheet as is included in their own 1/700 scale kits but parts could quite easily be used with those from other manufacturers.

The scales of 1/96 and 1/48 are widely used by those wishing to build larger models, particularly working ones, and so a number of fittings and other accessories are available for these from P S Ships (UK), Tom's Modelworks (US), and Scale Link (UK). Quaycraft (UK) specialise in ship's boats and have available suitable craft at 1/96, 1/72 and 1/48. Whatever the scale of model, it has to be painted and White Ensign Models produce their range of ColourCoats, which include the various camouflage colours worn by many of the 'Flower' class.

The Revell 1/72 kit has received much attention and so there are numerous accessories available for use at this scale. Probably the largest range is from Great Little Ships (David Parkins) in England and this includes over twenty different sets, comprising mainly etched brass but also some white metal and resin castings. The sets vary in scope and complexity from the 'Deck & Fittings Set' which includes a new forecastle deck, to pipe sets for the areas

Below: 1/700 scale etched brass fret fromWhite Ensign Models.

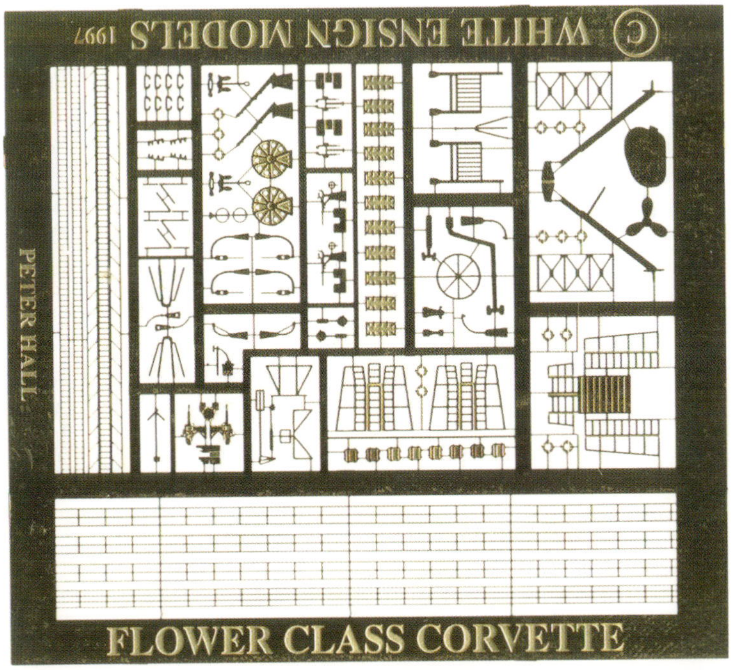

Bottom: Comparison between single Oerlikons: in 1/72 scale, Revell (front left), GLS (front centre), P S Ships (front right); at the back a 1/48 scale model from P S Ships.

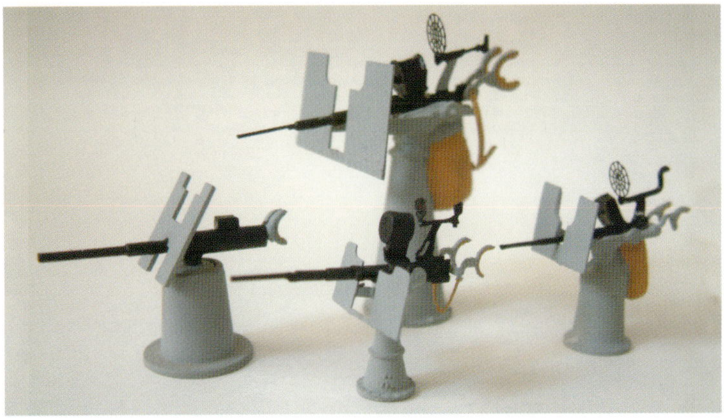

Above, left: Comparison between Hedgehog mortars: in 1/72 scale, Revell (front left), GLS (front centre), P S Ships (front right); at the back a 1/48 scale model from P S Ships.

Above, right: 1/72 RN crew from Hecker & Goros.

around the bridge and boiler room. There is also a 'Propeller and Rudder Set' and the armament is very well catered for, from the main 4in gun to the Lewis machine guns. All these sets are very detailed and can be used to greatly enhance the basic kit.

P S Ships also offer six packs of resin and white metal fittings, including parts for the bridge area, armament, carley floats and ship's boats, the latter being manufactured by Quaycraft.

Bob Pearson's corvette decals.

It is worthwhile noting that some of these fittings vary, not only in level of detail, but also significantly in size from the original parts supplied in the Revell kit. The accompanying photograph clearly shows the differences between the 20mm Oerlikon gun mounting, that from the kit being front left, the GLS version front centre and the P S Ships version on the right. A 1/48 scale model, also from P S Ships, is at the back. The other photograph shows the same arrangement of manufacturers for the Hedgehog A/S mortar.

The most obvious discrepancy with the Oerlikon gun mountings is the size and shape of the shield, that in the original kit being located much too high compared with the cannon. It is also important to confirm the precise shield shape for any particular vessel from photographs. In the case of the Hedgehog, the projectiles in the original kit are of entirely the wrong shape whereas those from both Great Little Ships and P S Ships are correct.

The final accessory is for those who wish to include crew members. The German firm of Hecker & Goros produce two packs, each containing three figures. The first is KSHG 206 which contains gun crew figures, two of which are wearing hard hats and the second is KSHG 209 which has an officer with binoculars and two ratings, all wearing heavy coats.

To complete the model, a set of decals, at scales of 1/350, 1/96 and 1/72, are available from Bob Pearson in Canada via his website at www.cbrnp.com/RNP/Flower. The sheet includes various artwork for eleven different Canadian vessels, including *Snowberry*. Each ship is represented by artwork for the 4in gun shield, ship's nameplates and pendant numbers, both for the sides of the hull and the stern.

Modelmakers' Showcase

When selecting the next project, the modelmaker faces a number of decisions. Should it be a static or a working model? If a static model, should it be a full hull or a waterline model? The following photographs are of models by both amateur and professional modelmakers and reflect the different decisions that these individuals have made and their approaches to the different challenges faced.

'A LOVELY BUNCH OF FLOWERS' 1/700 Scale

By CHRIS DRAGE

In this series of five models, Chris built two models 'direct from the box' and modified one of these kits to portray three other vessels in the class. All models are at 1/700 scale and come from White Ensign Models, who produce two different kits, HMS *Buttercup* and HMS *Bluebell*. Chris selected the model of *Buttercup* as the basis for his modifications, using four kits to produce three different models. The models represent HMS *Alisma* (K 185), HMCS *Snowberry* (K 166) and HMS *Loosestrife* (K 105) in addition to *Buttercup* (K 193) and *Bluebell* (K 80).

All models were enhanced by Chris, so the term 'direct from the box' is not strictly correct but more properly indicates that these two models were built to represent the vessels intended by the manufacturer. Chris produced full-hull models but displayed each one in a semi-diorama representing the bottom of a dry dock. Good references, both photographs and drawings, were essential to produce accurate representations of the different vessels which are all painted in different Western Approaches camouflage schemes.

K80
37

K185

K166

HMS *CAMPANULA* 1/700 Scale

By Mike McCabe

This model is based on the White Ensign Models *Bluebell* kit and represents the actual vessel in which Nicholas Montserrat, the author of *The Cruel Sea*, had served. There are a great number of fittings to be included in such a small model – just about 7cm long.

Mike scratch built items for the different equipment carried by *Campanula* when compared with the original *Bluebell*, including the radar lantern. Changes to the arrangement of carley floats and depth charges were also required. Although the model is displayed on a sea base, Mike added the underwater section of the hull so that, when viewed in rough water, the vessel's bottom could be seen in places.

The railings supplied with the kit were replaced by the even finer items available from Gold Medal Models.

K18

K18

HMS *CHARLOCK* 1:350 Scale

By IAN RUSCOE

This is a scratch-built model showing the ship moored alongside the quay being provisioned with stores and weapons. The basic hull is carved from a special resin compound which is ideal for this kind of work. The rest of the model is made from various gauges of plastic card and plastic square and round rod. The finer details are surplus photo etch parts taken from the spares box.

The overall model was spray painted with the detail painting done by hand. When the paint was dry, an oil paint wash of Raw Umber was applied to the model, the excess being removed using various sizes of broad flat brushes, in order to lightly stain the paint and hence produce the initial stage of weathering. To add the final bit of weathering artist's pastel chalks were used, these being ground up and applied using a brush.

HMCS *SNOWBERRY* 1:72 Scale

By TED TAYLOR

Ted has assembled a number of kits for display by different manufacturers and so the model represents one built 'straight from the box'. Being a display model, no attempt has been made at weathering and the vessel is shown as freshly painted in a Western Approaches camouflage scheme.

The crew members, included with the model, are displayed in 'action' poses and give a very good impression of the actual size of these vessels. The large amount of equipment and fittings squeezed into these vessels is also well illustrated.

K166

K166

'DUEL AT SEA' 1:72 Scale

By JOSEPH NEUMEYER

The amazing work of Joseph Neumeyer has already been featured in an earlier book in this series – *German S-Boats* by Steve Wiper. Joseph is a professional modelmaker and the owner of Dynamic Dioramas. More examples of his work can be found at www.dynamicdioramas.org. Here you will find land-based dioramas as well as more vessels at sea.

This particular diorama represents a battle between a 'Flower' class corvette and a smaller and much faster S-Boat in the English Channel in 1944. The model makes use of the accessories available from Great Little Ships (David Parkins).

HMS *ACANTHUS* 1:72 Scale

By MARK HUSBAND

Mark's model is from an original Matchbox kit. Additional wooden bulkheads have been fitted in the hull to improve the stiffness and to provide watertight compartments. To provide access to the interior, a forward section of the deck from the breakwater to the forecastle step slides out. The aft section of superstructure also lifts off and there is a small area of the quarterdeck which is removable.

Where appropriate, individual wood strips have been added, replacing the wood grain moulding of the kit and other additional details, such as oars in the ship's boat, have been added. A brass propeller, with stainless steel shafting, replaces the kit part and the model is ballasted as a fully loaded vessel, giving realistic scale speed and movement on the water.

K01
K01

K01

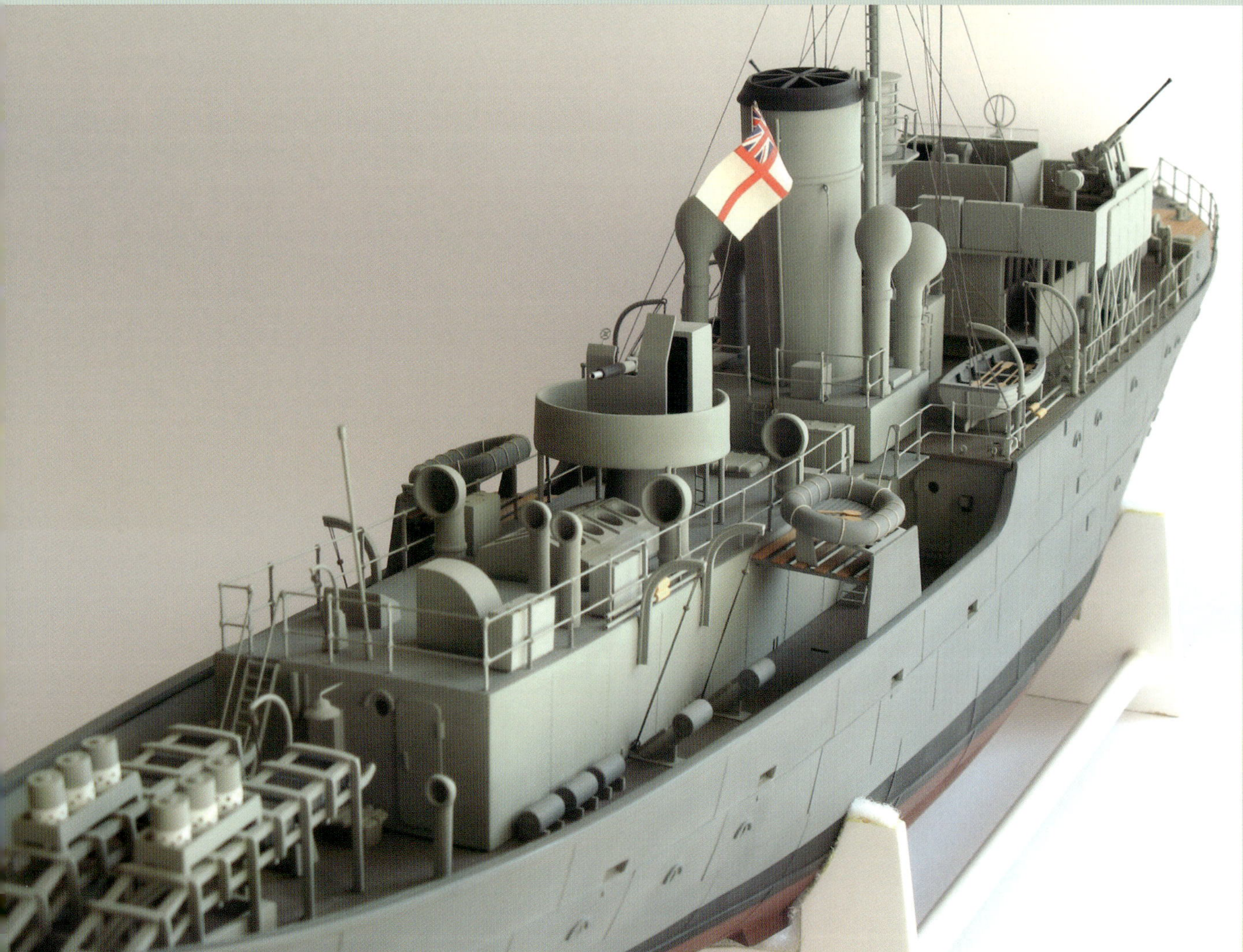

Illustrations by Bob Pearson

HMS *Aubretia* 1941
In Mountbatten Pink, which she is known to have worn while serving with EG2, and the illustration shows her with EG2's yellow/blue chequered funnel band.

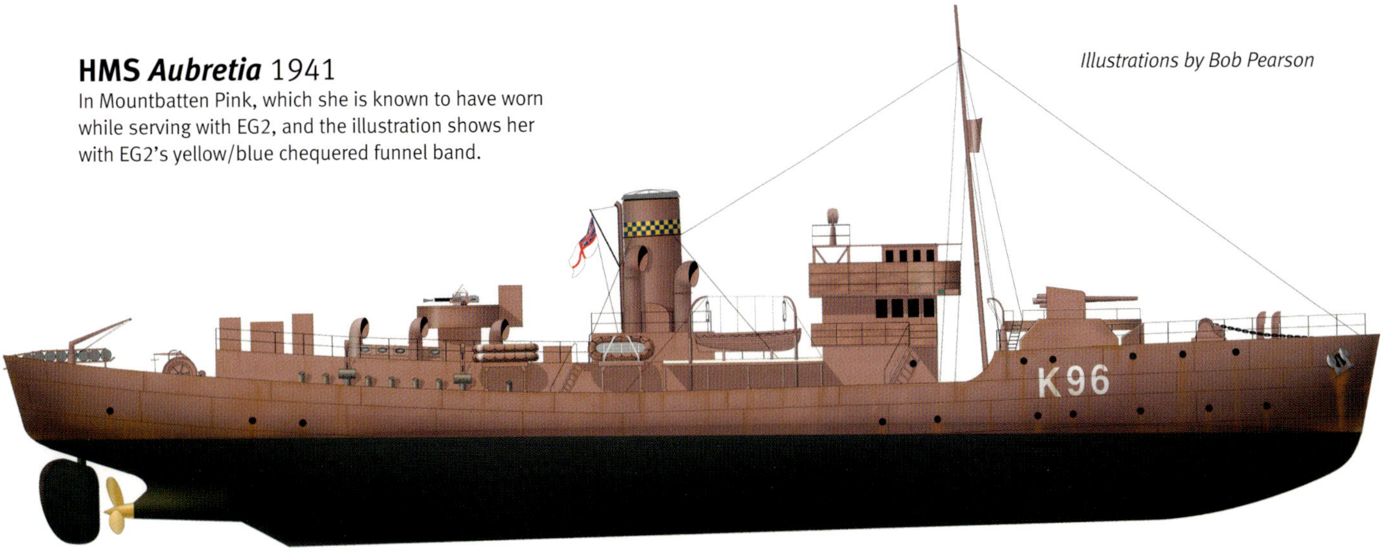

HMS *Burdock* 1941
An unofficial pattern of yellow and blue while serving in the South Atlantic in late 1941. HMS *Alisma* wore similar colours.

HMCS *Dauphin* 1941
Overall medium grey (AP507b) with light patches on bow, gunshield and bandstand. As built appearance of early RCN ships with mainmast sited where RN ships had the bandstand.

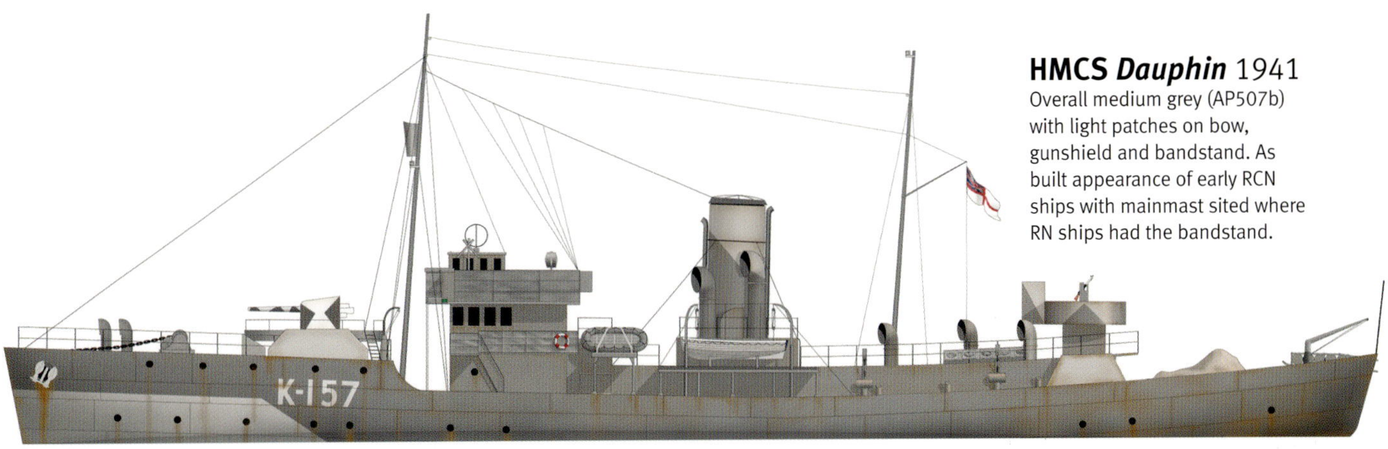

HMS *Pennywort* March 1942
Western Approaches (WA) white and B55.

Illustrations by Bob Pearson

HMS *Jonquil* April 1942
An Admiralty Disruptive pattern featuring MS4a, B5 and 507a.

HMS *Spirea* April 1942
A non-WA scheme of MS1, MS4 and MS4a. She has an extended forecastle and radar but retains the original mast position and bridge.

USS *Saucy* May 1942
Wearing Ms16 camouflage, which consists of white and Thayer blue.

USS *Tenacity* June 1942
Shown in Ms12 consisting of 5-N Navy Blue, 5-O Ocean Gray and 5-H Haze Gray.

Illustrations by Bob Pearson

HMCS *Arrowhead* June 1942

WA three-tone scheme. One of ten ordered in Canada for the RN, but turned over to the RCN, they retained 'Flower' names and were generally better equipped than other locally-built RCN units, although she lacks Hedgehog. The gunshield emblem is an Indian head over crossed arrows.

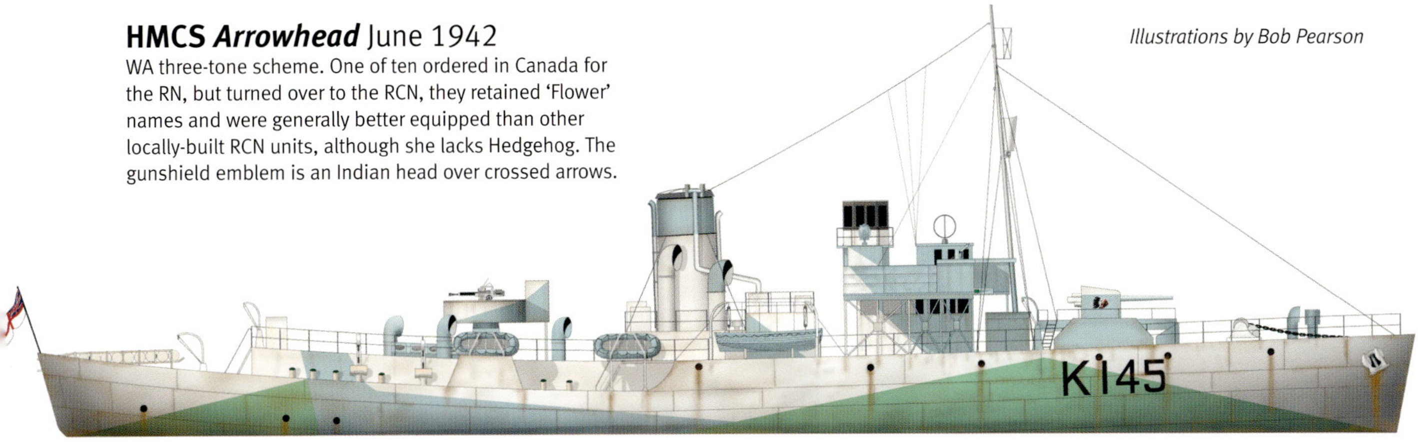

HMCS *Kamsack* c1942

Western Approaches white, WA blue and WA green.

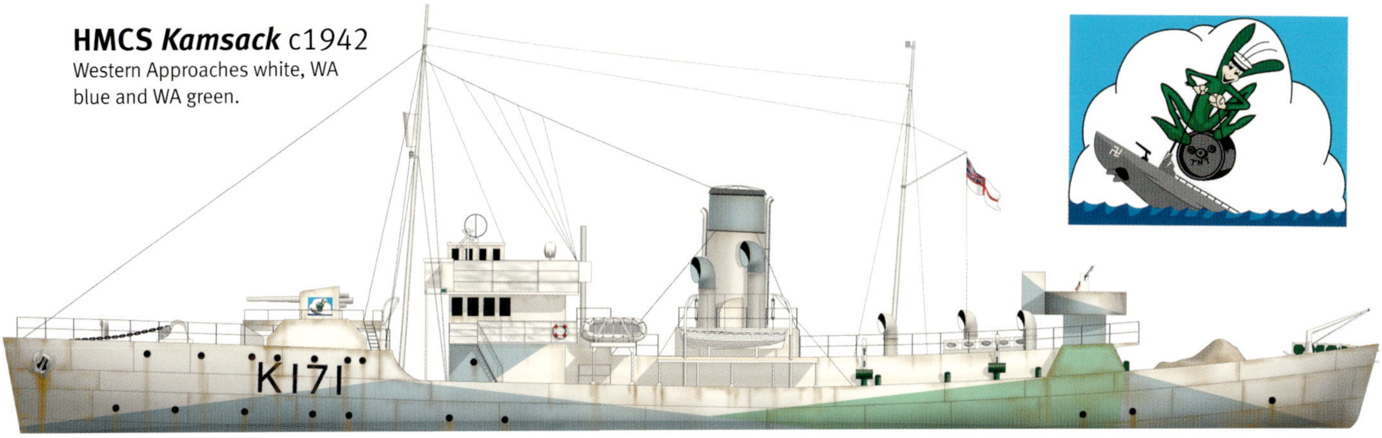

HMCS *Kamloops* 1942

Actual colours unknown, hence pattern shown in grey.

HMCS *Midland* 1942

Overall light grey (AP507c) with dark grey (AP507a) patterns.

Illustrations by Bob Pearson

HMS *Abelia* 1942
Western Approaches (WA) scheme in three pastel shades, off-white, light blue and light green. The ship is fitted for minesweeping and has one of the first Type 271 radar lanterns above the bridge.

HMCS *Shawnigan* 1942
Another WA pattern; the enlarged detail is the gunshield emblem.

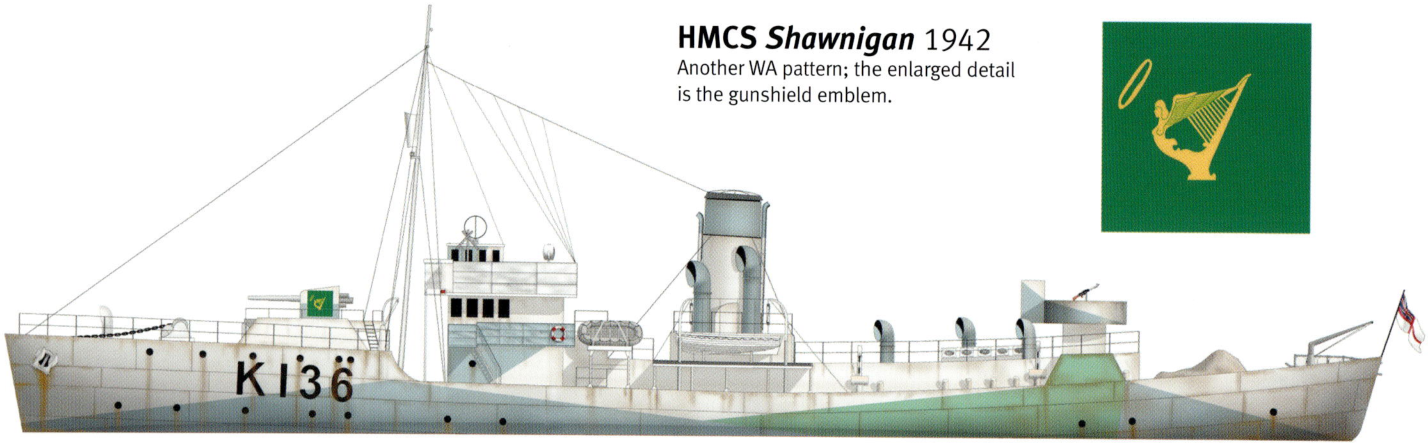

HMS *Bluebell* 1942
A two-tone WA scheme (she belongs to the 37th Escort Group as denoted by the number on the funnel). Note extended forecastle, new bridge with Hedgehog forward of it and mast re-sited abaft to improve visibility; there are two twin Lewis guns aft on the engine room casing.

HMS *Borage* 1942
Three-tone Western Approaches (WA) scheme. Fitted for 'LL' magnetic minesweeping, the ship also has an 'acoustic hammer' over the bow designed to make enough noise to set off acoustic mines ahead of the ship.

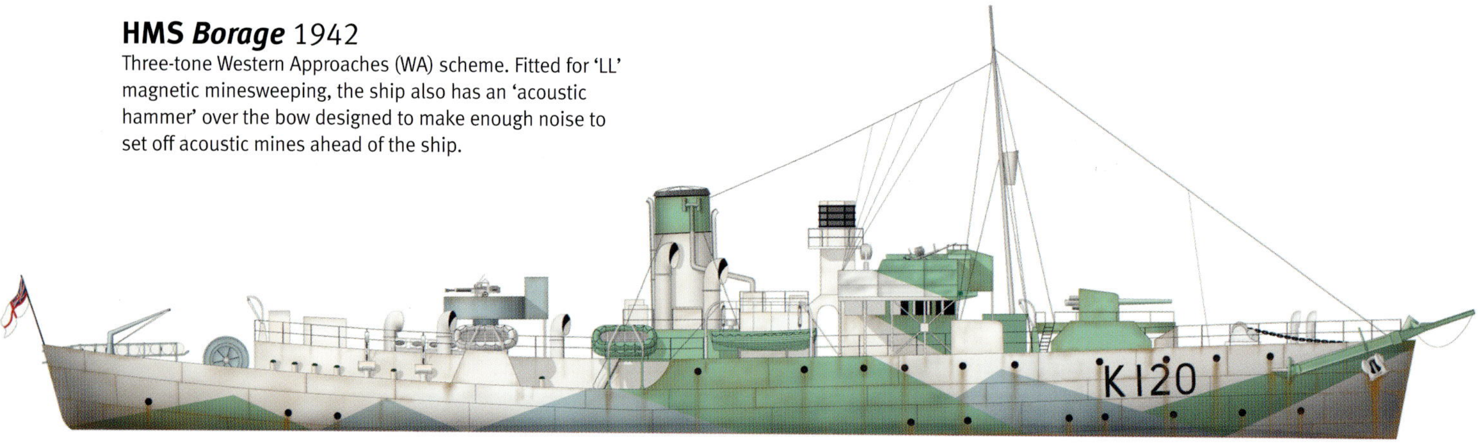

Illustrations by Bob Pearson

HMS *Honeysuckle* 1942
In non-standard colours of dark blue grey, medium blue grey, light blue, light green and white. Pendant number style and location is speculative.

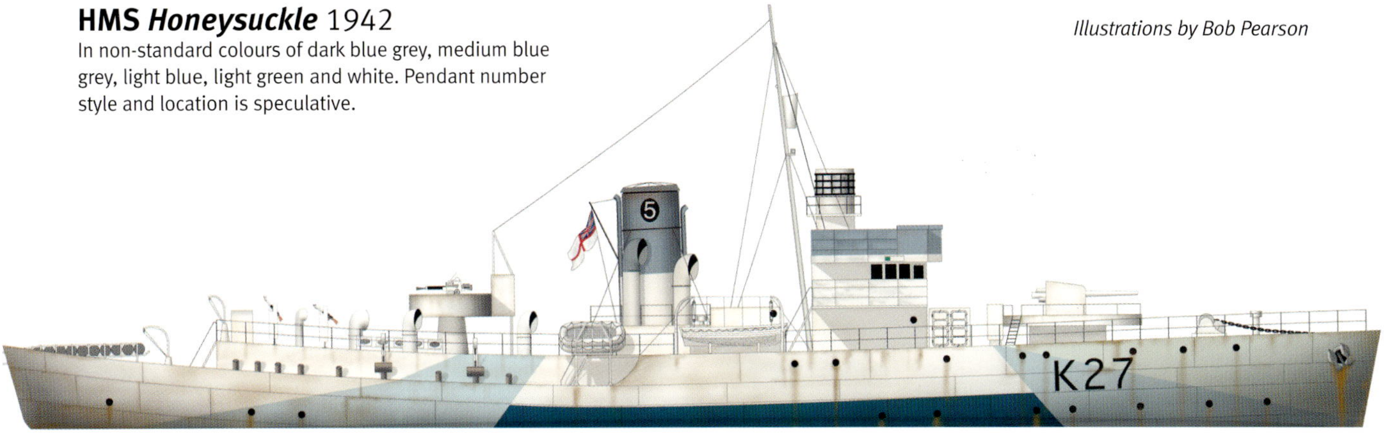

HMS *Poppy* July 1942
Wearing 507a and 507c.

HMS Campanula December 1942
In white, WA blue and black.

HMS *Clematis* early 1943
Shows the next major change in colours, in which the pastel WA blue and green were dropped in favour of B55. The ship has a quad 0.5in mount aft where the single 2pdr was usually sited.

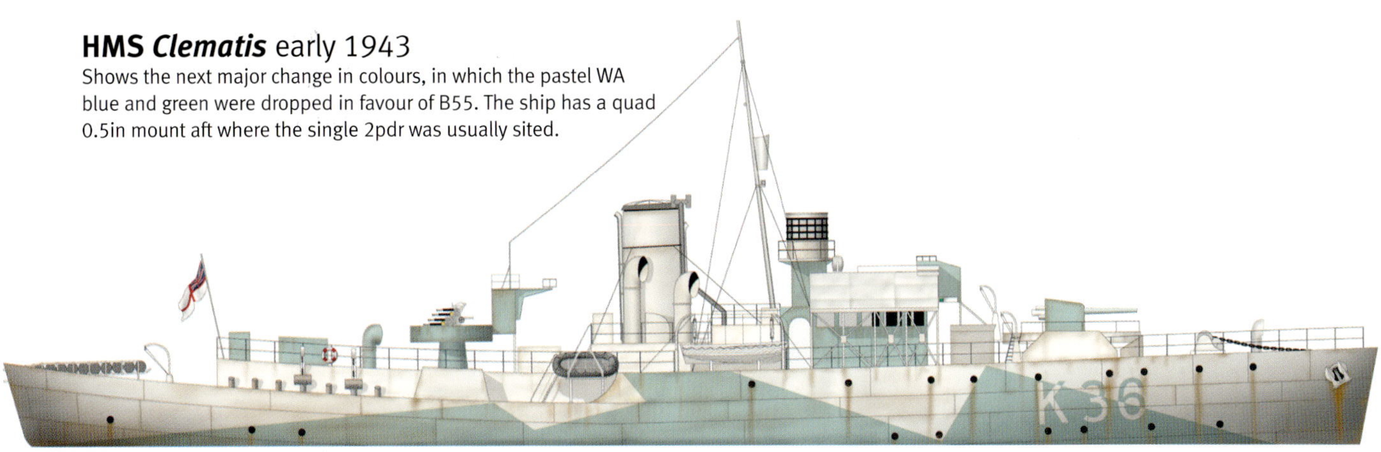

Illustrations by Bob Pearson

HMS *Gloxinia* February 1943

Used as a minesweeper in the Mediterranean, the ship is painted in two greys (probably AP505a and AP507c) with a false bow wave. The Mediterranean 'Flowers' had increased, and non-standard, AA weaponry (in this case a 4in HA on the bandstand), but missed out on many of the modifications applied to UK-based ships.

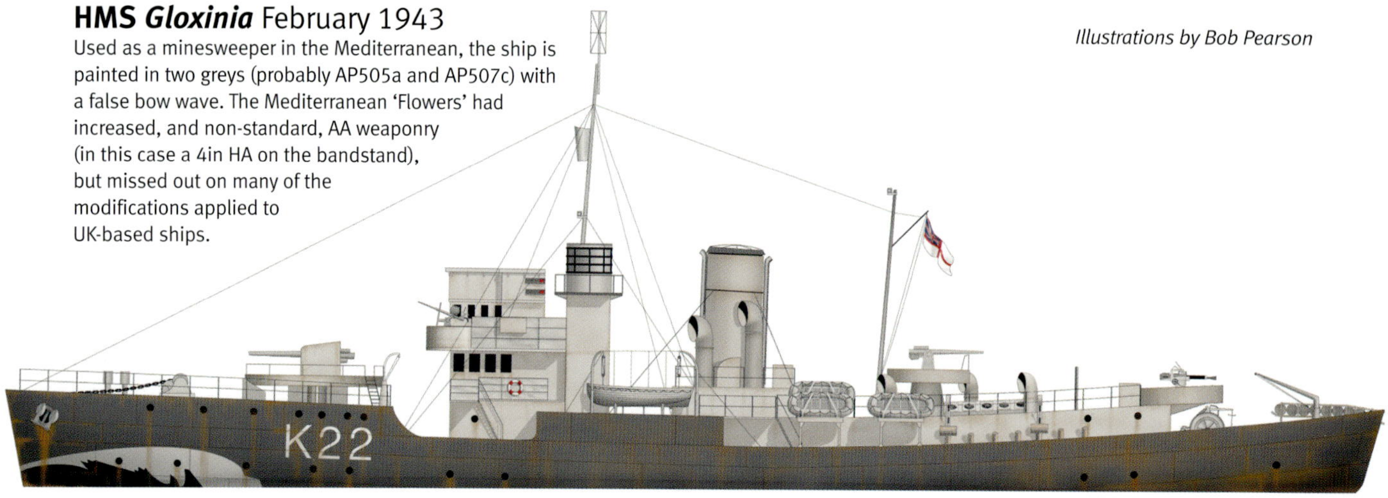

HMCS *Chicoutimi* 1943

Seen in three colours which are speculatively shown as 507a, 507b and 507c.

HMCS *Snowberry* May 1943

Another of the RN-ordered Canadian-built 'Flowers' in a three-tone WA pattern, but with modified bridge; the enlarged detail is the gunshield emblem.

USS *Intensity* September 1943

In Ms14 which was an overall Ocean Gray.

Illustrations by Bob Pearson

HMCS *Arvida* March 1944

A standard mid-war scheme of white and B55. On many RCN corvettes the gunshield art migrated to the front of the asdic house if rocket launchers were installed on the side of the gunshield.

HMCS *Cobourg* May 1944

In white and B55.

HMCS *Buctouche* 1944

White and B55. Her gunshield should really have a white cloud - it is shown as grey for contrast to the white page.

HMCS *Shediac* May 1944

Retaining the short forecastle at this late date, the ship was one of a small number of 'Flowers' fitted for ocean towage if required.

Illustrations by Bob Pearson

HMCS *Drumheller* 1944-5
White with either a grey or B55 midships panel.

HMCS *Chicoutimi* 1945
White and grey (or B55).

HMCS *West York* May 1945
White with a B55 panel.

HMS *Bluebell* 1945
In 507a, B5 and MS4a.

CORVETTE BUILDING LIST

P. No.	Name	Builder	Laid Down	Launched	Completed	Fate
Ordered 25/07/1939						
M 48	**ANEMONE**	Blyth Dry Dock	26/10/1939	22/04/1940	12/08/1940	Scrapped Norway 1964
M 86	**ARBUTUS**	Blyth Dry Dock	30/11/1939	5/06/1940	12/10/1940	Sunk by *U-136*. North Atlantic 5/02/1942
M 36	**ASPHODEL**	G Brown (Greenock)	20/10/1939	25/ 05/1940	11/09/1940	Sunk by *U-575* off Cape Finisterre 9/03/1944
M 96	**AUBRIETIA**	G Brown (Greenock)	27/10/1939	5/09/1940	23/12/1940	Scrapped Norway 1966
M 12	**AURICULA**	G Brown (Greenock)	25/11/1939	14/11/1940	5/03/1941	Mined Kourier Bay 5/05/1942 and sank
M 25	**AZALEA**	Cook Welton & Gemmell	15/11/1939	8/07/1940	27/01/1943	Mercantile. Lost 1955
M 66	**BEGONIA**	Cook, Welton & Gemmell	13/03/1940	18/09/1940	3/03/1941	USN *Impulse* 1942. Wrecked 1970
M 80	**BLUEBELL**	Fleming & Ferguson	25/10/1939	24/04/1940	19/07/1940	Sunk by *U-711* off Kola Inlet 17/02/1945
M 18	**CAMPANULA**	Fleming & Ferguson	26/10/1939	23/05/1940	6/09/1940	Scrapped 1947
M 09	**CANDYTUFT**	Grangemouth Dockyard	31/10/1939	8/ 07/1940	16/10/1940	USN *Tenacity*. Sold 1947
M 00	**CARNATION**	Grangemouth Dockyard	26/02/1940	3/09/1940	22/02/1941	RNethN *Frisio*. 1943-4/5. Scrapped 1966
M 75	**CELANDINE**	Grangemouth Dockyard	30/04/1940	28/12/1940	30/04/1941	Sold for scrapping 1948
M 36	**CLEMATIS**	Hill (Bristol)	11/10/1939	22/04/1940	27/07/1940	Sold for scrapping 1949
M 94	**COLUMBINE**	Hill (Bristol)	2/11/1939	13/08/1940	9/11/1940	Mercantile 1949. Scrapped 1966
M 45	**CONVOLVULUS**	Hill (Bristol)	17/01/1940	22/09/1940	26/02/1941	Scrapped 1947
M 32	**COREOPSIS**	Inglis (Pointhouse)	19/09/1939	23/05/1940	17/08/1940	RHS *Kreizis* 1943-52. Scrapped 1958
M 49	**CROCUS**	Inglis (Pointhouse)	26/10/1939	26/06/1940	20/10/1940	Mercantile 1946. Scrapped 1952
M 82	**CYCLAMEN**	Lewis (Aberdeen)	30/11/1939	20/06/1940	30/09/1940	Mercantile 1948. Scrapped 1966
M 07	**DAFFODIL**	Lewis (Aberdeen)	8/12/1939	3/09/1940	6/01/ 1941	*Dianella* 1940. Scrapped 1947
M 59	**DAHLIA**	Lewis (Aberdeen)	28/02/1940	31/10/1940	21/03/1941	Sold 1948 for scrapping
M 77	**DELPHINIUM**	Robb (Leith)	31/10/1939	6/06/1940	15/11/1940	Sold 1949 for scrapping
M 95	**DIANTHUS**	Robb (Leith)	31/10/1939	9/07//1940	17/03/1941	Mercantile 1949. Scrapped 1970
M 99	**GARDENIA**	Simons (Renfrew)	20/09/1939	10/04/1940	24/05/1940	Lost after collision with trawler off Oran 9/11/1942
M 16	**GERANIUM**	Simons (Renfrew)	21/09/1939	10/04/1940	24/06/1940	RDN *Thetis* 1945. Scrapped 1963
M 34	**GLADIOLUS**	Smith's Dock (Middlesboro)	19/10/1939	24/04/1940	24/06/1940	Torpedoed by *U-558* Western Approaches 16/10/1941
M 72	**GODETIA** (i)	Smith's Dock (Middlesboro)	4/01/1940	8/05/1940	15/07/1940	Lost by collision off Northern Ireland 6/09/1940
	LA BASTIAISE	Smith's Dock (Middlesboro)	18/01/1940	8/05/1940	22/06/1940	French Navy. Lost running trials off Hartlepool 22/06/1940
K 122	**LA DIEPPOISE**	Smith's Dock (Middlesboro)	30/01/1940	21/06/1940	26/08/1940	(Fr) RN *Fleur de Lys*. Sunk by *U-206* off Gibralar 14/10/1941
K 46	**LA MALOUINE**	Smith's Dock (Middlesboro)	13/11/1939	21/03/1940	29/07/1940	(Fr) RN 1940. Scrapped 1947
K 107	**LA PAIMPOLAISE**	Smith's Dock (Middlesboro)	23/03/1940	4/07/1940	26/09/1940	(Fr) RN *Nasturtium* 1940. Mercantile 1948. Scrapped
Ordered 31/08/1939						
K 03	**HELIOTROPE**	Crown (Sunderland)	23/10/1939	5/06/1940	12/09/1940	USN *Surprise* (1942/45). Chinese Navy 1950. Scrapped
K 64	**HOLLYHOCK**	Crown (Sunderland)	27/11/1939	19/08/1940	19/11/1940	Bombed IJN aircraft east of Ceylon 9/04/1942
K 27	**HONEYSUCKLE**	Ferguson (Port Glasgow)	26/10/1939	22/04/1940	14/09/1940	Scrapped 1950
K 39	**HYDRANGEA**	Ferguson (Port Glasgow)	22/10/1939	4/09/1940	3/01/1941	Mercantile 1948. Wrecked Formosa Strait 1957
K 23	**JASMINE**	Ferguson (Port Glasgow)	23/12/1939	14/01/1940	16/05/1941	Sold French Purchasing Commission 1948
K 69	**JONQUIL**	Fleming & Ferguson	27/12/1939	9/07/1940	21/10/1940	Mercantile. Lost in collision South Atlantic 1955
K 82	**LARKSPUR**	Fleming & Ferguson	26/03/1940	5/09/1940	4/01/1941	USN *Fury* (1942/45.) Mercantile 1946, Scrapped 1953
K 60	**LAVENDER**	A Hall (Aberdeen)	30/04/1941	27/11/1940	16/05/1941	Mercantile 1948, Scrapped 1964
K 05	**LOBELIA**	A Hall (Aberdeen)	27/06/1940	15/02/1941	16/07/1941	French Navy 1941/47. Mercantile. Scrapped 1970
K 54	**MARGUERITE**	Hall Russell (Aberdeen)	30/12/1939	8/07/1940	20/11/1940	Mercantile *Weather Observer* (1947). Scrapped 1961

Continued...

P. No.	Name	Builder	Laid Down	Launched	Completed	Fate
K 87	MARIGOLD	Hall Russell (Aberdeen)	26/01/1940	4/09/1940	28/02/1941	Torpedoed Italian aircraft off Algiers 9/12/1942
K 38	MIGNONETTE	Hall Russell (Aberdeen)	15/07/1940	28/01/1941	7/05/1941	Mercantile 1946. Wrecked off Lemnos 1948
K 11	MIMOSA	Hill (Bristol)	22/04/1940	18/01/1941	11/05/1941	French Navy 1941. Torpedoed *U-124* North Atlantic 9/06/1942
K 65	MYOSOTIS	Lewis (Aberdeen)	21/06/1940	28/01/1941	30/05/1941	Mercantile 1946. Scrapped 1969
K 74	NARCISSUS	Lewis (Aberdeen)	9/09/1940	29/03/1941	17/07/1941	Mercantile 1946. Wrecked near Ilheus 27/06/1969
K 19	NIGELLA	Philip (Dartmouth)	28/11/1939	21/09/1940	25/02/1941	Mercantile 1947. Wrecked Min River 1955
K 61	PENSTEMON	Philip (Dartmouth)	28/11/1939	18/01/1941	31/07/1941	Mercantile 1947. Wrecked Plettenberg Bay 1967
K 79	PETUNIA	Robb (Leith)	4/12/1939	19/09/1940	13/01/1941	Chinese Navy *Fu Po* (1946) Lost in collision 1947
K 47	POLYANTHUS	Robb (Leith)	19/03/1940	30/11/1940	23/04/1941	Torpedoed *U-957* south of Iceland 21/09/1943
K 91	PRIMROSE	Simons (Renfrew)	22/09/1939	8/05/1940	15/07/1940	Mercantile 1949 Scrapped 1966
K 14	PRIMULA	Simons (Renfrew)	23/09/1939	22/06/1940	27/08/1940	Mercantile 1946. Scrapped 1953
K 97	SALVIA	Simons (Renfrew)	26/09/1939	6/08/1940	20/09/1940	Torpedoed *U-568* west of Alexandria 24/12/1941
K 10	SNAPDRAGON (i)	Simons (Renfrew)	27/09/1939	3/09/1940	28/10/1940	Bombed German aircraft Central Mediterranean 19/12/1942
K 41	SUNFLOWER	Smith's Dock (Middlesboro)	24/05/1940	19/08/1940	25/01/1941	Scrapped 1947
K 67	SNOWBROP	Smith's Dock (Middlesboro)	4/02/1941	12/05/1941	30/07/1941	Ex French order. Mercantile conversion 1949 and scrapped
K 29	TULIP	Smith's Dock (Middlesboro)	30/05/1940	4/09/1940	18/11/1940	Ex French order. Mercantile 1950. Scrapped 1965
K 85	VERBENA	Smith's Dock (Middlesboro)	9/06/1940	1/10/1940	19/12/1940	Ex French order. Mercantile conversion but scrapped 1951
K 37	VERONICA	Smith's Dock (Middlesboro)	9/07/1940	17/10/1940	18/12/1941	Ex French order. USN *Temptress* (1942/45) Mercantile. Scrapped 1951
K 44	WALLFLOWER	Smith's Dock (Middlesboro)	23/07/1940	14/11/1940	7/03/1941	Ex French order. Mercantile 1949. Scrapped 1966
K 98	ZINNIA	Smith's Dock (Middlesboro)	20/08/1940	28/11/1940	30/03/1941	Ex French order. Torpedoed *U-564* west of Portugal 23/08/1941
Ordered 19/09/1939						
K 73	ARABIS (i)	Harland & Wolff (Belfast)	30/10/1939	14/02/1940	5/04/1940	USN *Saucy* 1942. RN *Snapdragon* (ii) 1945. Mercantile scrapped 1964
K 28	CALENDULA	Harland & Wolff (Belfast)	30/10/1939	21/03/1940	6/05/1940	USN *Ready* (1942/45). Mercantile then sold
K 31	CAMELLIA	Harland & Wolff (Belfast)	14/11/1939	4/05/1940	18/06/1940	Mercantile 1948. Scrapped 1965
K 88	CLARKIA	Harland & Wolff (Belfast)	30/10/1939	7/03/1940	22/04/1940	Scrapped 1947
K 50	ERICA	Harland & Wolff (Belfast)	22/02/1940	18/06/1940	9/08/1940	Mined off Benghazi 9/02/1943
K 43	FREESIA	Harland & Wolff (Belfast)	18/06/1940	3/10/1940	19/11/1940	Mercantile 1946. Wrecked under tow 1947
K 90	GENTIAN	Harland & Wolff (Belfast)	20/04/1940	6/08/1940	20/09/1940	Sold 1947 and scrapped
K 22	GLOXINIA	Harland & Wolff (Belfast)	21/03/1940	2/07/1940	22/08/1940	Sold 1947 and scrapped
K 69	HEATHER	Harland & Wolff (Belfast)	22/05/1940	17/09/1940	1/11/1940	Sold 1947 and scrapped
K 24	HIBISCUS	Harland & Wolff (Belfast)	14/11/1939	6/04/1940	21/05/1940	USN *Spry* (1942/45). Mercantile 1948. Scrapped 1955
K 84	HYACINTH	Harland & Wolff (Belfast)	20/04/1940	19/08/1940	3/10/1940	RHN *Apostolis* 1943. Scrapped 1961
K 33	KINGCUP	Harland & Wolff (Belfast)	19/07/1940	31/10/1940	30/12/1940	Mercantile 1946. Scrapped 1959
K 81	MALLOW	Harland & Wolff (Belfast)	14/11/1939	22/05/1940	2/07/1940	RYN *Nada* (1944). Sold 1950
K 76	ORCHIS	Harland & Wolff (Belfast)	18/06/1940	15/10/1940	29/11/1940	Mined off Normandy beaches 21/08/1944.
K 15	PANSY	Harland & Wolff (Belfast)	14/11/1939	20/04/1940	4/06/1940	*Heartsease* (1940), USN *Courage* (1942/45). Sold 1951 and lost 1959
K 40	PEONY	Harland & Wolff (Belfast)	24/02/1940	4/06/1940	2/08/1940	RHN *Sakhtouris* (1943). Scrapped 1952
K 55	PERIWINKLE	Harland & Wolff (Belfast)	30/10/1939	24/02/1940	8/04/1940	USN *Restless* (1942/45). Mercantile 1947. Scrapped 1953

P. No.	Name	Builder	Laid Down	Launched	Completed	Fate
K 63	**PICOTEE**	Harland & Wolff (Belfast)	21/93/1940	19/07/1940	5/09/1940	Torpedoed *U-568* south of Iceland 12/08/1941
K 71	**PIMPERNEL**	Harland & Wolff (Belfast)	19/07/1940	16/11/1940	30/12/1940	Sold 1948 and scrapped
K 78	**RHODODENDRON**	Harland & Wolff (Belfast)	22/05/1940	2/09/1940	18/10/1940	Mercantile 1950. Scrapped 1968
Ordered 21/09/1939						
K 01	**ACANTHUS**	Ailsa (Troon)	21/12/1939	26/05/1941	1/10/1941	RN *Andenes* (1941/46). Mercantile 1946. Scrapped 1971
K 58	**ACONITE**	Ailsa (Troon)	25/03/1940	31/03/1941	23/07/1941	French Navy *Aconit* (1941/47). Mercantile 1947. Scrapped 1967
K 17	**AMARANTHUS**	Fleming & Ferguson	4/05/1940	17/10/1940	12/02/1941	Mercantile 1946. Scrapped 195
K 51	**ROCKROSE**	Hill (Bristol)	28/12/1940	26/07/1941	4/11/1941	SAN *Protea* 1947. Mercantile 1965
K 04	**SAXIFRAGE**	Hill (Bristol)	1/02/1941	24/10/1941	6/02/1942	Mercantile 1947 and sold
K 08	**SPIRAEA**	Inglis (Pointhouse)	31/05/1940	31/10/1940	22/02/1941	Mercantile 1948 and sold
K 20	**STARWORT**	Inglis (Pointhouse)	11/06/1940	12/02/1941	26/04/1941	Mercantile 1948. Scrapped 1967.
K 57	**SUNDEW**	Lewis (Aberdeen)	4/11/1940	28/05/1941	19/09/1941	French Navy *Roselys* (1942/47). Scrapped 1948
K 35	**VIOLET**	Simons (Renfrew)	21/03/1940	30/12/1940	3/02/1941	Mercantile 1947. Scrapped 1970
K 53	**WOODRUFF**	Simons (Renfrew)	29/04/1940	28/02/1941	7/04/1941	Mercantile 1948. Scrapped 1959
Ordered 12/12/1939						
K 100	**ALYSSUM**	G Brown (Greenock)	24/06/1940	3/03/1940	17/06/1941	French Navy *Alysse* (1941). Torpedoed *U-654* W Atlantic 8/02/1942
K 114	**BELLWORT**	G Brown (Greenock)	17/09/1940	11/08/1941	20/11/1941	INS *Cliona* (1946). Scrapped 1970
K 120	**BORAGE**	G Brown (Greenock)	27/11/1940	22/11/1941	29/04/1942	INS *Macha* (1946). Scrapped 1970
K 134	**CLOVER**	Fleming & Ferguson	29/07/1940	30/01/1941	13/05/1941	Mercantile 1947. Chinese Navy *Kai Feng* 1952. Sold
K 140	**COLTSFOOT**	A Hall (Aberdeen)	4/09/1940	12/05/1941	1/11/1941	Mercantile 1947. Wrecked near Syra 21/11/1954
K 183	**IRIS**	Hall Russell (Aberdeen)	19/09/1940	9/06/1941	16/09/1941	*Coriander* (1940). French Navy *Comandante Detroyat* (1941/47). Scrapped 1948
K 105	**LOOSESTRIFE**	Hall Russell (Aberdeen)	9/12/1940	25/08/1941	25/11/1941	Mercantile (1947). Scrapped 1962.
K 93	**LOTUS** (i)	Hill (Bristol)	26/05/1941	17/01/1942	23/05/1942	French Navy *Comandante d'Estienne d'Orves* (1942/47). Scrapped 1951
K 144	**MEADOWSWEET**	Hill (Bristol)	12/08/1941	28/03/1942	8/07/1942	Mercantile 1951. Scrapped 1965
K 123	**OXLIP**	Inglis (Pointhouse)	9/12/1940	28/08/1941	28/12/1941	INS *Maev* (1946) Scrapped 1972
Ordered 15/12/1939						
K 126	**BURDOCK**	Crown (Sunderland)	13/06/1940	14/12/1940	27/03/1941	Sold 1947 for scrapping
K 108	**CAMPION**	Crown (Sunderland)	16/09/1940	20/06/1941	7/07/1941	Sold 1947 for scrapping
K 111	**PENNYWORT**	Inglis (Pointhouse)	11/03/1941	18/10/1941	5/03/1942	Sold 1948 for scrapping
K 130	**PHLOX**	Robb (Leith)	26/03/1941	16/01/1942	9/05/1942	*Lotus* (ii) (1942). Mercantile 1947. Wrecked 1966
K 137	**PINK**	Robb (Leith)	20/05/1941	16/02/1942	2/07/1942	Torpedoed *U-988* off Normany beaches. Hulk scrapped 1947
K 117	**RANUNCULUS**	Simons (Renfrew)	10/07/1940	25/06/1941	28/07/1941	French Navy *Renoncule* (1941/46). Mercantile 1947. Scrapped 1967
K 102	**ROSE**	Simons (Renfrew)	3/09/1940	22/09/1941	31/10/1941	RNN (1941/45). Lost in collision with frigate *Manners* 26/10/1944
K 128	**SAMPHIRE**	Smith's Dock (Middlesboro)	4/12/1940	14/04/1941	30/06/1941	Torpedoed Italian submarine *Platino* off Bougie 30/01/1943
K 142	**STONECROP**	Smith's Dock (Middlesboro)	4/02/1940	12/05/1941	30/07/1941	Mercantile 1947. Sold 1950
K 132	**VETCH**	Smith's Dock (Middlesboro)	15/03/1941	27/05/1941	11/08/1941	Mercantile 1948. Sold 1956
Ordered –/01/1940						
K 145	**ARROWHEAD**	Marine Industries (Canada)	11/04/1940	8/08/1940	15/05/1941	RCN (1941/45). Mercantile 1947. Scrapped 1959.
K 182	**BITTERSWEET**	Marine Industries (Canada)	17/04/1940	12/09/1940	15/05/1941	RCN (1941/45). Sold 1950 for scrapping).
K 150	**EYEBRIGHT**	Canadian Vickers (Montreal)	20/02/1940	22/07/1940	15/05/1941	RCN (1941/45). Mercantile 1950. Scrapped 1965.

Continued...

P. No.	Name	Builder	Laid Down	Launched	Completed	Fate
K 194	**FENNEL**	Marine Industries (Canada)	29/03/1940	20/08/1940	15/05/1941	RCN (1941/45)
K 159	**HEPATICA**	Davie Shipbuilding	24/02/1940	6/07/1940	15/05/1941	RCN (1941/45). Scrapped 1948
K 191	**MAYFLOWER**	Canadian Vickers (Montreal)	20/02/1940	3/07/1940	15/05/1941	RCN (1941/45). Scrapped 1948
K 166	**SNOWBERRY**	Davie Shipbuilding	24/02/1940	8/08/1940	15/05/1941	RCN (1941/45). Scrapped 1947
K 198	**SPIKENARD**	Davie Shipbuilding	24/02/1940	10/08/1940	15/05/1941	RCN (1941). Torpedoed *U-136* south of Iceland 11/02/1942.
K 172	**TRILLIUM**	Canadian Vickers (Montreal)	20/02/1940	26/06/1940	15/05/1941	RCN (1941/45). Mercantile 1950. Scrapped 1971
K 155	**WINDFLOWER**	Davie Shipbuilding	24/02/1940	4/07/1940	15/05/1941	RCN (1941). Lost in collision North Atlantic 7/12/1941
Ordered 1/02/1940						
K 129	**AGASSIZ**	Burrard Dry Dock	29/04/1940	15/08/1940	23/01/1941	RCN. Sold 1945 for scrapping
K 103	**ALBERNI**	Yarrow (Esquimalt)	19/04/1940	22/08/1940	4/02/1940	RCN. Torpedoed *U-480* off Isle of Wight 21/08/1944
K 127	**ALGOMA**	Port Arthur Shipbuilding	18/06/1940	17/12/1940	11/07/1941	RCN. Venezuelan Navy *Constitucion* (1946). Scrapped 1962
K 148	**AMHERST**	St John Shipbuilding	23/05/1940	4/01/1940	5/08/1941	RCN. Venezuelan Navy *Federacion* (1946). Scrapped 1956
K 113	**ARVIDA**	Morton (Quebec)	28/02/1940	21/09/1940	22/05/1941	RCN. Mercantile 1950 and sold
K 147	**BADDECK**	Davie Shipbuilding	14/08/1940	20/11/1940	18/05/1941	RCN. Mercantile 1946. Sold
K 175	**BANFF** (i)	Burrard Dry Dock	11/04/1940	18/07/1940	17/12/1940	RCN. *Wetaskiwin* (1941). Venezuelan Navy *Victoria* (1946)
K 138	**BARRIE**	Collingwood Shipyards	4/04/1940	23/11/1940	12/05/1941	RCN. Mercantile 1947. Argentinean Navy *Capitan Canepa* (1957)
K 165	**BATTLEFORD**	Collingwood Shipyards	30/09/1940	15/04/1941	31/07/1941	RCN, Venezuelan Navy *Libertad* (1946). Wrecked 12/04/1949
K 149	**BRANDON**	Davie Shipbuilding	10/10/1940	29/04/1941	22/07/1941	RCN. Sold and scrapped 1945
K 179	**BUCTOUCHE**	Davie Shipbuilding	14/08/1940	20/11/1940	5/06/1941	RCN. Sold and scrapped 1945
K 154	**CAMROSE**	Marine Industries	20/11/1940	5/05/1941	4/10/1941	RCN. Sold 6/47 and scrapped
K 171	**CARLETON**	Port Arthur Shipbuilding	20/11/40	5/5/1941	4.10.1941	RCN. *Kamsack* (1941). Venezuelan Navy *Carabobo* (1945). and wrecked on route 12/1945
K 116	**CHAMBLY**	Canadian Vickers (Montreal)	20/02/1940	29/07/1940	18/12/1940	RCN. Mercantile 1952. Scrapped 1966
K 156	**CHICOUTIMI**	Canadian Vickers (Montreal)	5/07/1940	16/10/1940	12/05/1941	RCN. Sold and scrapped 1946
K 131	**CHILLIWACK**	Burrard Dry Dock	3/07/1940	14/09/1940	8/04/1941	RCN. Sold and scrapped 1946
K 124	**COBALT**	Port Arthur Shipbuilding	1/04/1940	17/08/1940	25/11/1940	RCN. Mercantile 1953. Sold and scrapped 1961
K 180	**COLLINGWOOD**	Collingwood Shipyards	2/03/1940	27/07/1940	9/11/1940	RCN. Sold and scrapped 1950
K 157	**DAUPHIN**	Canadian Vickers (Montrial)	6/07/1940	24/10/1940	17/05/1941	RCN. Mercantile 1949. Sold for scrapping 1957
K 104	**DAWSON**	Victoria Machinery Depot	7/09/1940	8/02/1941	6/10/1941	RCN. Sold and scrapped 1946
K 167	**DRUMHELLER**	Collingwood Shipyards	4/12/1940	5/07/1941	13/09/1941	RCN. Sold and scrapped 1949
K 177	**DUNVEGAN**	Marine Industries	30/08/1940	11/12/1940	9/09/1941	RCN. Venezuelan Navy *Independencia* (1946). Scrapped 1953
K 106	**EDMUNDSON**	Yarrow (Esquimalt)	23/08/1940	22/02/1941	12/10/1941	RCN. Mercantile 1946. Scrapped 1961
K 163	**GALT**	Collingwood Shipyards	27/05/1940	28/12/1940	15/05/1941	RCN. Sold and scrapped 1946
K 176	**JASPER**	Victoria Machinery Depot	29/04/1940	7/08/1940	17/03/1941	RCN. *Kamloops* (1940). Scrapped 1945
K 125	**KENOGAMI**	Port Arthur Shipbuilding	20/04/1940	5/09/1940	29/06/1941	RCN. Sold 1950 for scrapping
K 160	**LETHBRIDGE**	Canadian Vickers (Montreal)	5/08/1940	21/11/1940	25/06/1941	RCN. Mercantile 1952. Scrapped 1966
K 115	**LEVIS**	G T Davie (Lauzon)	1/03/1940	4/09/1940	16/05/1941	RCN. Torpedoed *U-74* east of Cape Farewell 19/09/1941
K 134	**LOUISBURG** (i)	Morton (Quebec)	4/10/1940	27/05/1941	2/10/1941	RCN. Torpedoed Italian aircraft east of Oran 6/02/1943
K 151	**LUNENBURG**	G T Davie (Lauzon)	28/09/1940	10/07/1941	4/12/1941	RCN. Sold 1946 for scrapping
K 112	**MATAPEDIA**	Morton (Quebec)	2/02/1940	14/09/1940	9/05/1941	RCN. Sold 1950 for scrapping
K 139	**MONCTON**	St John Shipbuilding	17/12/1940	11/08/1940	24/04/1942	RCN. Mercantile 1953. Sold and scrapped 1966
K 164	**MOOSEJAW**	Collingwood Shipyard	12/08/1940	9/04/1941	19/06/1941	RCN. Sold 1949 and scrapped
K 170	**MORDEN**	Port Arthur Shipbuilding	25/10/1940	5/05/1941	6/09/1941	RCN. Sold 1950 and scrapped

P. No.	Name	Builder	Laid Down	Launched	Completed	Fate
K 101	**NANAIMO**	Yarrow (Esquimalt)	27/04/1940	28/20/1940	26/04/1941	RCN. Mercantile 1953. Scrapped 1966
K 118	**NAPANEE**	Kingston Shipbuilding	20/03/1940	31/08/1940	12/05/1941	RCN. Sold 1946 for scrapping
K 178	**OAKVILLE**	Port Arthur Shipbuilding	21/12/1940	21/06/1941	18/11/1941	RCN. Venezuelan Navy *Patria* 1946 and sold
K 119	**ORILLIA**	Collingwood Shipyards	4/03/1940	15/09/1940	25/11/1940	RCN. Sold 1951 for scrapping
K 146	**PICTOU**	Davie Shipbuilding	12/07/1940	5/10/1940	29/04/1941	RCN. Mercantile 1946 Scrapped 1963
K 161	**PRESTCOTT**	Kingston Shipbuilding	31/08/1940	7/01/1941	26/06/1941	RCN. Sold 1946 for scrapping
K 133	**QUESNEL**	Victoria Machinery Depot	9/05/1940	12/11/1940	23/05/1941	RCN. Sold 1945 for scrapping
K 121	**RIMOUSKI**	Davie Shipbuilding	12/07/1940	3/10/1940	26/04/1941	RCN. Sold 1950 for scrapping
K 169	**ROSTHERN**	Port Arthur Shipbuilding	18/06/1940	30/11/1940	17/06/1941	RCN. Sold 1946 for scrapping
K 181	**SACKVILLE**	St John Shipbuilding	28/05/1940	15/05/1941	30/12/1941	RCN. Surveying vessel 1953. Museum ship 1990
K 158	**SASKATOON**	Canadian Vickers (Montreal)	9/08/1940	6/11/1940	9/06/1941	RCN. Sold 1946 for scrapping.
K 136	**SHAWINIGAN**	G T Davie (Lauzon)	4/06/1940	16/05/1941	19/09/1941	RCN. Torpedoed *U-1228* Cabot Strait 24/11/1944
K 110	**SHEDIAC**	Davie Shipbuilding (Lauzon)	5/10/1940	29/04/1941	8/07/1941	RCN. Mercantile 1954. Sold for scrapping
K 152	**SHERBROOKE**	Marine Industries (Sorel)	5/08/1940	25/10/1940	5/06/1941	RCN. Sold 1947 for scrapping
K 153	**SOREL**	Marine Industries (Sorel)	24/08/1940	16/11/1940	19/08/1941	RCN. Sold 1945 for scrapping
K 162	**SUDBURY**	Kingston Shipbuilding	25/01/1941	31/05/1941	15/10/1941	RCN. Mercantile sold 1950
K 141	**SUMMERSIDE**	Morton (Quebec)	4/10/1940	17/05/1941	11/09/1941	RCN. Sold 1946 for scrapping
K 168	**THE PAS**	Collingwood Shipyards	7/01/1941	16/08/1941	21/10/1941	RCN. Sold 1945 and scrapped
K 174	**TRAIL**	Burrard Dry Dock	20/07/1940	17/10/1940	30/04/1941	RCN. Sold 1950 for scrapping
K 173	**WEYBURN**	Burrard Dry Dock	21/12/1940	26/07/1941	26/11/1941	RCN. Mined Strait s of Gibraltar 22/02/1943

Ordered 8/04/1940

P. No.	Name	Builder	Laid Down	Launched	Completed	Fate
K 184	Unnamed	Harland & Wolff (Belfast)	19/08/1940	28/11/1940	3/02/1941	French Navy. RN *Abelia* (1940). Mercantile 1948. Scrapped 1966
K 185	Unnamed	Harland & Wolff (Belfast)	19/08/1940	17/12/1940	13/02/1941	French Navy. RN *Alisma* (1940). Mercantile 1948. Lost 1954
K 186	Unnamed	Harland & Wolff (Belfast)	17/09/1940	15/01/1941	1/03/1941	French Navy. RN *Anchusa* (1940). Mercantile 1946. Scrapped 1960
K 187	Unnamed	Harland & Wolff (Belfast)	17/09/1940	16/01/1941	28/03/1941	French Navy. RN *Armeria* (1940). Mercantile 1948. Scrapped 1961
K 188	Unnamed	Harland & Wolff (Belfast)	15/10/1940	12/02/1941	9/04/1941	French Navy. RN *Aster* (1940). Scrapped 1946
K 189	Unnamed	Harland & Wolff (Belfast)	15/10/1940	15/02/1941	12/05/1941	French Navy. RN *Bergamot* (1940). Mercantile 1947. Sold 1955
K 190	**BROOM**	Harland & Wolff (Belfast)	16/11/1940	12/03/1941	9/06/1941	*Vervain* (1941). Torpedoed *U-1276* south of Ireland 20/02/1945
K 192	**BRYONY**	Harland & Wolff (Belfast)	16/11/1940	15/03/1941	16/06/1941	Mercantile 1947. Sold
K 193	**BUTTERCUP**	Harland & Wolff (Belfast)	17/12/1940	10/04/1941	24/04/1942	RNN *Nordkyn* (1942). Mercantile 1956. Scrapped 1970
K 195	**CHRYSANTHEMUM**	Harland & Wolff (Belfast)	17/12/1940	11/04/1941	26/01/1942	French Navy *Comandante Drogou* (1942/47). Mercantile 1947. Portuguese Navy *Carvalho Araujo* (1959). Sold
K 196	**COWSLIP**	Harland & Wolff (Belfast)	16/01/1941	28/05/1941	9/08/1941	Mercantile conversion abandoned 1948 and scrapped
K 197	**EGLANTINE**	Harland & Wolff (Belfast)	16/01/1941	11/06/1941	27/08/1941	RNN *Soroy* (1941). Mercantile 1956 and scrapped
K 199	**FRITILLARY**	Harland & Wolff (Belfast)	15/02/1941	22/07/1941	1/11/1941	Mercantile (1947). Scrapped 1955
K 200	**GENISTA**	Harland & Wolff (Belfast)	15/02/1941	24/07/1941	8/12/1941	Mercantile 1947. Scrapped 1961
K 201	**GLORIOSA**	Harland & Wolff (Belfast)	–	–	–	Cancelled 23/01/1941
K 202	**HAREBELL**	Harland & Wolff (Belfast)	–	–	–	Cancelled 23/01/1941
K 203	**HEMLOCK**	Harland & Wolff (Belfast)	–	–	–	Cancelled 23/01/1941
K 204	**IVY**	Harland & Wolff (Belfast)	–	–	–	Cancelled 23/01/1941
K 205	**LING**	Harland & Wolff (Belfast)	–	–	–	Cancelled 23/01/1941
K 206	**MARJORAM**	Harland & Wolff (Belfast)	–	–	–	Cancelled 23/01/1941

Continued...

P. No.	Name	Builder	Laid Down	Launched	Completed	Fate
Ordered 28/06/1940						
K 207	**MONKSHOOD**	Fleming & Ferguson	1/10/1940	17/04/1941	31/07/1941	Mercantile 1948. Scrapped 1965
K 208	**MONTBRETIA**	Fleming & Ferguson	16/10/1940	27/05/1941	29/09/1941	RNN (1941). torpedoed *U-624* North Atlantic 18/11/1942
Ordered 3/08/1940						
K 212	**NETTLE**	A Hall (Aberdeen)	24/12/1940	23/09/1941	23/02/1942	*Hyderabad* (1941). Sold 1948 for scrapping
K 214	**POPPY**	A Hall (Aberdeen)	6/03/1941	20/11/1941	12/05/1942	Mercantile 1946. Scrapped 195
K 214	**POTENTILLA**	Simon (Renfrew)	28/02/1941	18/12/1941	5/02/1942	RNN (1942/44). Sold 1946 for scrapping
K 209	**SWEETBRIAR**	Smith's Dock (Middlesboro)	4/04/1941	26/06/1941	8/09/1941	Mercantile 1949. Scrapped 1966
K 210	**THYME**	Smith's Dock (Middlesboro)	30/04/1941	25/07/1941	23/10/1941	Mercantile 1946 Sold 1958
K 211	**ZENOBIA**	Smith's Dock (Middlesboro)	19/05/1941	22/08/1941	2/11/1941	*Snowflake* (1941). Mercantile 1947. Scrapped 1962
Ordered 24/08/1940						
K 226	**DART**	Crown (Sunderland)	15/01/1941	24/09/1941	23/02/1942	*Godetia* (ii) (1941). Scrapped 1947
Ordered 24/10/1940						
K 216	**ETTRICK**	Fleming & Ferguson	10/02/1941	28/07/1941	26/12/1941	*Tamarisk* (ii) (1941), RHN *Tombazis* (1943/52). Scrapped 1963
Ordered 29/10/1940						
K 72	**CHELMER**	G Brown (Greenock)	16/04/1941	30/05/1942	28/11/1942	*Balsam* (1941). Sold 1947 for scrapping
Ordered 3/12/1940						
K 218	**BRANTFORD**	Midland Shipbuilding	24/02/1941	6/09/1941	15/05/1942	RCN. Mercantile 1950. Sold 1956
K 229	**DUNDAS**	Victoria Machinery	19/03/1941	25/07/1941	1/04/1942	RCN. Sold 1945 for scrapping
K 240	**KITCHENER** (i)	Yarrow (Esquimalt)	16/06/1941	26/08/1941	20/03/1942	RCN. *Vancouver* (ii) (1941). Sold 1945 for scrapping
K 220	**MIDLAND**	Midland Shipbuilding	24/02/1941	25/06/1941	17/11/1941	RCN. Sold 1945 for mercantile conversion
K 228	**NEW WESTMINSTER**	Victoria Machinery Depot	4/02/1941	14/05/1041	31/01/1942	RCN. Mercantile 1950. Sold 1954
K 223	**TIMMINS**	Yarrow (Esquimalt)	14/12/1940	26/06/1941	10/02/1942	RCN. Mercantile 1949. Sold
Ordered –/03/1941						
K 231	**CALGARY**	Marine Industries	22/03/1941	23/08/1941	16/12/1941	RCN. Sold 1946 for scrapping
K 244	**CHARLOTTETOWN**	Kingston Shipbuilding	7/06/1941	10/09/1941	13/12/1941	RCN. Torpedoed *U-517* Gulf of St Lawrence 11/09/1942
K 273	**FORT WILLIAM**	Marine Industries (Sorel)	22/03/1941	25/10/1941	28/04/1942	RCN. *Le Malbaie* (1941). Sold and scrapped 1946
K 233	**FREDERICTON** (i)	Port Arthur Shipbuilding	28/04/1941	18/09/1941	26/05/1942	RCN. *Port Arthur* (1941). Sold for scrapping 1945
K 245	**FREDERICTON** (ii)	Marine Industries (Sorel)	22/03/1941	2/09/1941	8/12/1941	RCN. Mercantile 1946 Scrapped 1962
K 237	**HALIFAX**	Halifax Shipyards	26/04/1941	4/10/1941	26/11/1941	RCN. Mercantile 1945. and sold
K 242	**QUEBEC**	Morton (Quebec)	7/06/1941	12/11/1941	24/05/1942	RCN. *Ville de Quebec* (1942). Mercantile 1946
K 234	**REGINA**	Marine Industries (Sorel)	22/03/1941	14/10/1941	22/01/1942	RCN. Torpedoed *U-667* English Channel 8/08/1944
K 225	**VANCOUVER** (i)	Marine Industries (Sorel)	28/02/1941	18/11/1941	28/06/1942	RCN. *Kitchener* (ii). Sold 1949 for scrapping
K 238	**WOODSTOCK**	Collingwood Shipyards	23/05/1941	10/12/1941	1/05/1942	RCN. Mercantile 1951 and sold
Ordered 6/10/1941						
K 277	**COMFREY**	Collingwood Shipyards	6/01/1942	28/07/1942	21/11/1942	USN *Action* (1942). Mercantile 1947, wrecked 6/04/1972
K 279	**DITTANY**	Collingwood Shipyards	--/ –/1942	31/10/1942	31/05/1943	USN *Beacon*, cancelled. Mercantile, 1950, scrapped 1966

P. No.	Name	Builder	Laid Down	Launched	Completed	Fate
K 284	**FLAX**	Kingston Shipbuilding	28/02/1942	15/06/1942	8/12/1942	USN *Brisk* (1942). Mercantile 1947, sold 1964
K 285	**HONESTY**	Kingston Shipbuilding	–/–/1942	28/09/1942	18/05/1943	USN *Caprice*, cancelled. Mercantile conversion 1948
K 282	**LINARIA**	Midland Shipbuilding	–/–/1942	18/11/1942	22/06/1943	USN *Clash*, cancelled. Mercantile 1948 and sold
K 287	**MANDRAKE**	Morton (Quebec)	–/11/1941	22/08/1942	6/04/1943	USN *Haste* (1942). Mercantile 1949, scrapped 1971
K 288	**MILFOIL**	Morton (Quebec)	–/11/1941	22/08/1942	31/03/1943	USN *Intensity* (1942). Mercantile 1950. Scrapped 1966
K 289	**MUSK**	Morton (Quebec)	23/11/1941	22/08/1942	22/12/1942	USN *Might* (1942). Mercantile 1950 and sold
K 290	**NEPETA**	Morton (Quebec)	23/07/1942	29/11/1942	20/07/1943	USN *Pert* (1942). Mercantile 1950 and sold
K 291	**PRIVET**	Morton (Quebec)	14/08/1942	4/12/1942	16/08/1943	USN *Prudent* (1942). Italian Navy *Elbano* 1949. Stricken 1970
Ordered 24/10/1941						
K.....	**AMARYLLIS**	Fleming & Ferguson	–	–	–	Re-ordered 9/12/1943 as *Allington Castle*
Ordered 6/12/1941						
K 286	**ROSEBAY**	Kingston Shipbuilding	1/10/1942	11/02/1943	28/07/1943	USN *Splendor*, cancelled. Mercantile 1947, scrapped 1954
K 280	**SMILAX**	Collingwood Shipyards	–/–/1942	24/12/1942	21/06/1943	USN *Tact*, cancelled. Argentinian Navy *Republica* 1949. Scrapped 1968
K 281	**STATICE**	Collingwood Shipyards	–/–/1942	10/04/1943	20/09/1943	USN *Vim*, cancelled. Mercantile conversion cancelled 1951. Scrapped 1961
K 285	**WILLOWHERB**	Midland Shipbuilding	–/–/1942	24/03/1943	–/–/1943	USN *Vitality*, cancelled. Fate as *Statice* above
Ordered 8/12/1941						
K 274	**BETONY**	A Hall (Aberdeen)	26/09/1942	22/04/1943	31/08/1943	RIN *Sind* (ii) (1945). RThN *Prase* (1947). Wrecked 1951
Ordered –/2/1942						
K 15	**ATHOLL**	Morton (Quebec)	15/08/1942	4/04/1943	14/10/1943	RCN. Sold 1952 and scrapped
K 686	**FORT FRANCIS**	Collingwood Shipyards	10/12/1943	30/08/1944	18/11/1944	RCN. *Ferus* (1943). Mercantile 1945. Wrecked 1949
K 338	**LINDSAY**	Midland Shipbuilding	30/09/1942	4/06/1943	15/11/1943	RCN. Mercantile 1946, and sold
K 401	**LOUISBURG** (ii)	Morton (Quebec)	11/01/1943	13/07/1943	13/12/1943	RCN. Dominican Navy *Juan Alejandro Acosta* 1947. Discarded 1978
K 520	**NORSYD**	Morton (Quebec)	14/01/1943	31/07/1943	22/12/1943	RCN. Mercantile 1945. Israeli Navy *Haganah* 1950. Scrapped 1956
K 339	**NORTH BAY**	Collingwood Shipyards	24/09/1942	27/04/1943	25/10/1943	RCN. Mercantile 1946 and scrapped
K 340	**OWEN SOUND**	Collingwood Shipyards	11/11/1942	15/06/1943	17/11/1943	RCN. Mercantile 1946 and sold
K 537	**RIVIERE DU LOUP**	Morton (Quebec)	5/01/1943	2/07/1943	21/11/1943	RCN. Dominican Navy *Juan Bautista Maggiolo* 1947. Discarded 1972
Ordered 26/02/1942						
K 275	**BUDDLEIA**	A Hall (Aberdeen)	30/11/1942	19/06/1943	10/11/1943	RCN *Giffard* (ii) (K 402 – 1943). Scrapped 1952
Ordered –/04/1942						
K 333	**COBOURG**	Midlands Shipbuilding	25/11/1042	14/07/1943	11/05/1944	RCN. Mercantile 1945. Lost by fire 1971
K 335	**FRONTENAC**	Kingston Shipbuilding	19/02/1943	2/06/1943	26/10/1943	RCN Sold 1945
K 415	**HAWKESBURY**	Morton (Quebec)	20/07/1943	16/11/1943	14/06/1944	RCN. Mercantile 1950. Scrapped 1956
K –	**INGERSOLL**	–	–	–	–	RCN. Cancelled –/12/1943
K 343	**St LAMBERT**	Morton (Quebec)	8/07/1943	6/11/1943	27/05/1944	RCN. Mercantile 1946. Scrapped 1957

Continued...

P. No.	Name	Builder	Laid Down	Launched	Completed	Fate
K 687	**SEA CLIFF**	Collingwood Shipyards	29/05/1943	20/12/1943	9/05/1944	RCN. *Guelph* (1943). Mercantile 1945. Scrapped 1964
K 368	**TRENTONIAN**	Kingston Shipbuilding	19/02/1943	1/09/1943	1/12/1943	RCN. Torpedoed *U-1004* off Falmouth 22/02/1945
K 346	**WHITBY**	Marine Industries	1/04/1943	18/09/1943	6/06/1944	RCN. Mercantile 1946-62 and sold
Ordered 15/05/1942						
K 306	**BUGLOSS**	Crown (Sunderland)	26/11/1942	21/06/1943	8/11/1943	RIN *Assam* (ii) (1945/48) and sold
K 307	**BULRUSH**	Crown (Sunderland)	22/02/1943	11/10/1943	8/02/1944	RCN *Mimico* (ii) (K 485 -1943). Mercantile 1950 and sold
Ordered –/06/1942						
K 358	**ASBESTOS**	Morton (Quebec)	20/07/1943	22/11/1943	16/06/1944	RCN. Sold Dominican Navy (1948) Wrecked 1949 on route
K 332	**BELLEVILLE**	Kingston Shipbuilding	21/01/1944	17/06/1944	19/10/1944	RCN. Dominican Navy *Juan Bautista Cambiaso* (1947). Scrapped 1972
K –	**BRAMPTON**	–	–	–	–	RCN. Cancelled –/12/1943
K 540	**BUCKINGHAM**	Morton (Quebec)	8/11/1943	11/05/1944	25/09/1944	RCN *Beauharnois* (ii) (1944). Mercantile 1946. Israeli Navy *Wedgewood* (1950). Scrapped 1956
K 440	**LACHUTE**	Morton (Quebec)	24/11/1943	9/06/1944	26/10/1944	RCN. Dominican Navy *Christobal Colon* (1947). Wrecked 31/08/1979
K –	**LISTOWEL**	–	–	–	–	RCN. Cancelled –/12/1943
K –	**MEAFORD**	–	–	–	–	RCN. Cancelled –/12/1943
K 341	**PARRY SOUND**	Marine Industries (Sorel)	11/06/1943	13/11/1943	30/08/1944	RCN. Mercantile 1950, scrapped 1962
K 342	**PETERBOROUGH**	Kingston Shipbuilding	14/09/1943	15/01/1944	1/06/1944	RCN. Dominican Navy *Gerardo Jansen* (1947)Scrapped 1972
K 688	**POINTE CLAIRE**	Morton (Quebec)	23/11/1943	24/06/1944	10/11/1944	RCN. *Merrittonia* (1944). Sold 1945 and wrecked
K –	**RENFREW**	–	–	–	–	RCN. Cancelled –/12/1943
K –	**SIMCOE**	–	–	–	–	RCN. Cancelled –/12/1943
K 345	**SMITHS FALLS**	Kingston Shipbuilding	21/ 01/1944	19/08/1944	28/11/1944	RCN. Mercantile 1945. Scrapped 1962
K 457	**STELLARTON**	Morton (Quebec)	16/11/1943	27/04/1944	29/09/1944	RCN. Chilean Navy *Casma* (1946). Scrapped 1966
K 455	**STRATHROY**	Marine Industries (Sorel)	18/11/1943	15/06/1944	20/11/1944	RCN. Chilean Navy *Chipana* (1946). Scrapped1969
K 394	**THORLOCK**	Marine Industries (Sorel)	25/09/1943	15/05/1944	13/11/1944	RCN. Chilean Navy *Papudo* (1946). Scrapped 1967
K 369	**WEST YORK**	Marine Industries (Sorel)	23/07/1943	25/01/1944	6/10/1944	RCN. Mercantile 1946. Sunk 1960 following collision
Ordered 22/07/1942						
K 385	**ARABIS** (ii)	G Brown (Greenock)	26/02/1943	28/10/1943	16/03/1944	RNZN (1944/48). Scrapped 1951
K 348	**BURNET**	Ferguson (Port Glasgow)	2/11/1942	31/05/1943	23/09/1943	RIN *Gondwana* (1945), RThN *Bangpakong* (1947). Stricken 1984
K 360	**CEANOTHUS**	Ferguson (Port Glasgow)	5/02/1943	30/08/1943	1/12/1943	RCN *Forest Hill* (ii) (K 487 – 1943). Scrapped 1947
Ordered 25/07/1942						
K 382	**CANDYTUFT**	Inglis (Pointhouse)	27/02/1943	28/09/1943	5/01/1944	RCN *Longbranch* (ii) (K 487 - 1943). Mercantile 1947. Scuttled off Canada 1966
K 395	**CHARLOCK**	Ferguson (Port Glasgow)	6/04/1943	16/11/1943	10/03/1944	RIN *Maharatta* (ii) (1946). Wrecked 1947
Ordered –/06/1943						
K –	Unnamed	–	–	–	–	RCN. Cancelled –/12/1943
K –	Unnamed	–	–	–	–	RCN. Cancelled –/12/1943
K –	Unnamed	–	–	–	–	RCN. Cancelled –/12/1943

Armament

GUNS

The 'Flower' class carried the planned main gun armament from the start. Fortunately, there were plenty examples in store of the 45-calibre 4in Mark IX BL (breech loading) gun on the CP (centre pivot) Mark I mounting. These had been produced during the Great War to arm the multitude of *Aberdare* class minesweeping and convoy sloops.

The gun fired a 31-pound shell out to a maximum range of 13,840 yards. The mounting weighed a total of 4 tons 13 hundredweight (cwt), with a crew of seven. It fired a semi armour piercing (SAP) shell, and was more than capable of destroying a U-boat in good conditions. However, it had a slow rate of fire, and lacking any type of fire control required good teamwork. A similar mounting was built in Canada for the vast building programme there. In photographs the mounting can be seen with both the curved and square splinter shield, and it was also carried by anti-submarine trawlers. The accompanying drawings are based on the original Vickers Armstrong drawing and a copy of the gunnery manual, dated October 1917.

The secondary armament, as authorised, was the single 40mm (2-pounder) Mark VIII HV (high velocity) gun on the manually operated Mark VIII mounting. This standard pom-pom had a muzzle velocity of 2400ft/sec and a rate of fire of 115rpm (rounds per minute) using belted ammunition. With a crew of two, its maximum elevation was 70 degrees. Predominantly an anti-aircraft weapon, the gun itself was complex, with over 400 parts, but it did not see general service until early 1941 due to delays in production of the new mounting. The mounting weighed 1 ton 3 hundredweight (cwt).

Early 'Flowers' had to go to sea with what close-range armament was available – single or twin 0.303in Lewis machine guns, or the ingenious steam-powered Holman

Below: The gun crew practise loading the 4in BL on *Dianthus* in August 1942. BL (breech loading) denoted a gun with separate shell – in this photo about to be rammed into the open breech - and charge, of bagged cordite, shown in its leather container on the shoulder of the man to the left. *(IWM A11946)*

continued on p.81

4-inch (45 calibres) Mark IX Breech Loading gun on CP Mark I mounting of 1917
Originally fitted to *Aberdare* class minesweepers in the First World War, the guns were stored after those ships went out of service. The guns were classed as 'breech loading' because they used separate ammunition. The mounting had two basic shapes of shield with curved and square fronts. Many retained open sight-ports, but others had hinge-down covers over them, and by 1944 many carried rocket flare rails on the sides.

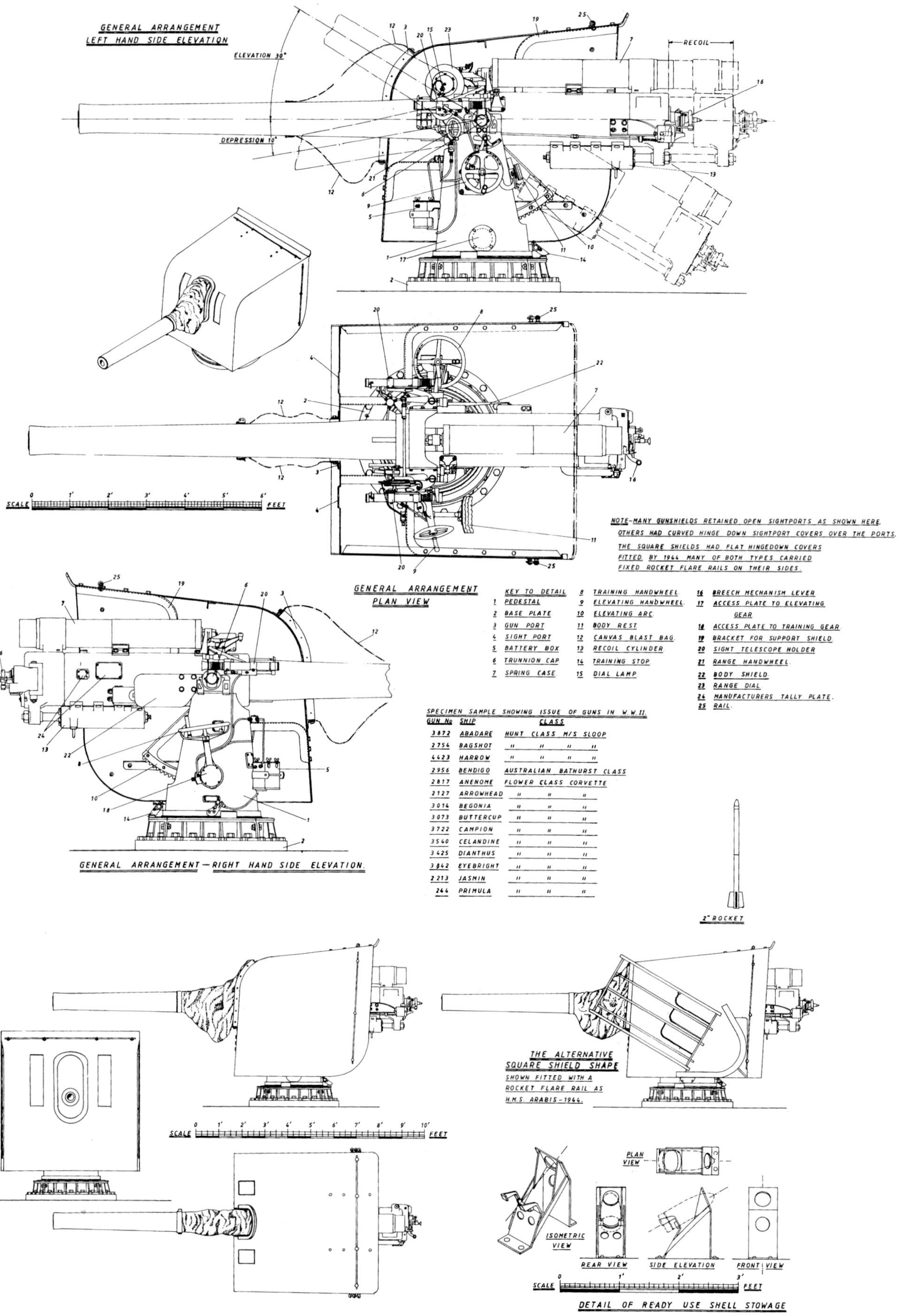

4-INCH MARK IX BL ON CP MARK I MOUNTING

GUN

Construction	Steel and wire
Bore	4.00 inches
Weight inc breech mechanism	2.125 tons
Length oa	184.6 inches
Length of bore	177.4 inches
Length of chamber	25.493 inches
Length of rifling	149.475 inches
Muzzle velocity	2642 feet per second
Working pressure	18.5 tons per square inch
Approx life	3600 equivalent full charges
Max range	13, 840 yards at 30° elevation
Weight of projectile	31 pounds
Propellant charge	7.914 pounds
Volume of chamber	470.3 cubic inches

MOUNTING

Weights	*Tons*	*Hundredweight*	*Quarters*	*Pounds*
Carriage and fittings	0	13	0	0
Gun and mechanism	2	2	2	0
Cradle and fittings	1	0	1	14
Base plate	0	15	2	0
Total	**4**	**13**	**1**	**14**
Spray shield and supports	0	14	1	13

Max force of recoil @ 30° elevation	17.1 tons
Max force of recoil	15.5 tons
Recoil (working)	18.0 inches
Recoil (metal to metal)	20.0 inches
Speed of elevation	2° per handwheel revolution
Speed of training	3° per handwheel revolution
Diameter of base plate	47.5 inches
Elevation	30°
Depression	-10°
Gun crew	7
Width of shield at back	71.5 inches
Diameter of holding down bolts	Pitch centre 44.5 inches

A Canadian-built Mark VIII 2pdr on the single Mark VIII mounting. *(Author's collection)*

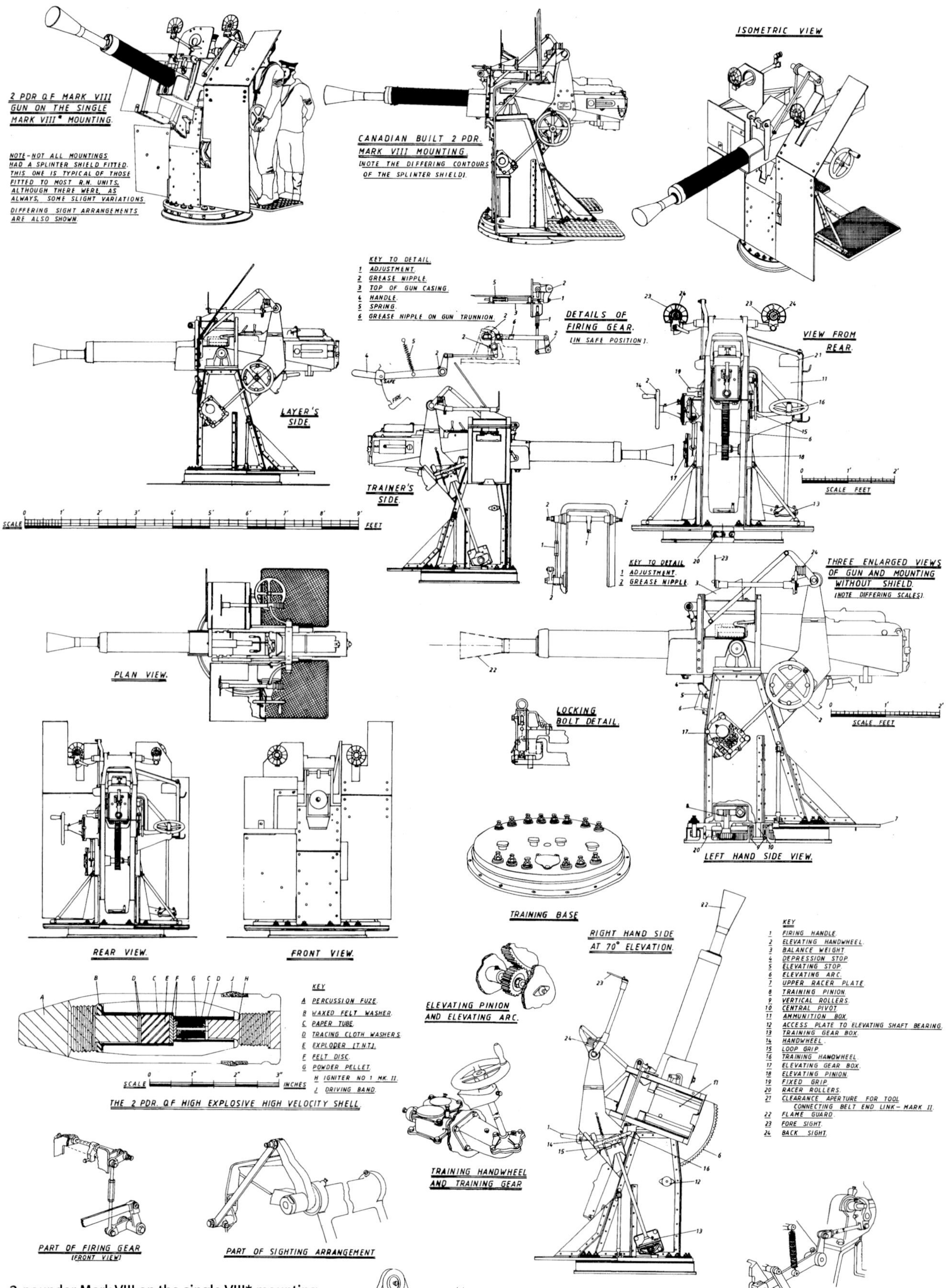

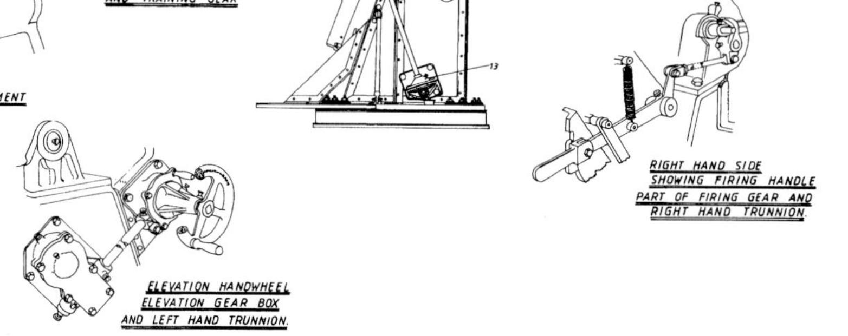

2-pounder Mark VIII on the single VIII* mounting
The single 'pom-pom' was the standard heavy AA gun in 'Flowers', although the earliest often had to make do with lighter weapons because of shortages of the 2pdr. Not all mountings were fitted with shields, which varied in detail, particularly the Canadian-built examples.

The front and shield of the 2pdr Mark VIII* mounting. *(Author's collection)*

2-POUNDER MARK VIII ON THE SINGLE VIII* MOUNTING

GUN	
Bore	1.57 inches
Weight	784-918 pounds
Length of barrel	62 inches
Length of gun	oa 115.6 inches
Length of rifling	54.84 inches
Twist of rifling	1 in 30
Number of grooves	12
Muzzle velocity	2400 feet per second
Length of recoil	7.5 inches average
Capacity of water jacket	22 pints
Approximate life	5000 equivalent full charges
Max range	6800 yards at 2300 fps
Ceiling	13,000 feet at 2300 fps
Weight of projectile	1.684 pounds
Propellant charge	0.2793 pounds
Rate of fire	115 rounds per minute

MOUNTING	
Weight without gun and shield	1 ton 3 cwt 12 pounds
Weight of shield	5.5 hundredweight
Elevation	70°
Depression	-10°
Working radius	6 feet

The single 2pdr on the Mark VIII mounting in *Penstemon*, in this case without a gunshield. *(IWM A7370)*

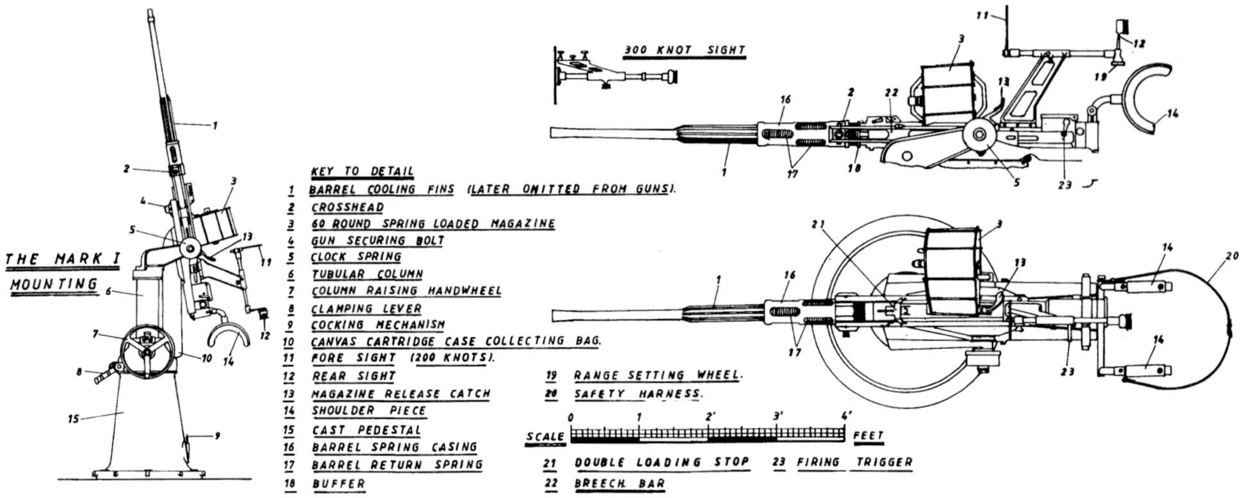

20-millimetre Oerlikon cannon on Mark I mounting

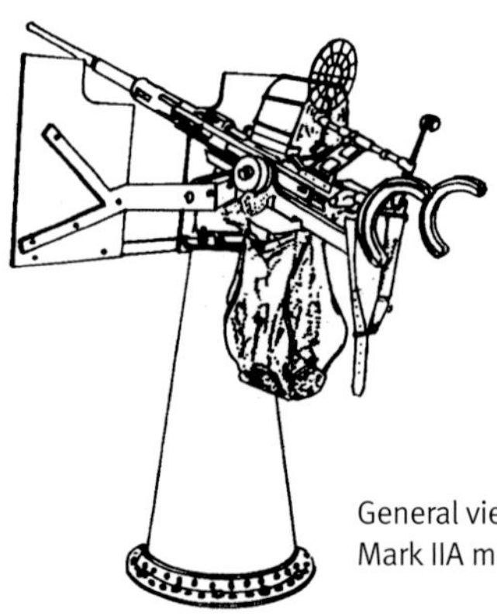

General view of 20mm Mark IIA mounting

20-MILLIMETRE OERLIKON CANNON

Bore	0.7874 inches
Weight	141-150 pounds
Length of gun	87 inches
Length of bore	55.118 inches
Length of rifling	49.61 inches
Twist of rifling	1 in 36
Number of grooves	9
Muzzle velocity	2750 feet per second
Approximate life	9000 equivalent full charges
Max range	4800 yards at 2725 fps
Ceiling	10,000 feet at 2725 fps
Weight of projectile	0.272 pounds
Propellant charge	0.0628 pounds
Rate of fire	465-480 rounds per minute

0.303-INCH LEWIS MACHINE GUN MARK III

Weight (unloaded)	26 pounds
Length of gun	50.5 inches
Muzzle velocity	2450 feet per second
Magazine	Pan of 47 or 97 rounds
Cyclic rate	550 rounds per minute

0.303-inch Lewis machine gun Mark III on twin mounting
Of American origin, the Lewis light machine gun was made under licence in Britain and widely used in the First World War. It was issued to many warships in the early years of the Second World War, on a twin mounting with or without a shield.

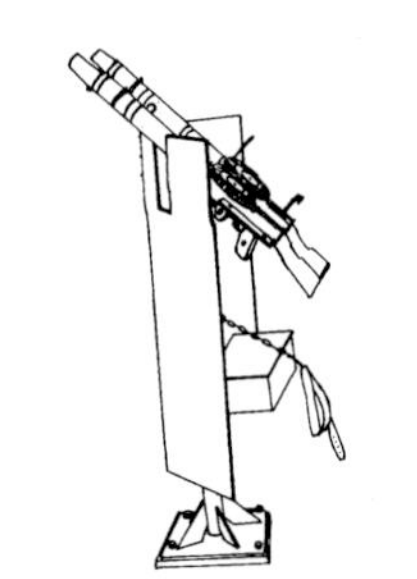

SHOWING BOX FOR READY USE REPLACEMENT MAGAZINES AND CHAIN AND SUPPORTING BODY BELT FOR THE GUNNER.

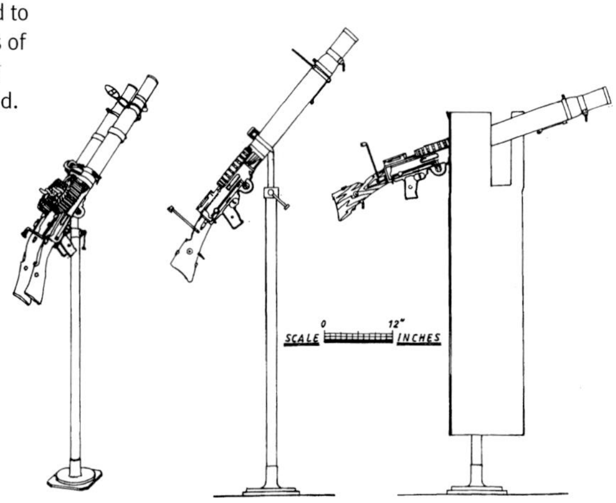

TWIN LEWIS GUN WITHOUT AND WITH SHIELD

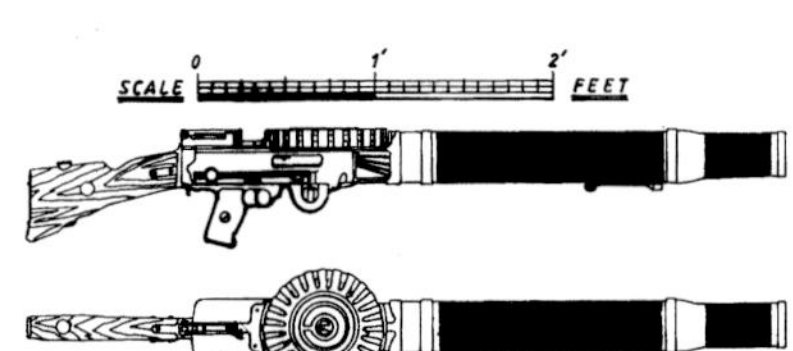

Above: The most important addition to the original close-range armament was the 20mm Oerlikon. This is a Mark I mounting with hand raising gear on the bridge wing of *Celandine*, July 1942. *(IWM A10780)*

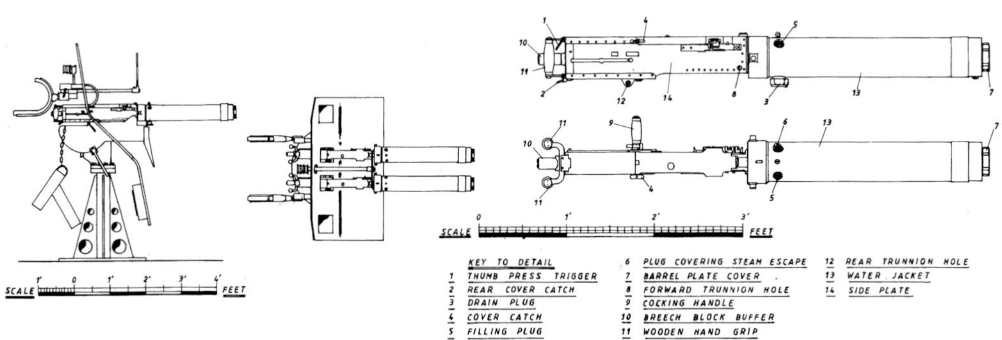

Above: The 0.5in Browning (Colt) machine gun on twin Mark IX mounting, 1942
An American weapons supplied under Lend-Lease and fitted in small numbers in RN warships, it was recoil-operated and fed by articulated link belts. A cartwheel sight had 100-, 200- and 300-knot rings, for an effective range of 1000 yards. It was water-cooled, with a rotary hand pump and 9-gallon tank provided for each gun. With a muzzle velocity of 2560 feet per second, each gun fired at a rate of 500-800 rounds per minute, the mounting allowing a maximum elevation of 78 degrees and a depression of -15.

Below: The 0.303in Hotchkiss Mark I* machine gun
A licence-built version of a French design adopted by the British army during the First World War, the Hotchkiss was replaced by the lighter Lewis. However, the desperate shortage of light AA weapons in 1940 led to many of them being taken out of storage and issued to corvettes, trawlers and defensively equipped merchant ships. Its cyclic rate was 500 rounds per minute, with a muzzle velocity of 2425 feet per second.

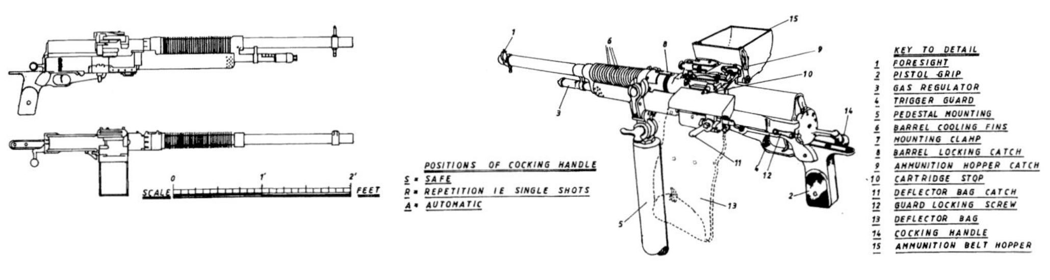

Projector, which fired a Mills grenade into the path of approaching aircraft – that at least was the theory, but it seldom produced the right result. The 0.303in Lewis guns were augmented by a number of Hotchkiss 0.303in machine guns from store and 0.300in Savage Lewis guns were supplied by the USA, which used the 0.300in rimless round and were not interchangeable.

A real improvement was the introduction of the 20mm Oerlikon gun on the Mark I or II manual mounting from late 1941. The 'Flowers' were not at the front of the queue, but it was gradually introduced during refits when it was fitted on the extended bridge wings. This potent weapon, with a calibre of 0.8in, a muzzle velocity of 2725ft/sec and a rate of fire of 465-480rpm from the 60-round magazine, had a maximum range of 6250 yards at 45 degrees. The crew of two comprised the gunlayer and magazine loader. This Swiss-designed gun had been discussed by the Admiralty in 1938, but there was concern that the weapon fired whilst the breech was still open, and it was thought unsafe. However, it was eventually decided that it could be built under licence and once production was underway, it was to be found on both warships and merchant ships.

When the Americans entered the war, they too built it under licence and it appeared in increasing numbers on most types of warship. In late 1941 it was carried by the Mark I mounting with hand raising gear, the Mark IIA mounting on a fixed pedestal and the Mark IIIA, another fixed pedestal mounting but with a few differences from the Mark IIA. Other improved mountings followed in later production. With the gun in full production and interchangeable between the RN and USN, it was found on the twin Mark V (power-operated) mounting, replacing the 2pdr pom-pom in some corvettes, particularly in 'Modified Flowers'.

The quadruple 0.5in Vickers heavy machine gun on the 'M' Mark III mounting of 1938 (the 'M' denoting multiple) consisted of four 0.5in guns mounted vertically, one above the other. Each gun was in a separate trunnion, but linked together so that all elevated and depressed together. Gunlaying was by handwheel and gearing, worked by the gunlayer standing on the left. The gun had a muzzle velocity of 2520ft/sec approx and fired at about 700rpm. Training could be free, by body weight, or by the trainer using a geared handwheel on the right of the mounting. The guns all fired together and could be fired by either man.

The half-inch solid rounds from the four barrels could together deliver 800 rounds in approximately 20 seconds and the belted ammunition could be replaced within 30 seconds. The mounting took up little space and was reliable, but the round fired was not usually lethal unless it hit the pilot or a vital part of the aircraft. Owing to the vibration produced during firing, the handbook suggested that frequent inspection of all screws, bolts, and split pins was advisable, between breaks in action. It was not particularly good at destroying aircraft, although it made a lot of noise!

In 1943-44 a small number of 'Flowers' had their bridge Oerlikons replaced by two 6pdr Hotchkiss QF (quick firing) guns on the non-recoil mounting. The theory was that the 4in gun was too slow, and the 6pdr with its higher rate of fire would increase the chances of sinking a surfaced U-boat. The gun dated from 1884 when it had been

6-POUNDER HOTCHKISS QF MARK I ON NON-RECOIL MOUNTING

GUN	
Bore	2.244 inches (57mm)
Weight inc breech mechanism	1060 pounds
Length of gun	97.63 inches
Length oa	109.72 inches
Length of bore	105.47 inches
Length of chamber	16.5 inches
Muzzle velocity	2380-2356 feet per second
Max range	11,300 yards
Weight of complete round	9 pounds 7 $\frac{5}{16}$ ounces
Propellant charge	1.27 pounds
Volume of chamber	73.5 cubic inches
MOUNTING	
Weight	8 hundredweight
Weight of shield (if fitted)	8 hundredweight
Elevation	10°
Depression	-10°
Gun crew	2 (gunlayer & breechworker/loader)
Number of of holding down bolts	8
Diameter of holding down bolts	1.25 inches

6-pounder Hotchkiss QF Mark I gun on non-recoil mounting 1941
Originally introduced in 1884 for defence against torpedo boats, the gun was mounted in the fighting tops of capital ships and cruisers. A limited number were drawn from store in the middle years of the war and fitted on the very basic mounting shown here in the bridge wings of a few corvettes. An Admiralty Confidential Book of April 1944 lists twenty corvettes so fitted, although one (HMCS *Brandon*) is credited with 3pdrs.

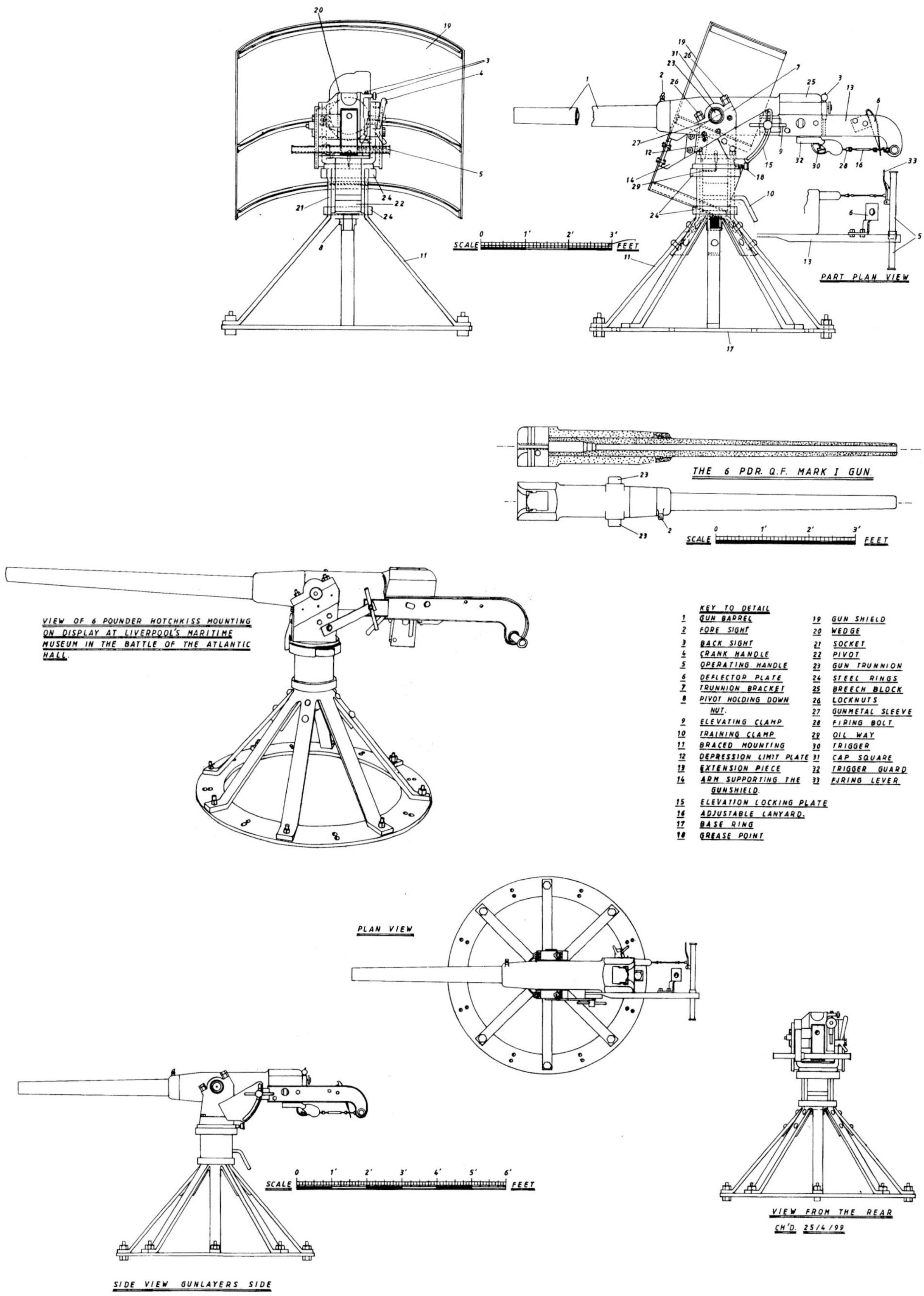

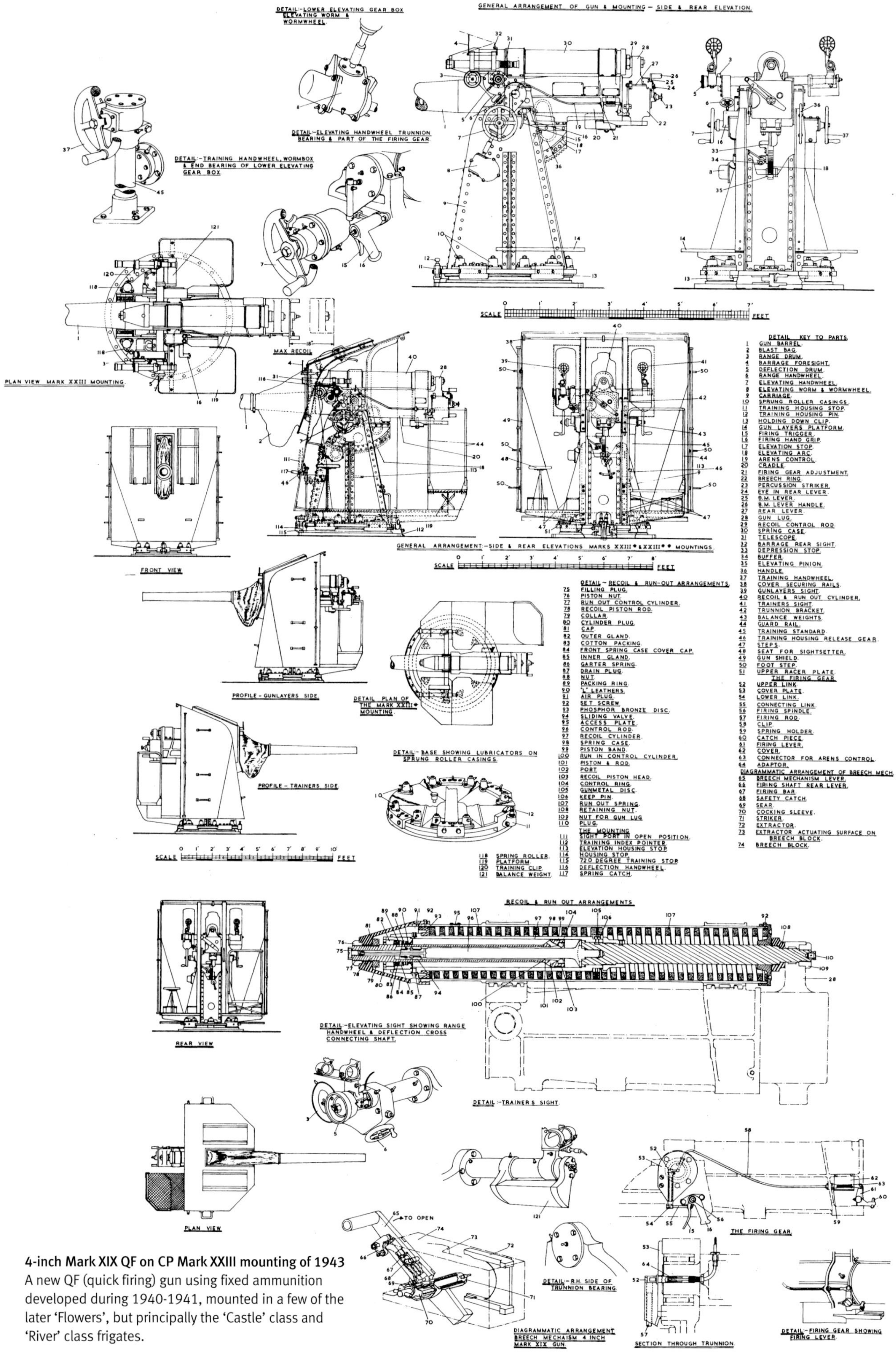

4-inch Mark XIX QF on CP Mark XXIII mounting of 1943
A new QF (quick firing) gun using fixed ammunition developed during 1940-1941, mounted in a few of the later 'Flowers', but principally the 'Castle' class and 'River' class frigates.

4-INCH MARK XIX QF ON CP MARK XXIII MOUNTING

GUN	
Weight inc breech mechanism	1 ton 5 hundredweight 1 quarter 12 pounds
Length oa	166 inches
Muzzle velocity	1275 feet per second
Max range	9500 yards
Weight of complete round	48.5 pounds
MOUNTING	
Weight	3 ton 4 hundredweight 1 quarter 14 pounds
Height	8 feet 1 inch
Width	5 feet 5 inches
Recoil (working)	16.5 inches
Recoil (metal to metal)	18.0 inches
Max force of recoil	7.5 tons
Diameter of base plate	47.5 inches
Elevation	60°
Depression	-10°
Number of holding down bolts	24

introduced as a defence against enemy torpedo boats. It required the same crew as the 20mm mounting, a gunlayer and breechworker/loader. It was not normally fitted with a gun shield. The bore of the gun was 2.244in (57mm) with a muzzle velocity of 2380-2356ft/sec. The gun weighed 7½cwt and the shell weighed 9lbs 7⁹⁄₁₆ozs complete. The gun mounting was a simple frame of angled plates. Its higher rate of fire was commendable, but there is no record of success in its intended task.

By late 1943 the existing stock of 4in BL guns was running low, so a new 4in gun of modern construction was introduced: the 4in Mark XIX gun on the CP Mark XXIII mounting. This gun had been under development during 1940-41, the first guns being proved in 1941. It fired a fixed ammunition, 35lb HE (high explosive) shell as used in the QF 4in Mark XVI gun. The muzzle velocity was limited by the gun mounting to 1300ft/sec, the range requirement being 8000 yards at 45 degrees elevation (the gun was actually capable of a range of 9700 yards).

In order to assist production it was decided that experienced gun-makers should be allowed to build the breech ring without shrinkage in view of the revised factors of safety. 'E' steel (17-ton yield) was approved for the gun, but it was finally decided to raise the yield to 33 tons in production, which initially was slow. Classes receiving this weapon included the 'Military' class A/S trawlers, a few of the 'Modified Flowers', 'River' and 'Castle' class escorts, and the 1942 'Battle' class fleet destroyer, where it functioned as a starshell mounting. Later large orders were placed for the RCN and RAN.

By late 1942 most 4in gun mountings had 2in rocket flare frames attached to the gun shield to port and starboard from which flares could be launched. The 2in flare round consisted of three portions: the rocket head Mark NIII, rocket motor Mark IX and four tail fins Mark NI. Its weight was 21½lb, its diameter 2½in and the rocket was 51in long. It was used for illuminating potential target areas during darkness or overcast conditions.

The rocket was fired and burst after travelling 5400 yards and attaining a height of 1600ft, the time of flight taking about 26.5 seconds. The round (rocket) left the launcher frame about 0.01 seconds after firing, combustion continued for 1.2 seconds, the parachute flare was ejected at 5400 yards range, and then burned for 70 seconds. The illumination intensity was about 100,000 candle power. It was suggested that it was better that the ship was upright when flares were fired. Direction was achieved by turning the gun mounting to the required bearing, so if a target was revealed by the light the gun would be able to aim quickly, although wind would affect the direction of travel.

ANTI-SUBMARINE WEAPONS

In 1939 the current feeling in the RN was that the enemy submarine threat could be contained. Perhaps as a result of unrealistic A/S exercises, it was argued that Asdic (later known as sonar) could accurately detect all submarines and that the depth charge then in use, with the Mark II depth charge thrower, would destroy the target. This was not a view shared by A/S specialists, but there were not many of these in the higher reaches of the Admiralty.

The depth charge and its thrower had in fact changed little from its inception in 1917, and Asdic was effective only against a submerged submarine whose presence had previously been revealed or suspected. Asdic contact was lost as the target was approached, a rule of thumb being that the depth of the target was one-third of the distance at which contact was lost. There

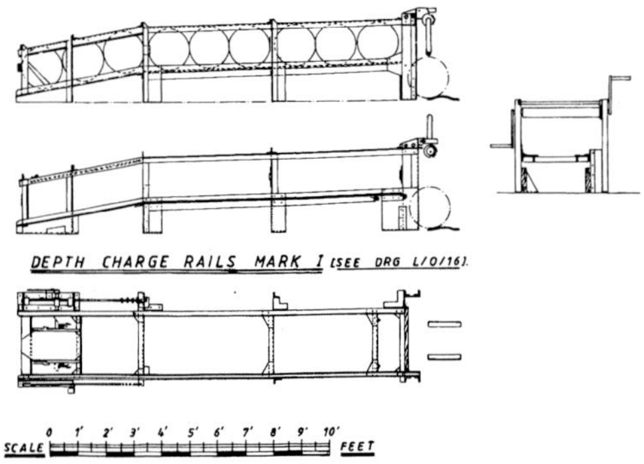

Depth charge rails Mark I
The standard over-the-stern chute.

was also the 'dead time' whilst the charges sank down to the supposed depth of the submarine. The single Asdic detection set, one rail and two throwers found in the modern destroyer turned out to be totally inadequate for the new war.

The standard Mark VII depth charge was not very different from the original design of 1917. It weighed 410lb in the shape of a cylinder 28in long and 17½in in diameter, with a central tube which contained the fuse and primer. It held 396lb of explosive and could be set to explode at 50ft increments from 50ft to 300ft, the supposed maximum diving depth of submarines). Its sinking rate was 10ft per second.

Depth charges were either rolled over the stern from rails, or fired each side of the ship by the Mark II projector designed by Thornycroft in 1917. Here the charge was placed on a steel carrier, with its timber stalk placed in the thrower barrel. When fired by explosive charge the depth charge with the carrier was thrown out to a distance of 40 yards. But each time the carrier was lost.

The standard pattern was the five-charge in which three DCs were released from the rail and two projected one on each beam to result in a diamond with a central charge, thus

X
X X X
X

Prior to 1939 the Anti-Submarine school at Portland (HMS *Osprey*) had realised that 'dead time' was an inherent problem, but lack of government funding prevented any real development.

As a result of operational experience, changes were made to try to bracket the target so that the U-boat's changes of depth

Continued on p.89

Depth charge rails and stowage on the quarterdeck of the Canadian corvette *Athol* at Halifax, NS in January 1944. *(Public Archives of Canada)*

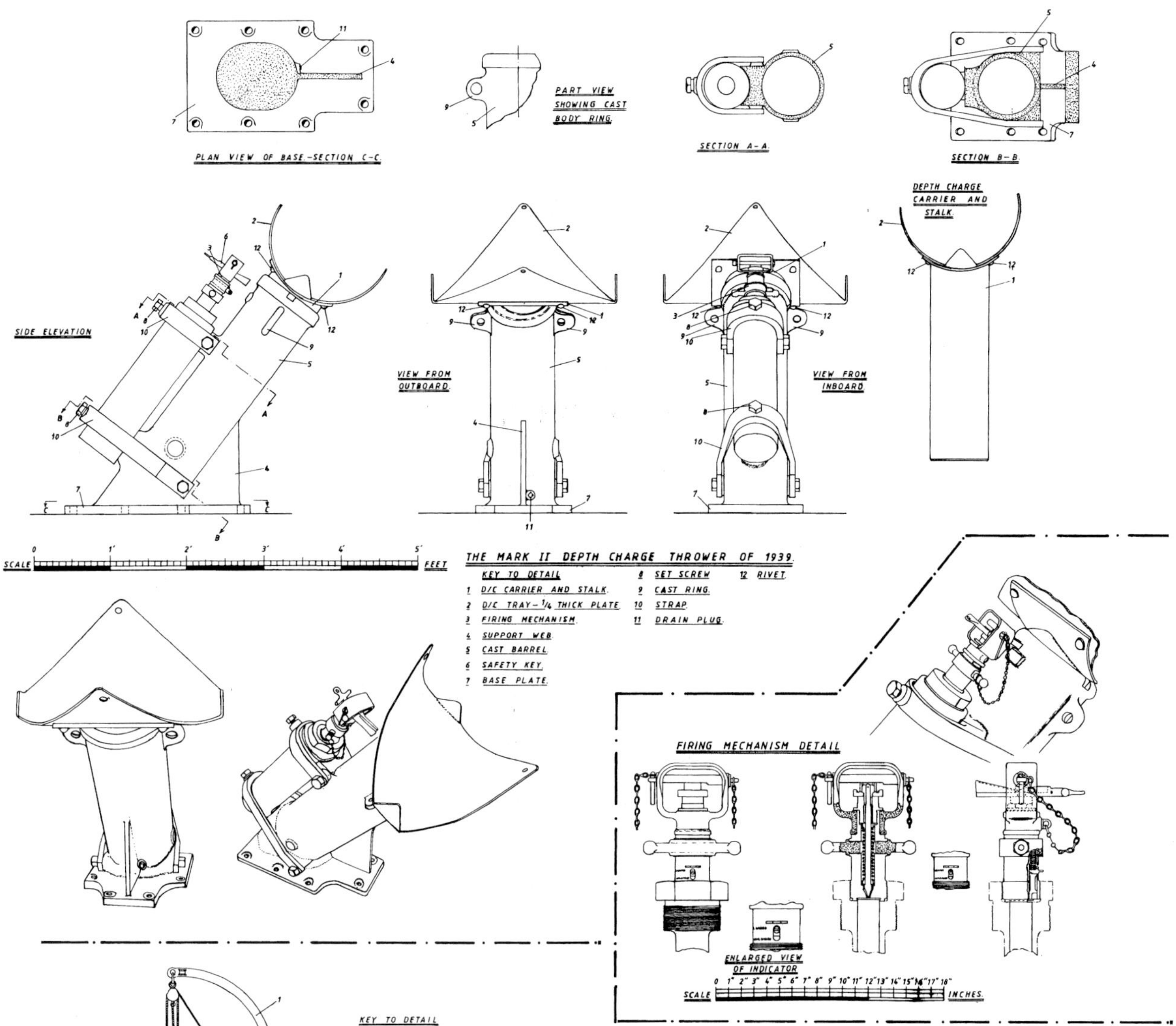

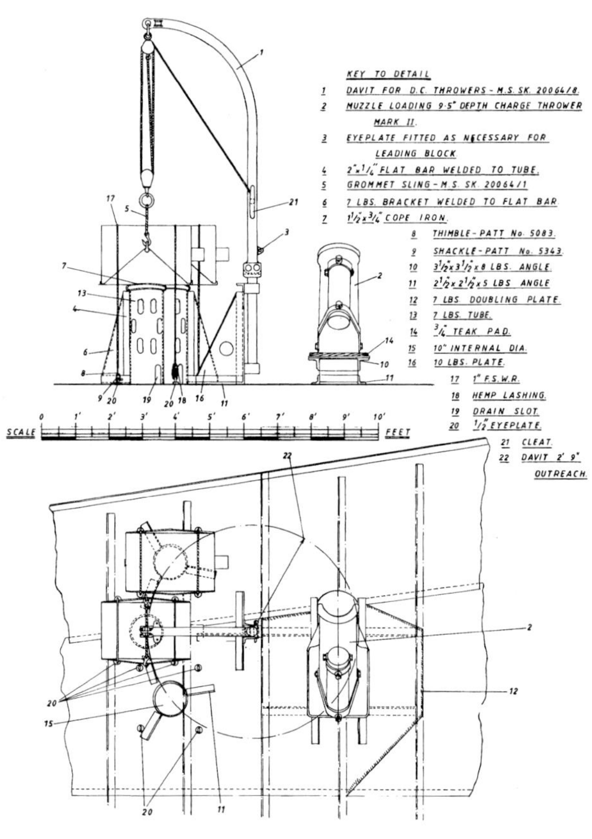

Arrangement of thrower and davit

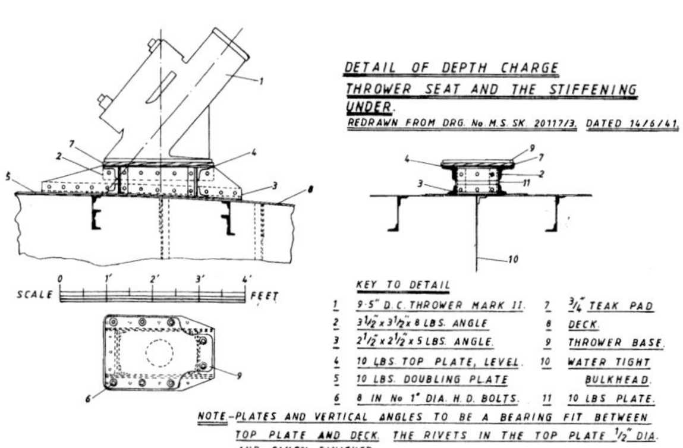

Depth charge thrower Mark II, 1939
The usual thrower on 'Flowers' for most of the war, the basic design of the Mark II dated from 1917, weighed about 10cwt including the carrier and could throw a standard Mark VII depth charge 40 yards. Its main drawback was a separate carrier which required space for stowage and was expended when a DC was fired. The improved Mark IV thrower was not introduced into 'Flowers' until late in the war.

The depth charge thrower Mark IV of 1943, modified for electro-hydraulic firing
More powerful than the Mark II it replaced, this projector could fire a standard charge out to 61 yards, some 20 yards further than the Mark II, but its main advantage was a built-in carrier, ending the wasteful practice of expendable carriers. The new equipment, which included the Mark I stowage rack, was fitted to all new ships from mid 1942 onwards, and also retro-fitted to earlier units as they came in for refit.

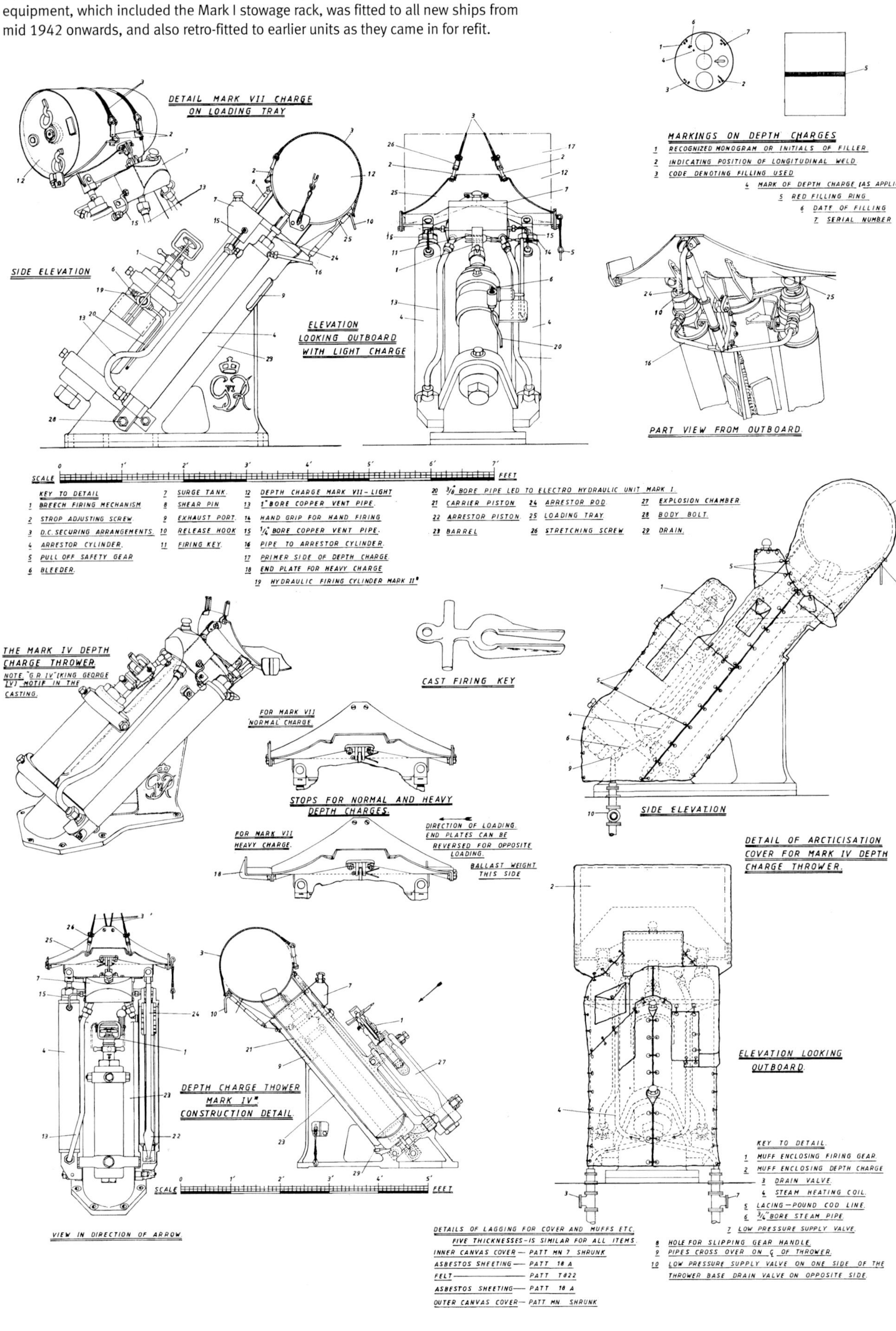

Mark VII Depth Charge and Mark I* depth charge stowage rack for Throwers Marks IV and V, 1943

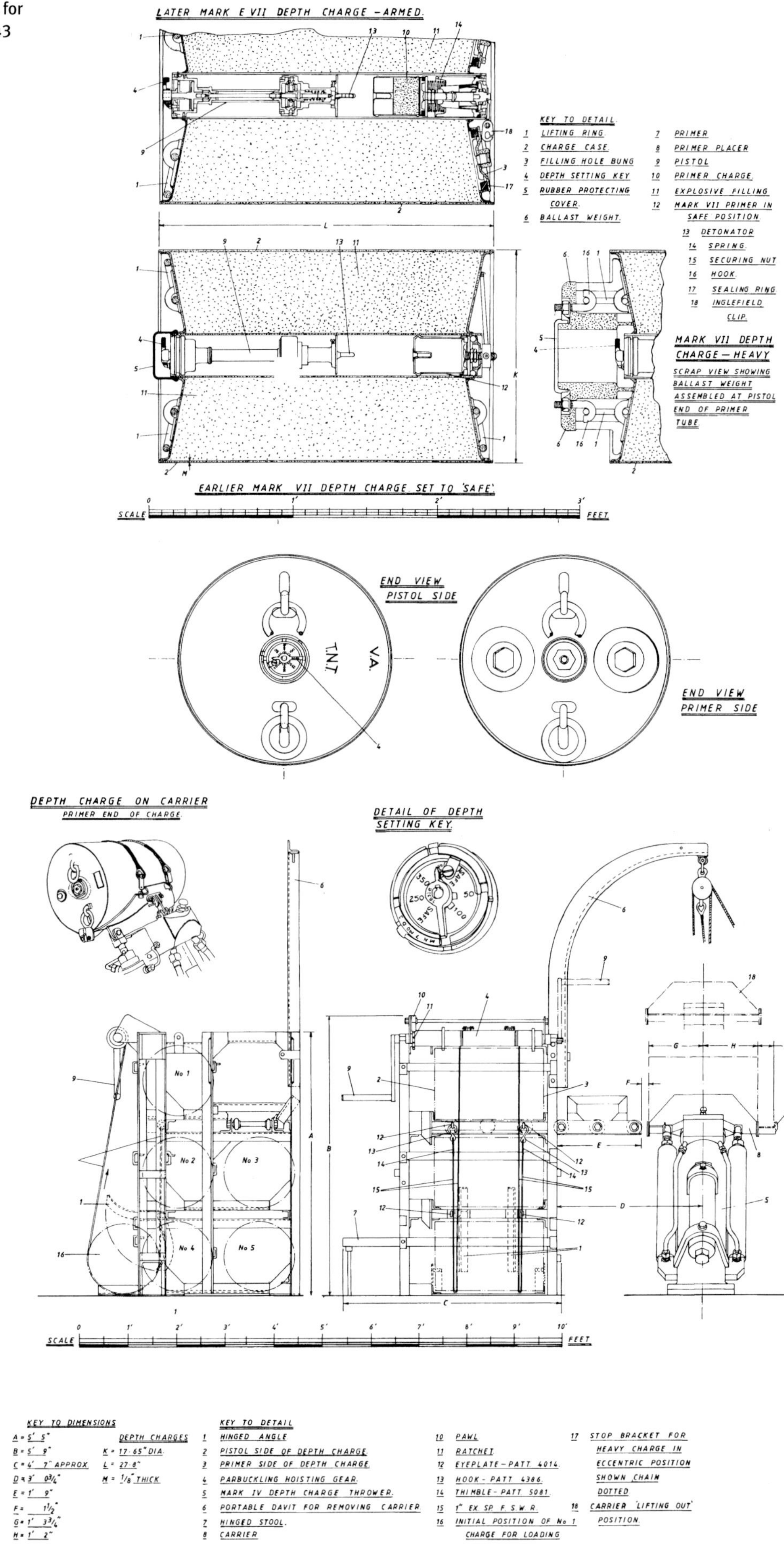

Hedgehog spigot mortar 1942

An ahead-throwing weapon firing twenty-four contact-fused bombs designed to overcome the problem of the Asdic blind spot when the attacking ship passes over the target. In 'Flowers' the weapon was usually sited on the starboard side just ahead of the bridge and one deck up from the forecastle. Unloaded it weighed about 2.1 tons and the frame was 6ft 9in (later 7ft 5in) long by 5ft wide. It fired its bombs about 200 yards, falling in an oval pattern that measured roughly 140 by 120 yards.

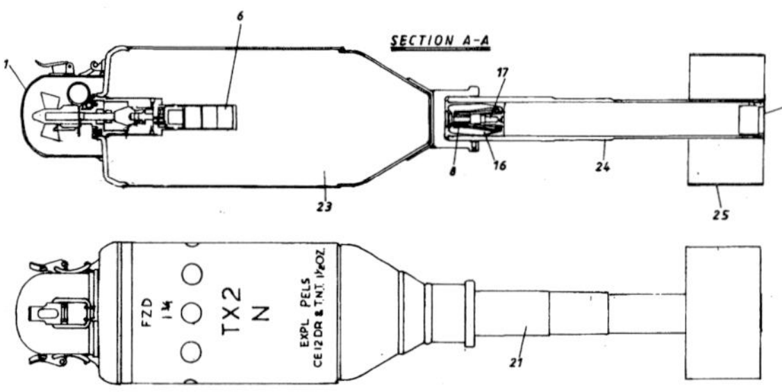

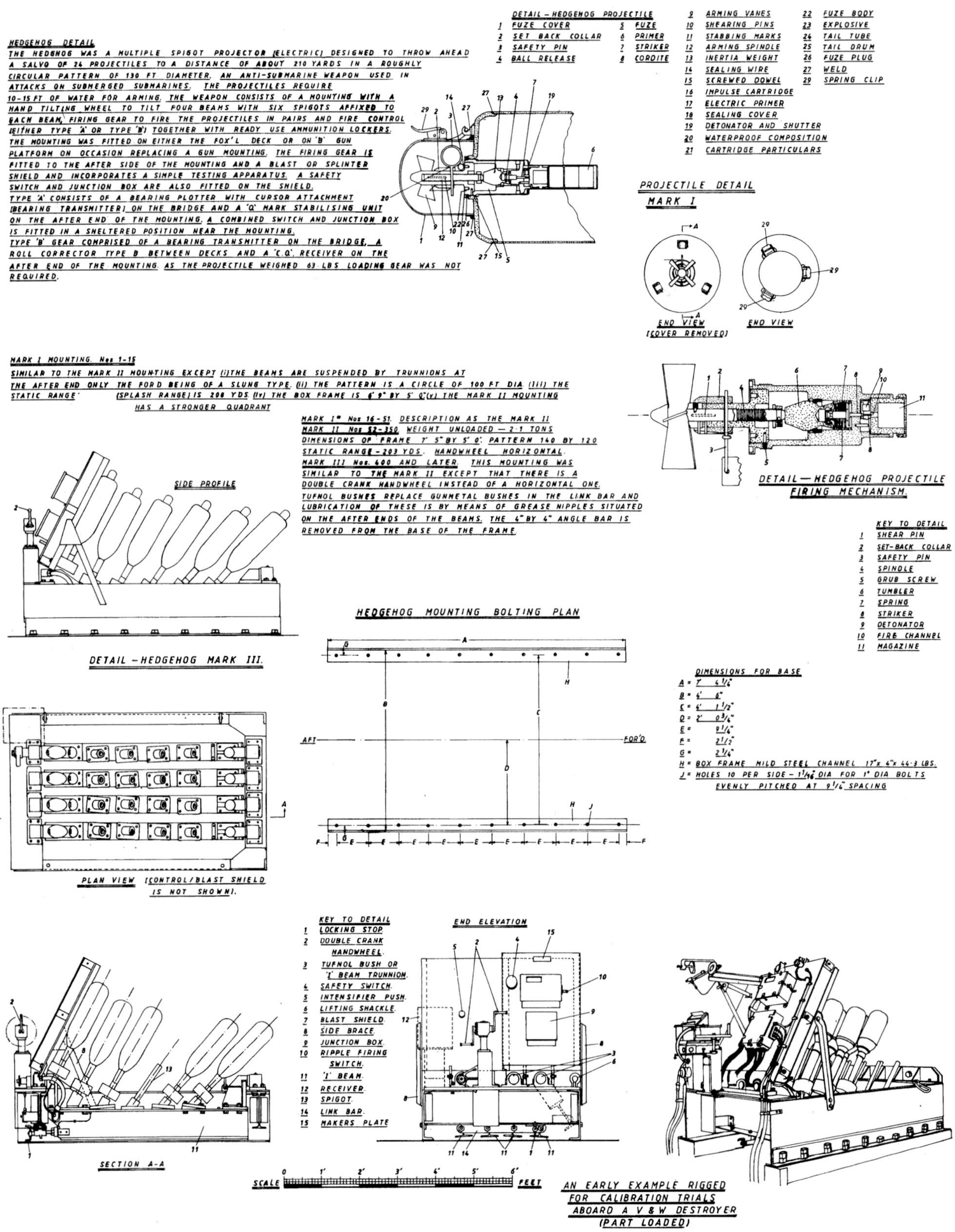

in the last few moments could be forestalled. With the installation of a second rail and four throwers a double diamond (ie, one diamond above the other) could be laid. The DC Mark VII Heavy was introduced. This was the standard Mark VII but with a 150lb cast-steel weight attached to increase the sinking rate to 16.5ft per second. At the same time new depth pistols were provided, to give depth settings of 50ft, 100ft, 150ft, 250ft, 350ft and 500ft, while the heavy charge could be set to explode at 140ft, 225ft, 300ft, 385ft and 500ft. However, it was soon obvious that the German submarine service had not read the script, as they usually attacked on the surface at night, where they could not be detected by Asdic, so there was an urgent requirement to solve this problem (see the section on surface search radar for the solution).

The problems inherent with the Mark II thrower were resolved in 1942 by the introduction of the Mark IV thrower, after extensive trials in the destroyer *Winchelsea* and the new twin-screw corvettes ('Rivers') *Rother*, *Spey* and *Swale* from late 1941 to mid 1942. In this new design the depth charge carrier was an integral part of the thrower and was retained by hydraulic rams. Furthermore, the depth charge was thrown 60 yards – a big improvement over the earlier 40. Since space was no longer required for the disposable carriers, a new DC stowage rack could be provided adjacent to the thrower, where six depth charges were stowed. The Mark IV was fitted to new construction from mid 1942 and retro-fitted in earlier ships as refit periods allowed. Later a lighter version which threw the charge to 80 yards, the Mark V, was produced, but this was not fitted to the 'Flowers'.

As mentioned earlier, the limitations of Asdic led to the revival of pre-war interest in a means of firing the Mark VII charge ahead of the ship, or delivering a multi-charge pattern of smaller projectiles. A number of projects were pursued. The Thornycroft Projector, which threw a Mark VII charge some 250 yards ahead of the ship was tried but although successful, was not put into production, apparently because of the uncertain trajectory of a conventional DC in flight. The Fairlie Mortar, a ten-barrelled mortar to fire a 20lb contact-fused charge, was considered but it was thought that the charge was too small and it was increased to 35lb. Later, after much more work, it emerged as the very potent triple-barrelled Squid.

The immediate result of the original specification was Hedgehog, an ahead throwing weapon carrying a 20lb charge and using the principle of the spigot mortar. In this the mortar bomb, which included the propellant in its own tail, was placed on a spigot, thus obviating the requirement for a heavy tube or barrel. The requirement was updated to increase the charge to 35lb, but using the same principle.

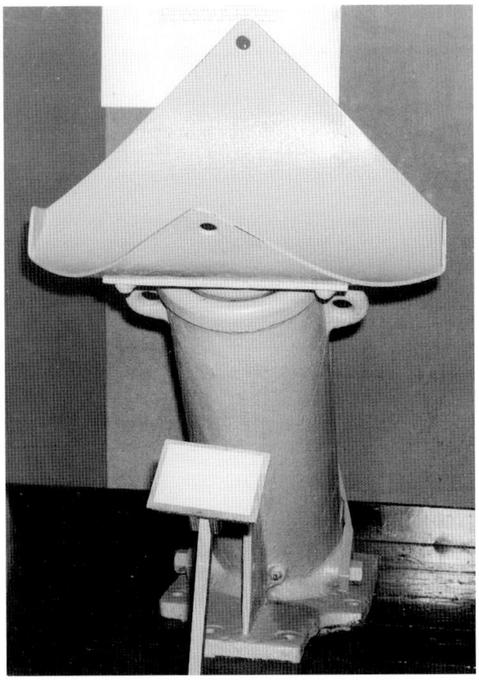

An example of the Mark II depth charge thrower and its carrier ('arbor') on display at the Priddy's Hard armament museum. *(Author's collection)*

Carried initially on the gun ring in lieu of 'A' gun in escort vessels, the mounting consisted of four trunnioned beams in the fore-and-aft direction, each holding six spigots. The twenty-four bombs were fired in a ripple sequence (to reduce deck load) and angling of the spigots produced a 120ft radius circle 200 yards ahead of the firing ship. The contact-fused bomb had an arming propeller in its nose which turned and armed the charge as it passed through the air and water; it weighed 62lb and carried a 35lb Torpex charge with a sinking rate of 22ft per second. The first production mounting (Mark I) was ready in September 1941 and land firing trials with dummy ammunition was carried out at the Whitchurch range in the presence of the Prime Minister and a large number of Admiralty departments.

Sea trials were carried out in HMS *Westcott* in late 1941. The Hedgehog was fitted in Liverpool, replacing 'A' gun on the forecastle. A limited amount of live ammunition was despatched from the filling factory and arrived on board just in time for the ship to sail at the appointed time. A number of single rounds and a full live salvo were fired at a wreck in Liverpool Bay which provided an excellent Asdic target, and what was more important, a hard surface on which the fuse could fire with certainty. All the rounds exploded in a satisfactory manner.

The ship then proceeded to the Clyde to carry out a considerable programme of firing trials with dummy ammunition. These included exercises with a submarine during which eight full salvoes were fired, with hits registered in five out of the eight – so if live rounds had been used she would have been sunk five times. In the last successful attack, the submarine surfaced with a projectile stuck in her casing. As a result of these trials it was decided to proceed with the fitting of Hedgehog throughout the escort fleet. The time of flight of the projectile in the air was approximately 7.5 seconds, with the sinking rate given as: 50ft = 2 seconds, 90ft = 4 seconds, 140ft = 6 seconds, 175ft = 7.5 seconds and thereafter sinking at about 23ft per second. The underwater advance was approx 8 yards, almost all of which was gained in the first 50ft of depth.

At least two salvoes of live ammunition were to be stowed in ready-use lockers fitted close to the mounting. The remainder were stowed (boxed) in the magazine or shell room. As the total weight of the projectile was only 63lb, special loading gear was not required (simply a strong back). Canvas covers with suitable arrangements were provided for the mounting (with a complete salvo loaded). Control equipment comprised the instrument panel on the mounting, the 'Q' Mark II Stabilising Unit (Type A) or CQ Receiver (Type B), and the bearing transmitter on the bridge. For ships operating in Arctic regions, a special framework and cover were provided, with a steam coil for heating fitted beneath the mounting. The cover allowed sufficient space so that when fully loaded it could be maintained. The crew consisted of the captain of the mount, firing number, trainer, communications number and three loaders, one of whom stood by the safety switch.

The Hedgehog became operational in early 1942, but for almost two years, despite such promising trials, results were poor – around a 10 per cent success rate, which was put down partly to the lack of depth-finding Asdic, partly to inexperience, and partly due to reluctance to use the weapon (it only exploded on contact, so there was no comfort from the huge eruption of water found with the depth charge). However, by 1944 with better Asdic, and its use in the shallower waters of the Channel and Continental Shelf, the success rate rose to 40 per cent.

The mounting itself was modified after the first 50 units had been produced, rearranging the spacing of the beams to give a new pattern of bombs 120ft long by 140ft wide at 200yd centre. Power stabilisation of the mounting was successfully introduced in the smaller split version which was found on some sloops. It was produced in the Mark I, II and III versions, and most were updated to Mark III.

The 'Flower' class usually mounted the Hedgehog to starboard in front of the bridge with the bomb ready-use locker to port. The Hedgehog and its fittings required a five- to six-week refit period in ships.

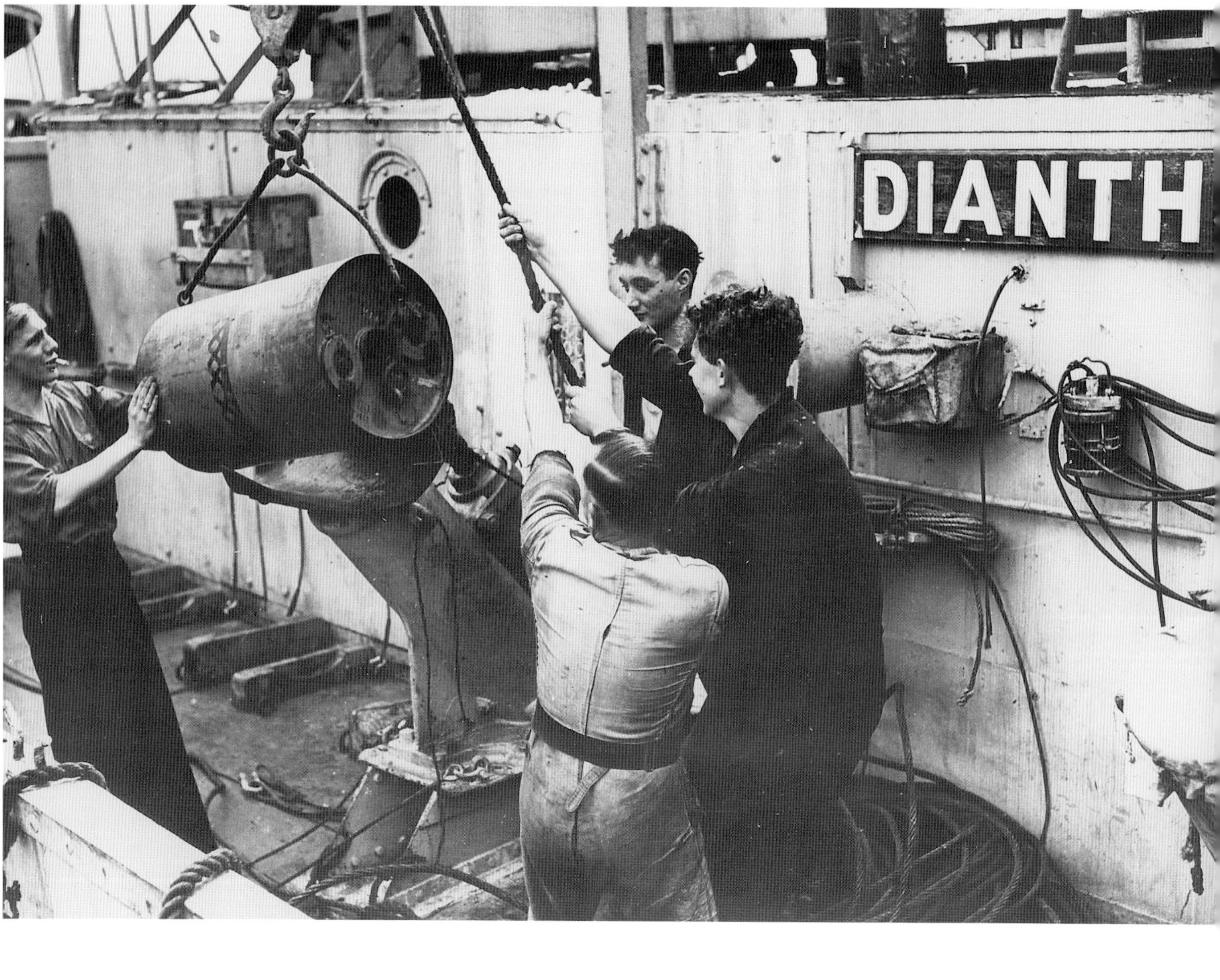

Reloading a Mark II depth charge thrower on *Dianthus* in August 1942. This is a harbour shot, but carrying out this procedure on the heaving deck in any kind of a seaway must have called for great skill and teamwork. *(IWM A11948)*

Surface Search Radar Type 271

The 'Flowers' were the most numerous escort for ocean convoys and one of their major disadvantages was lack of speed. A surfaced U-boat with its 17kt maximum could normally outrun them, and Asdic was of very little use unless they were underwater. As the surfaced U-boat normally attacked in darkness, it was difficult to detect by the Mark I eyeball. Normally the first indication that the convoy was under attack was when a merchant ship was torpedoed, and then there may have been more than one of a wolf-pack in close vicinity. What was required was a means of seeing in the dark, and providing a picture of the tactical situation. Star shells or parachute flares did provide some relief, but frequently merely revealed the location of the convoy to the enemy.

Very fortunately, research had commenced in 1934 with radio waves, and a committee of scientists under the chairmanship of Sir Henry Tizard was set up to study the possibilities of countering heavy air attacks. The first thoughts were to investigate a death ray, where aircraft engines would be affected by radio waves, but it was soon realised that the possibility of detecting aircraft by radio waves was a more promising avenue; indeed, earlier research had suggested that this was possible.

A historic experiment was carried out on 26 February 1935 when it was found that an aircraft flying in the 50-metre beam from the BBC's radio station at Daventry, produced a detectable echo in the receiver when it was 8 miles away. It was a rough demonstration of the distance at which an aircraft would produce an echo. It was then suggested that with the right research and funding, and within five years at the most, it would be possible to send fighters out to

Bluebell in an undated but mid-war photo after refit. The Type 271 lantern is uncovered, revealing the framework. *(Author's collection)*

Type 271 aerial and protective lantern

Views of Type 271P aerial
1. Transmitting aerial
2. Receiving aerial
3. 271 transmitter
4. Support pedestal
5. Roof of radar office
6. Direct drive handwheel for training aerials
7. Dipole

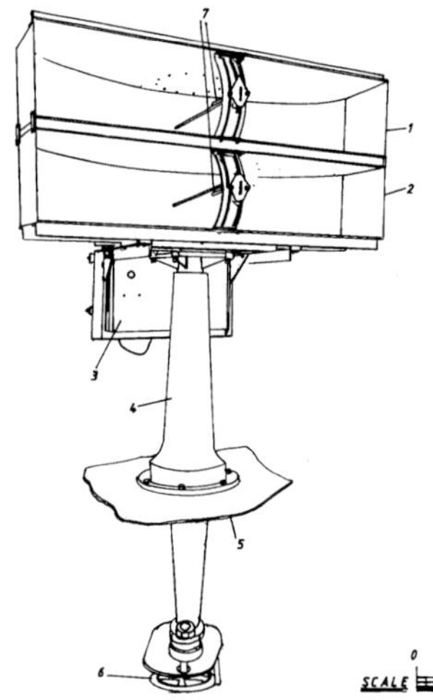

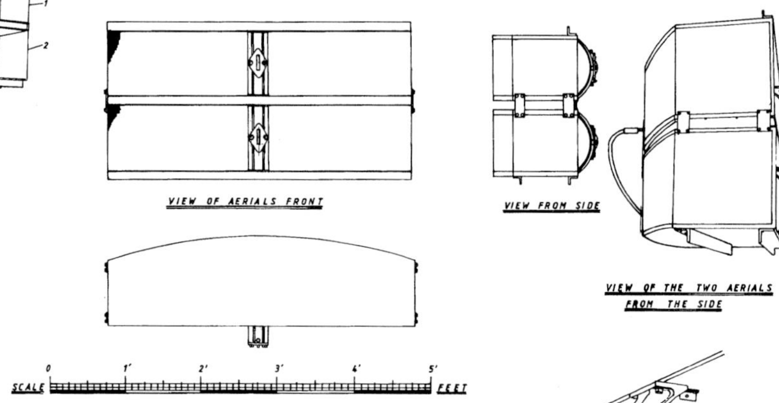

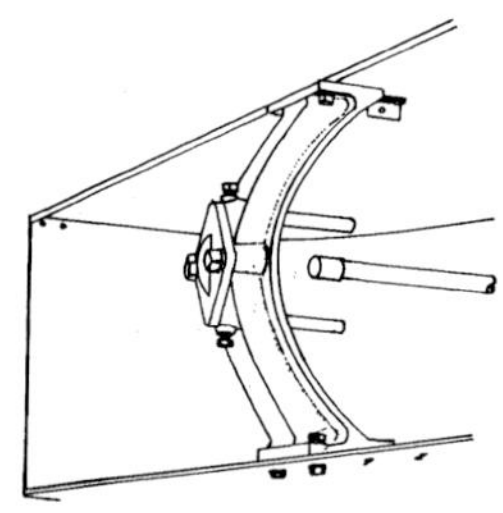

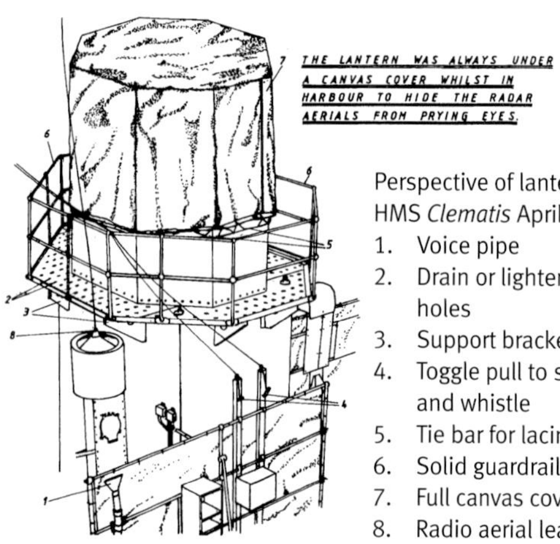

Perspective of lantern in HMS *Clematis* April 1942
1. Voice pipe
2. Drain or lightening holes
3. Support brackets
4. Toggle pull to siren and whistle
5. Tie bar for lacing bar
6. Solid guardrails
7. Full canvas cover
8. Radio aerial lead

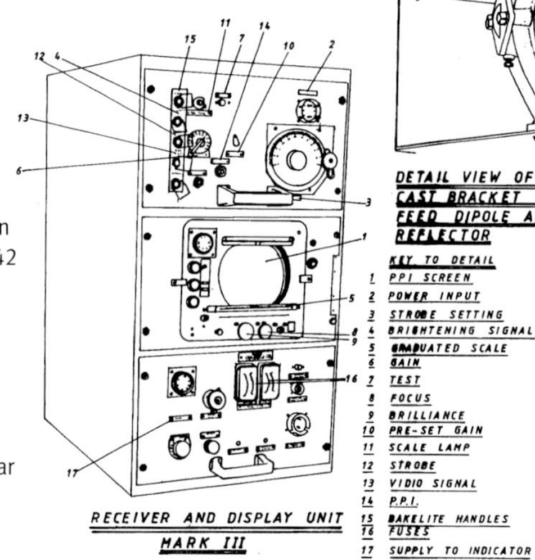

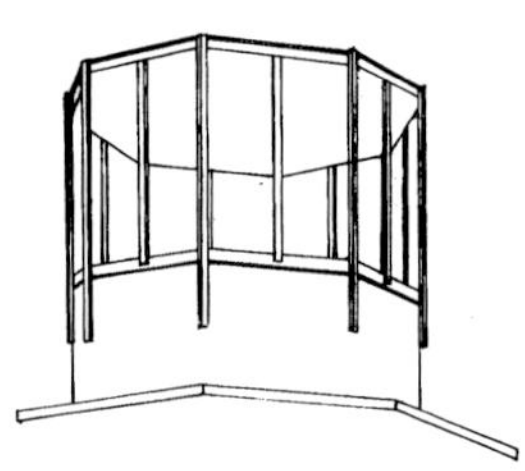

Early pattern lantern, HMS *Stonecrop* 1941

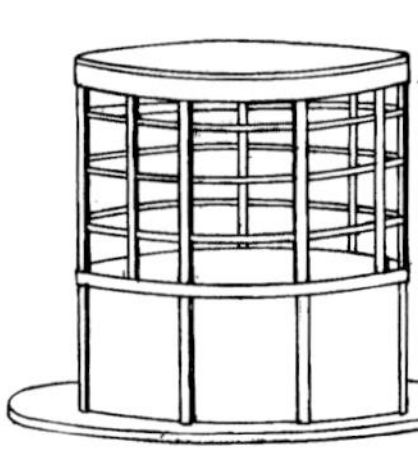

Later pattern lantern, HMCS *Guelph* early 1944

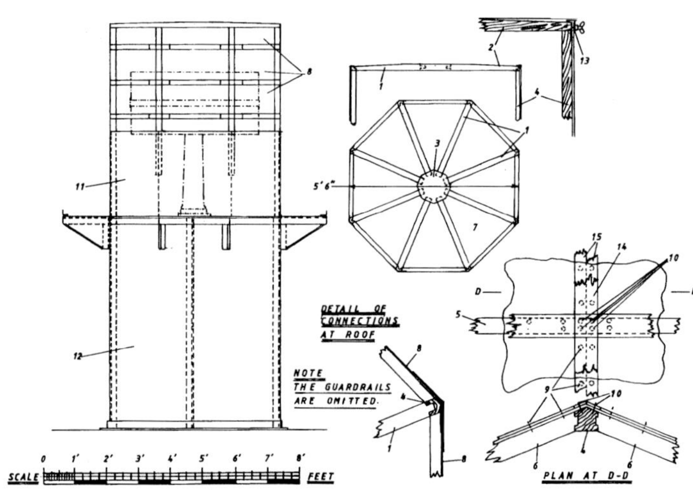

Lantern construction details
1. Radial beams of 2½in by 2in teak
2. Roof held in place with angle lugs, bolted with butterfly nuts
3. Wood centre piece 2½in thick
4. Wood stiffeners 2in by 2in
5. Teak securing battens 1½in by ½in
6. Teak stay 2in by 1½in
7. 3-pound roof
8. ⁵⁄₁₆in Perspex
9. Wood dowels
10. Metal 1in screws
11. Aerial lantern
12. Type 271 radar office
13. 5-pound strap
14. 2in by 2in teak stiffeners
15. Securing battens 1in by ½in

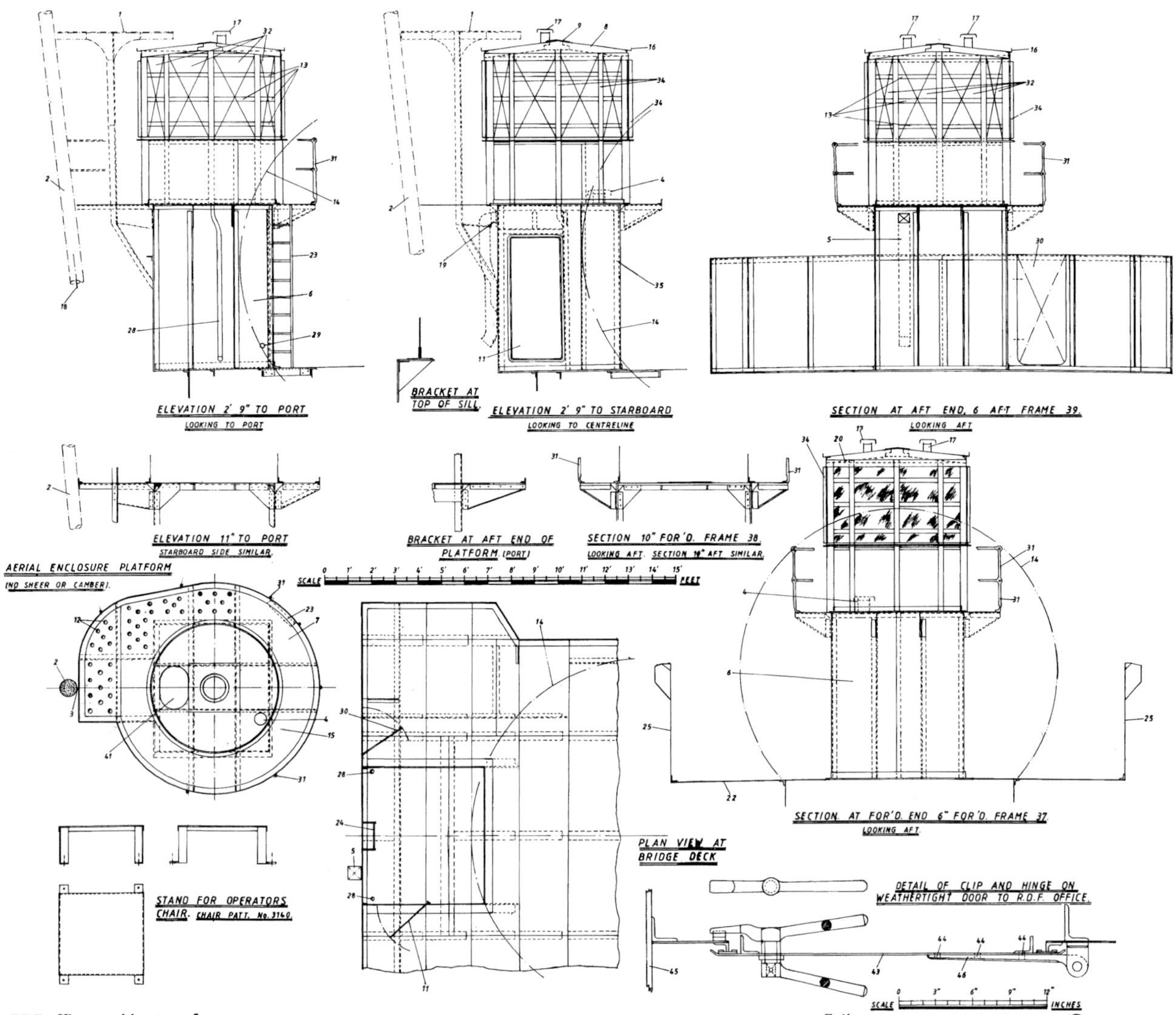

RDF office and lantern for Type 271 from May 1942

By late 1941 the source of excessive side echoes with the first Type 271 installations had been traced to the wooden pillars of the earlier hexagonal lantern and the improved cylindrical version shown here was introduced.

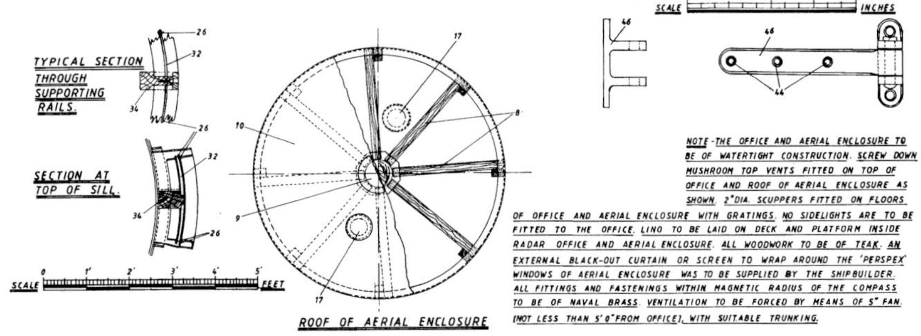

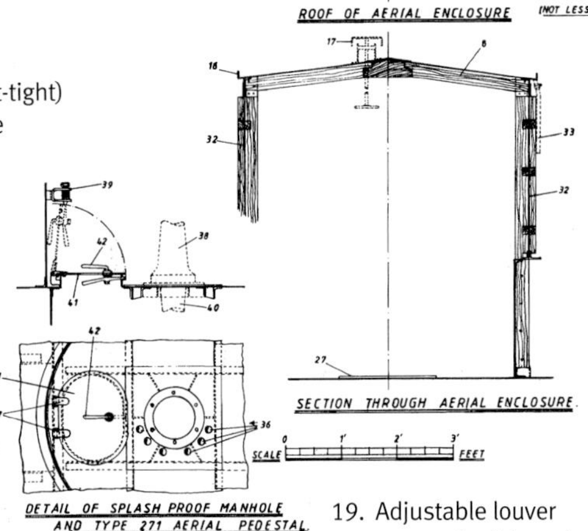

1. Searchlight platform
2. Mast (7in outside diameter)
3. Platform 1in clear of mast
4. 6in diameter mushroom vent (light-tight)
5. 6in by 5in vent trunk to radar office
6. Radar operator's office
7. Aerial enclosure platform
8. 3½in by 2½in teak radial beams
9. 3-pound mild steel galvanised cap
10. 3-pound mild steel galvanised roof
11. Weather-tight steel door
12. 2in lightening holes
13. 2in by 1½in teak inner support rails
14. Magnetic radius of standard compass at platform level
15. No lightening holes in front of platform over instruments
16. 2in by ³⁄₁₆in flat bar welded round top forming 1in rain gutter
17. 4in mushroom top exhaust vents, port and starboard
18. Centre of mast heel – Frame 40 at forecastle deck; rake 1⅛in per foot
19. Adjustable louver
20. 7-pound mild steel curtain ring (portable)
21. Aerial screen
22. Bridge deck
23. 15in teak ladder
24. 12in ladder
25. Bulwark
26. Rubber insertion
27. 15-pound doubling
28. 2in scupper, port and starboard
29. 2in voice pipe
30. 20-pound steel weatherproof door
31. 1in diameter stanchions
32. Screen ⁵⁄₁₆in Perspex
33. 1in rubber drain pipe
34. 3½in by 2½in teak uprights
35. 2in by 2in by ½in naval brass corner bar
36. Six 1½in diameter holes for cable glands
37. Light type hinges
38. Pedestal unit for Type 271 aerial
39. Automatic door catch
40. Pedestal for hand control
41. Manhole
42. Light type clip
43. 5-pound mild steel door plate
44. ½in diameter rivets
45. Mild steel door hinge

intercept aircraft at about 60-100 miles from the coast. A research station costing £12,300 was set up at Orfordness, and other secret work was carried out, so by the summer of 1935 the original RDF (Radio Direction Finding, later to be called Radar) early warning device had reached an advanced stage of development.

The idea was that RDF stations should form a chain at twenty-mile intervals along the east and south-east coast. Cover was required from the Tyne to Southampton, so that twenty stations had to be constructed. Fortunately, the project had high priority so the money was found and this programme formed the basis for the radar defence of Britain in the first years of war. Contracts were given to Metropolitan-Vickers for twenty sets of transmitting equipment and to Cossors for a similar number of receiving equipment, the designs to be based on the performance specifications prepared at Bawdsey research station. By the end of 1937 RDF was considered by the Air Staff to have proved itself, and the first stage in the development of radar was complete.

During the Munich crisis of 1938 the Thames Estuary Chain went into continuous operation and limited cover was given to the Forth-Clyde, Tyne and Humber areas by mobile sets hurriedly installed at three of the sites chosen for the final chain. By the end of May the whole chain was handed over to the RAF. In January 1939 it was decided that cover was needed north to Scapa Flow and west to Portland, and four more stations were built. When war was declared in September, Britain was guarded by an RDF chain of nineteen stations stretching from Netherbutton in the Orkneys to Ventnor in the Isle of Wight. The system had been fully tested in August, and was to prove invaluable next year in the Battle of Britain.

It had been demonstrated that early radar worked successfully in the manner of 'floodlighting', but it had severe limitations in providing precise data, like measuring the angles of bearing, so was no use for controlling anti-aircraft fire or naval gunnery. The answer lay in producing shorter wavelengths. A really sharp beam from a really small aerial was a great prize, and it was realised that greater power was the key.

Experimental work began in the autumn of 1939 on various aspects of the problem of centimetric radio. By 1940 the Telecommunications Research Establish-ment (TRE) was able to embark on a programme that was divided between basic research and the application of centimetric methods for airborne radar. Further development was done on magnetron transmitters, receivers, aerials and reflectors and the waveguides to feed them. Among the devices under development was AI (Air Interception) equipment to be carried in night fighters, ASV (Air to Surface Vessels) equipment to locate ships and surfaced submarines, IFF (Identification Friend or Foe) to be installed in all aircraft, and the naval Type 281, a high power aircraft warning set for use in ships.

As German submarine forces grew steadily stronger during 1940, the improvement of anti-submarine tactics became more urgent. As mentioned earlier, the primary problem was that of location. A U-boat running awash presented a very small visual target, and at night or in poor visibility was effectively invisible.

Luck was to play a part in the radar story. In early October 1940 Commanders Fawcette and Bayldon of the Admiralty were visiting TRE and saw the 10-centimetre experimental work. The idea of using centimetric waves for submarine detection was noticed from casual observations of small ships, such as motor launches or MTBs. The equipment being used was a GEC H1189 magnetron at the transmitter and two 3ft paraboloid mains for the transmitting and receiving aerials, and very clear echoes of such vessels about five times noise were obtained at 7-8 miles.

On 7 November a deputation from the Admiralty and Signal School attended a demonstration. A boat called *Titlark* was obtained and they were able to detect it very clearly up to 8 miles off. On the 9th a message was received that a submarine would pass Swanage on its way to Portsmouth on the 11th. A test was carried out and HMS *Usk* gave very large echoes at up to 5 miles. As she turned the signal fluctuated but the broadside view gave echoes about twice those of the stern view. *Usk* was still very obvious at 7 miles. Beyond 7 miles the echo became more difficult to follow, but it could still be made out at 9 miles. Towards the end of this trial the submarine's position was masked by local mist so it was not possible to be sure that the aerial system was being accurately directed. The experiment was carried out from a house about 26ft above sea level, in fairly smooth sea conditions.

These events provided the impetus and it was decided that the Admiralty Signal School should develop a 10cm set for naval use. It was decided that even if the equipment proved to be unsatisfactory, production should go ahead, and components were ordered for 150 sets. The Captain in charge also decided that the laboratory manufacture twenty-four copies of the experimental prototype, and ruled that no modifications could be accepted unless they were essential or could be introduced without delaying urgent production. Components for the 150 sets were ordered on trust. This new equipment was to be called Type 271 and operated at a wavelength of approximately 10cm.

Because of the urgency of the requirement, the equipment was reduced to its simplest form possible. The essential limitation was the need to mount the aerials vertically above the radar office and as close as possible. In the proposed form it could not be fitted in destroyers but would be suitable for use in corvettes. It was decided to fit a prototype set aboard HMS *Orchis*, due to complete on 23 March 1941.

Sea trials were carried out in April. The intention was primarily to establish the effective ranges on submarine and other targets under realistic sea conditions, so were carried out in both rough and smooth water. When limiting ranges were approached even in fairly smooth water, echoes, which tended to fluctuate rapidly, were sometimes absent for several seconds at a time. In rough water with small targets, these periods increased owing to the effect of intervening waves. The pitching and rolling of the ship did not appreciably effect performance, however. With the aerials 37ft above the sea, the reduction of useful ranges on a small target, such as a submarine was about 20 per cent. This was attributed to the effect of intervening waves blocking the visual path, or to the reduction in effective height of the conning tower due to waves. It was considered that at a greater height this effect would be less serious.

The initial results looked very promising. The maximum range when showing only 8ft of periscope was 1300 yards. The maximum range in smooth water was 5000 yards, with a comfortable working range of 4200 yards. The maximum range in rough water was 4400 yards, but although the echo was quite unmistakable, the submarine had been lost when giving a good echo at 3200 yards due to a 90-degree alteration of the ship's heading and it was not picked up again until 4400 yards.

The weather was too rough to allow a further trial because as a result of a collision the submarine was in a somewhat unseaworthy condition. *Orchis* was rolling often to 20 degrees and on occasion 30. The conclusion was that with constant awareness of the ship's head, the radar operator could have followed the submarine comfortably to 3500 yards in rough weather. The submarine trimming down did not appreciably affect the range. There was a much improved echo when the submarine was beam-on rather than end-on.

There was the added bonus that buoys showed up at 2000–2500 yards, so almost any buoys large enough to mark a channel or harbour could be spotted with certainty. In rough weather the Mull of Kintyre and Ailsa Craig were noticed at the extreme end of the trace on the indicator at about 28,000 yards. Even with the set switched on from cold, land was easily identified. It was found that a small dredger was picked up at 7500 yards, a small convoy at 16,000 yards and a liner at 20,000.

Other practical information was obtained. The radar office deckhead had to be stiffened before the pedestal was fitted. No guys were fitted to the office or aerial lantern and these would have been of advantage. Grab rails needed to be provided adjacent to the operator's chair. A voice pipe between the office and compass house and office and aerial compartment was fitted, but another was required on the outside bridge. The office door faced forward. In rough weather water cascaded through the top of the door and fell just short of the power board and rectifier. In anticipation of this, duckboards had been fitted and drain holes drilled in the deck. The duckboards were objectionable because anything dropped was lost for a short time, but unless a watertight door was fitted, they were essential. Under sea-going conditions in cold weather a radiator was essential to reduce the humidity. The switch at the office door for electric light needed to be waterproof – the one supplied failed early in the trials and was found to be full of water and corroded.

The trials had proved most useful, and improvements followed quickly. When a magnetron of ten to fifteen times the power of the present NT98 became available, and when remote control of the aerial enabled the height of the aerials to be doubled, these two factors gave the equipment nearly twice the effective range. In April 1942 the corvette *Vetch* made a first sighting of a U-boat at 7500 yards. By September 1942 the number of radar-fitted corvettes was thirty-two. Such was the desire for secrecy that in harbour a canvas screen was placed over the teak lantern to hide the shape of the antennas from prying eyes (an accurate analysis of dimensions would allow the enemy to deduce the operating wavelength). As experience was gained at sea, improvements were frequently made to equipment.

Some corvettes had other radar sets at their masthead: 286M (fixed) or 286P (rotating) These were useful for station-keeping but not very effective against U-boats. Early Canadian built ships had SW-1 and -2 of a generally similar performance. But it was the introduction of Type 271 radar that did most to mitigate the shortcomings of the slow corvette and was a standard fitting to the improved twin-screw corvettes of the 'River' class.

Appearance

The *Wetaskiwin* (ex-*Banff*) was one of the first Canadian-built 'Flowers' to complete, in December 1940. Shown here two months later at Esquimalt, British Columbia, she was fitted as a conventional (Oropesa) minesweeper, the extra gear on the quarterdeck requiring modification to the superstructure aft. The usual pronunciation of the ship's name as 'Wet Ass Queen' indicates what the crew thought of her seakeeping. *(Public Archives of Canada)*

Seen in September 1942, *Lotus* was a magnetic/acoustic sweeper conversion. The mast is still stepped before the bridge, which itself has been extended – note the Oerlikons in the wings. The second *Lotus* was one of a few corvettes whose hulls were modified during building to incorporate more sheer and flare. *(Ministry of Defence)*

Two views of *Buttercup* as completed in April 1942 for acoustic and magnetic mine-sweeping. The gear for the 'LL magnetic sweep' was carried on the quarterdeck, while the acoustic 'hammer' was deployed from the large A-frame over the bows. *(Ulster Folk & Transport Museum)*

Modifications to existing units (extended forecastle) 1941
Redrawn from a Smith's Dock original plan dated January 1941.

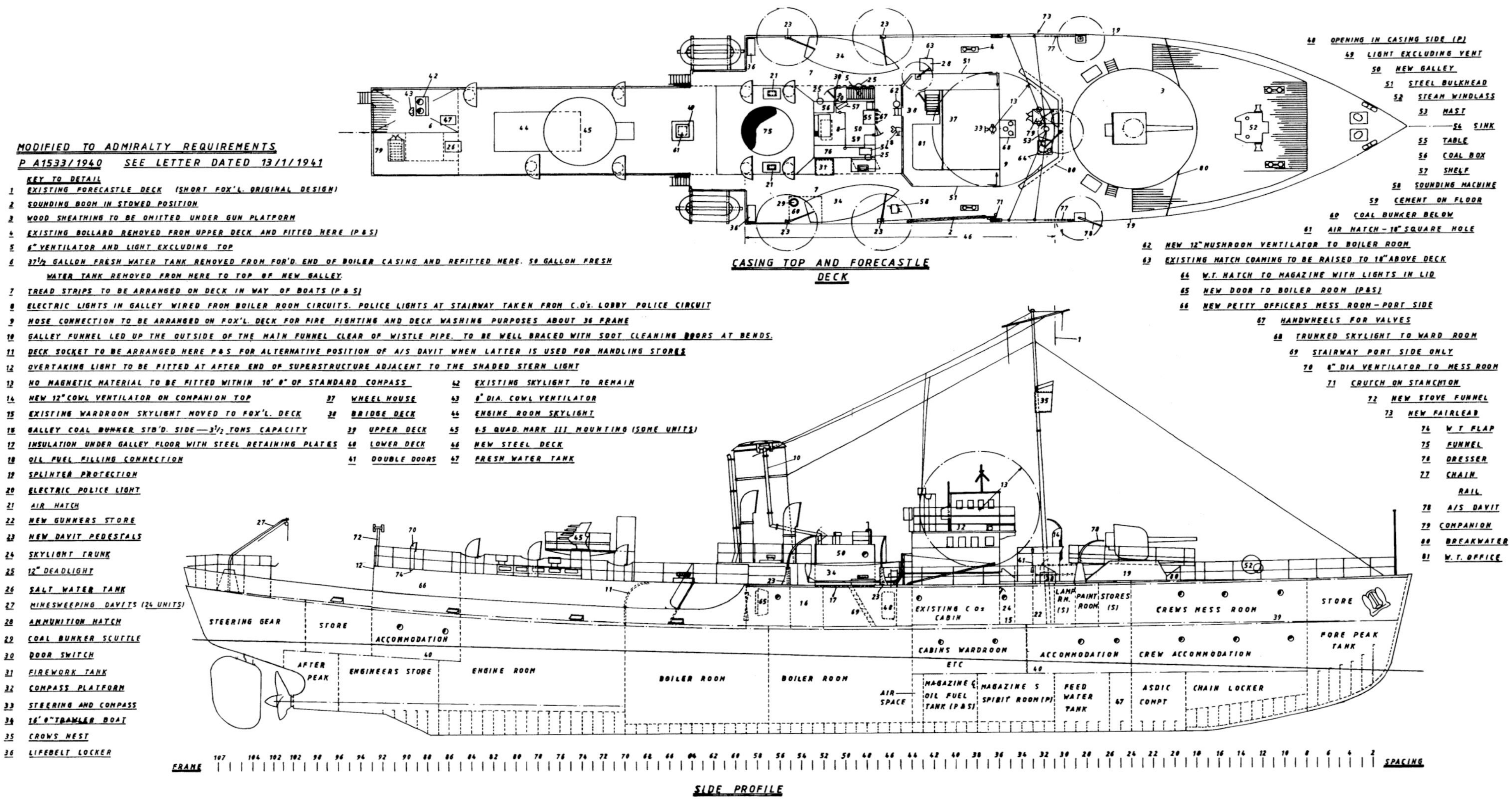

Modifications to compass platform 1940-41

Measures to protect the crew against machine gun attack from aircraft: protective plating added to shell plating in crew's washplace, crew shelters fore and aft, 2pdr gun platform, wheelhouse and engine room canopy. In addition, as shown here, there was to be of a bulletproof cruciform 'conning tower' on the compass platform. This drawing relates to *Primrose*, *Primula*, *Salvia* and *Snapdragon* (left-hand plan) and *Violet*, *Woodruff*, *Ranunculus* and *Rose* (right).

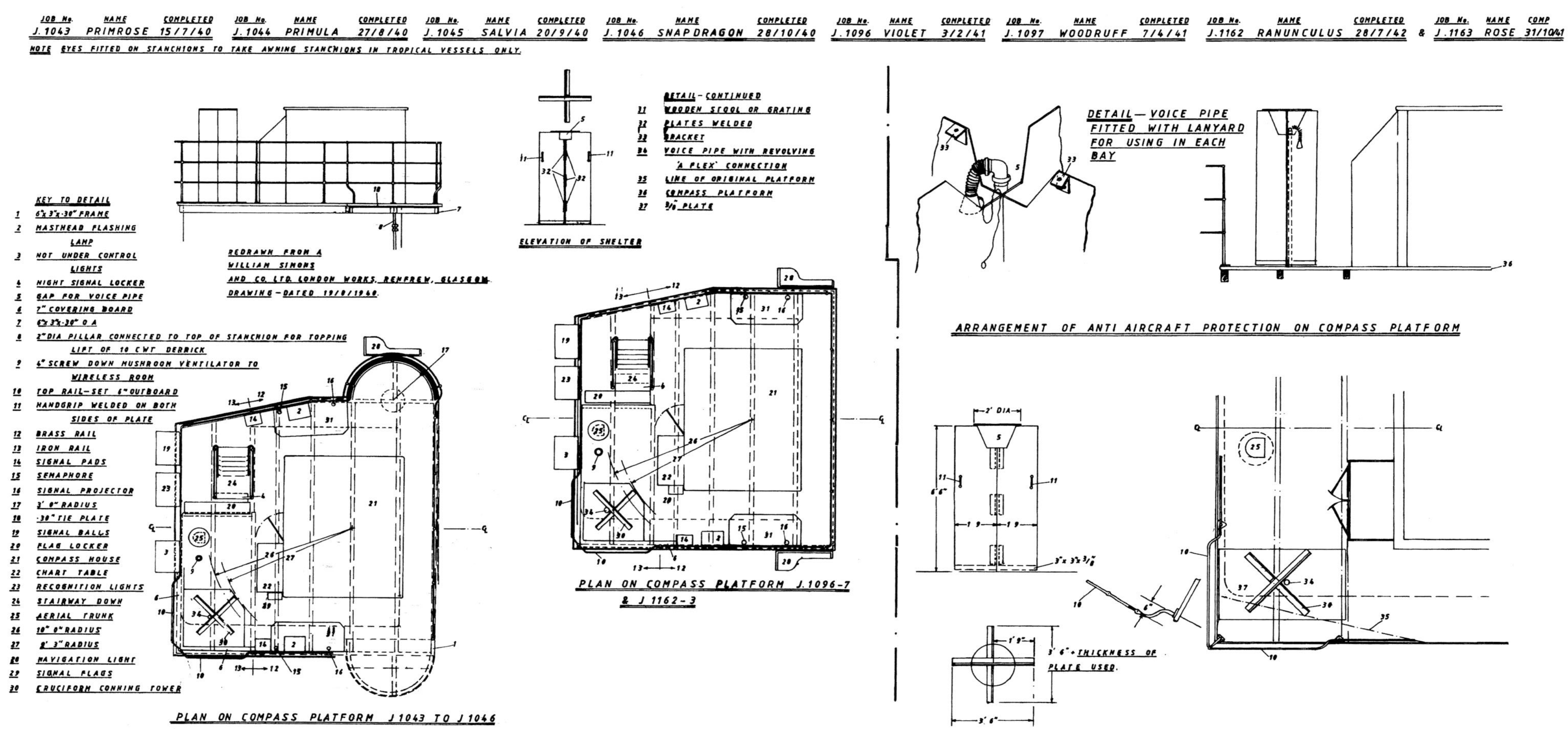

The bridge of the *Violet* as built. The wooden pilot house and extensive canvas screening gives the bridge a decidedly mercantile appearance. *(The Ballast Trust)*

Below: The more warship-like open bridge of *Clematis* in April 1942. She is still waiting for Oerlikons to replace the twin Lewis guns in the bridge wings, but she has Type 271 (with its lantern covered as was usual in port) *(IWM A8078)*

Two views of the recently refitted *Alisma* in April 1943. She retained the short forecastle and the mast stepped before the bridge, but the latter has been extended and carries single Oerlikons in the wings. The ship was fitted for conventional wire minesweeping *(IWM A8490 & A8492)*

The development of the 'Flower' class bridge
These six drawings show the basic patterns of bridge modified as the war progressed.

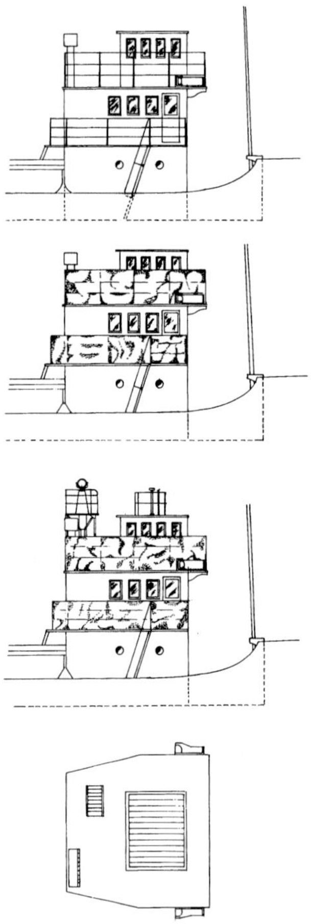

Type A: The original pattern followed mercantile practice with a teak bridge on two levels – wheelhouse and chartroom below and compass house above, the latter housing the A/S control and a watchkeeper's shelter. The open rails were covered only by canvas dodgers at first, then splinter mats and eventually bulletproof crew shelters, and an air lookout position was added to the compass house roof.

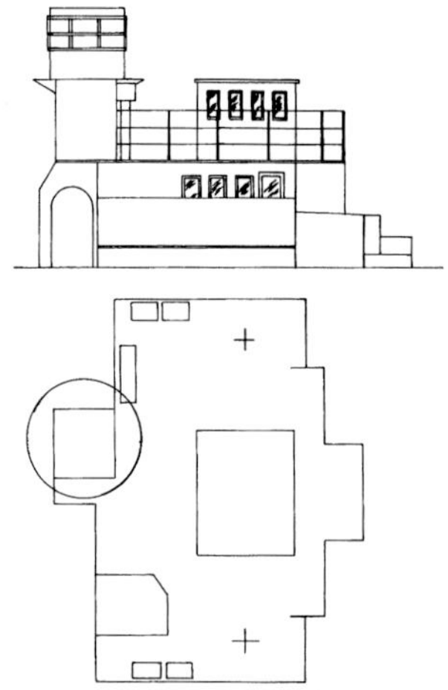

Type B: The compass platform wings were extended to mount close-range weapons, and later a platform for the Type 271 radar was added aft, usually offset to port (but occasionally to starboard), the first so fitted being *Orchis* in May 1941.

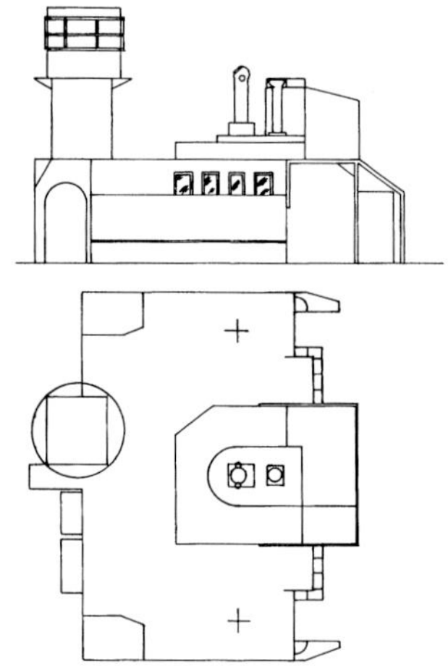

Type C: The compass house was removed, leaving an open bridge, which was better for air lookout. An Asdic office was added to the front of the bridge, all the extra weight requiring more bracing.

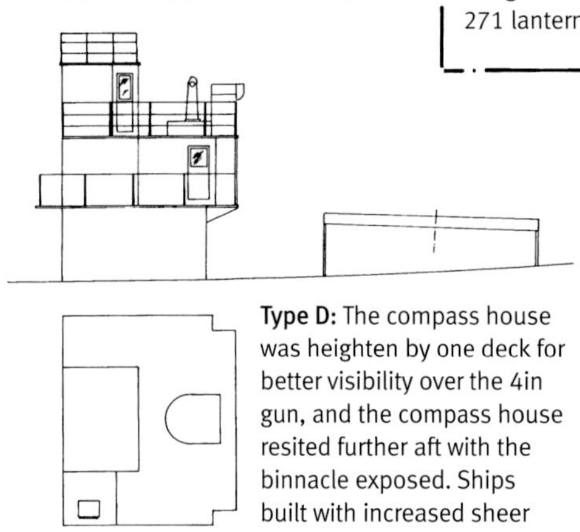

Type D: The compass house was heighten by one deck for better visibility over the 4in gun, and the compass house resited further aft with the binnacle exposed. Ships built with increased sheer had bridge types D-G, and some earlier units were so modified during major refits.

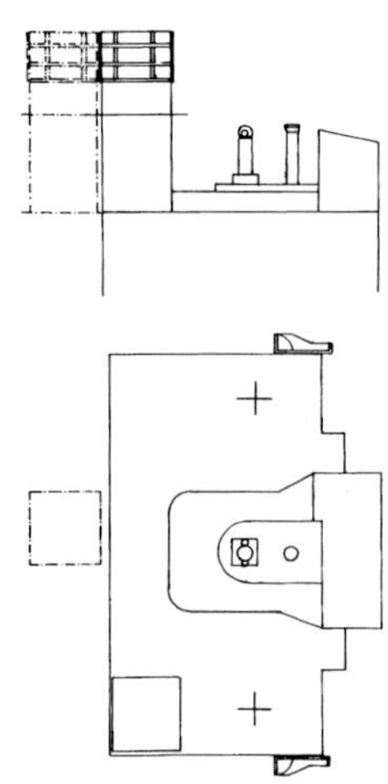

Types F & G: In 'F' the compass house was removed and the Asdic office now overhangs the bridge front; 'G' was similar except that the Type 271 lantern was carried on separate supports abaft the bridge instead of on the compass platform.

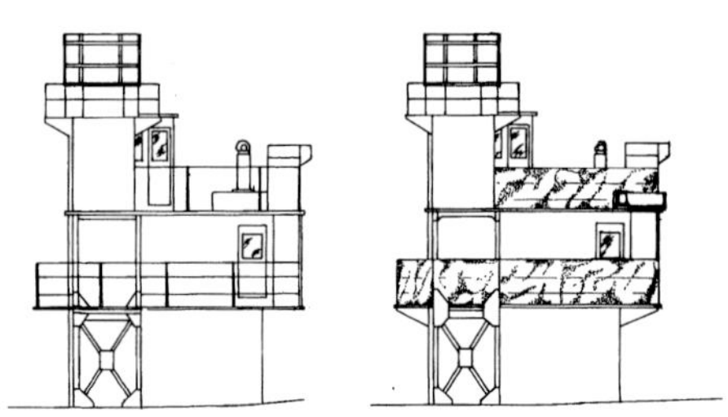

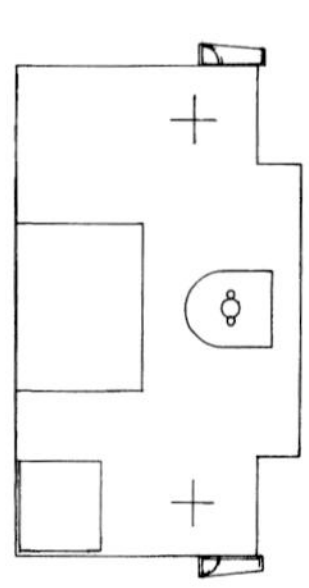

Type E: The compass platform was widened to carry the now-standard 20mm Oerlikons and the Type 271 lantern was fitted in the after starboard corner (although occasionally to port).

Type C bridge of HMS *Clematis* April 1942
(see photo on page 100)

1. Canvas cover over lantern
2. Drain holes in deck
3. Signal halyards secured to cleats
4. Twin 0.303in Lewis guns, port and starboard
5. 20in signal projector (canvas covered)
6. 10in signal projector
7. Ready-use ammunition locker
8. Aerial lead trunk
9. Voice pipe
10. Splinter mat
11. Canvas dodger
12. A/S office
13. Wind deflector
14. Binnacle
15. Pelorus
16. Fixed toughened glass windscreen

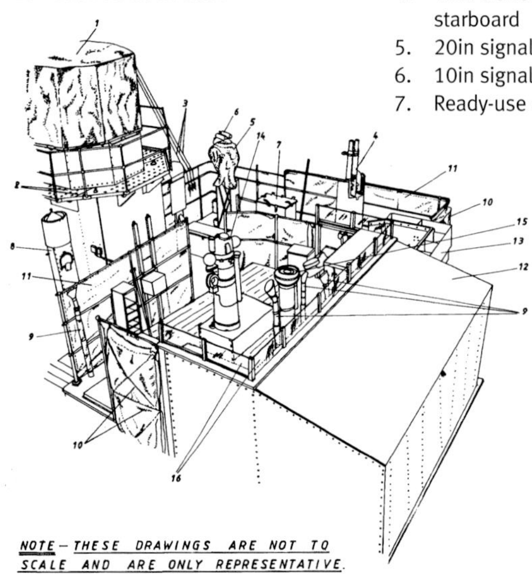

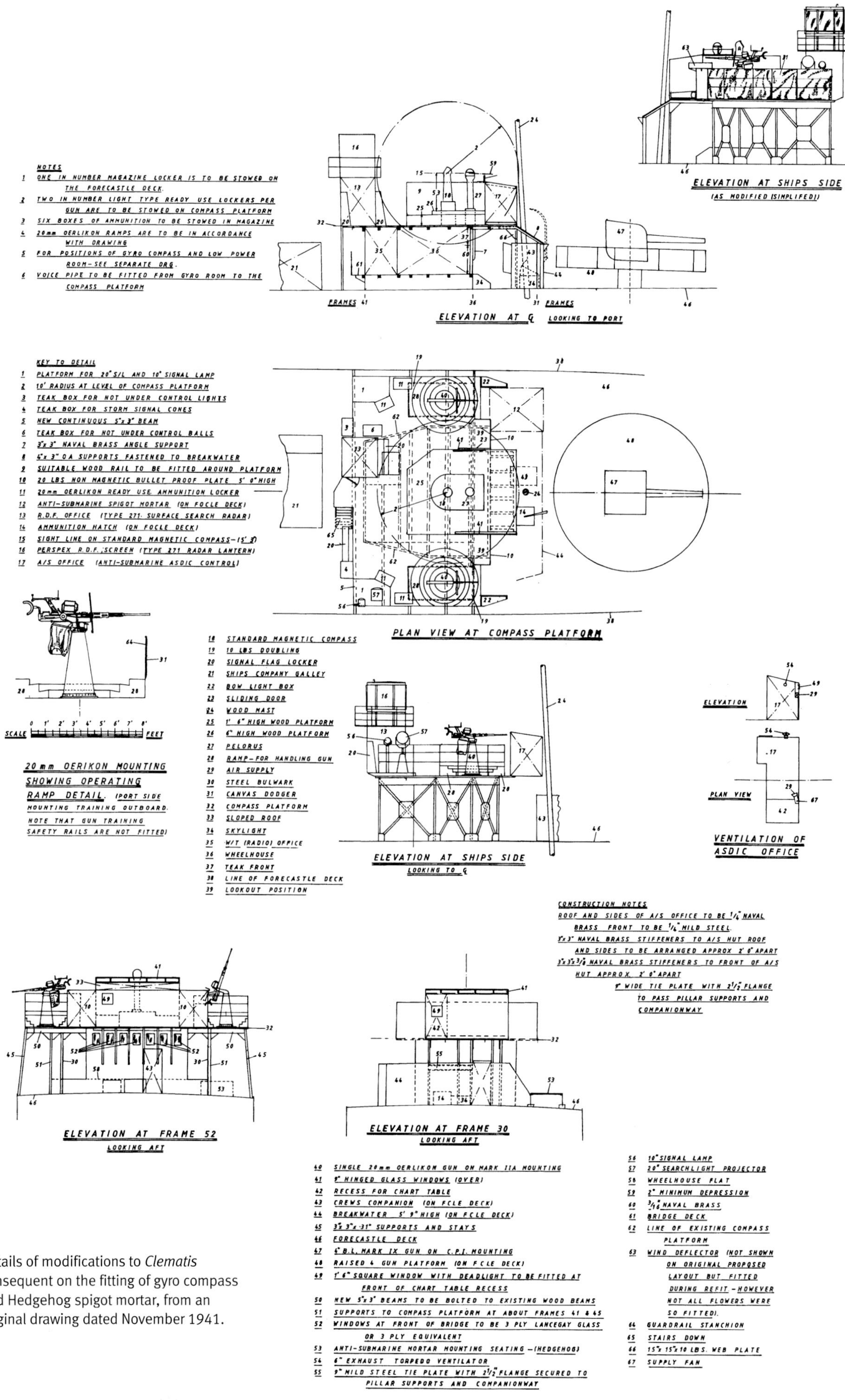

Details of modifications to *Clematis* consequent on the fitting of gyro compass and Hedgehog spigot mortar, from an original drawing dated November 1941.

Opposite, top: Looking across the bridge of the Canadian *Ville de Quebec* at Halifax, NS in October 1942. The ship has Oerlikons in the bridge wings (with safety rails to prevent the guns firing on dangerous arcs), but as yet no Type 271. The central position of the pigeon-holed flag locker suggests that traditional methods of communication were still in vogue. Some of the makeshift splinter protection can be seen lashed to the bridge front. *(Public Archives of Canada)*

Below: Bow detail of *Pink* in June 1943. Modified for minesweeping, the ship has been fitted with massive brackets aft of the anchors to support the A-frame that carried the acoustic 'hammer'. Although not easy to see in this view, *Pink* was one of the 'Flowers' that adopted a modified hull form, with greater sheer and flare *(IWM A17025)*

Below: There was a shortage of salvage tugs in some theatres, so a number of 'Flowers' were fitted for ocean towage. This is one of them, *Anemone*, seen on 29 July 1942 after refit with long forecastle and extended bridge. *(Ministry of Defence)*

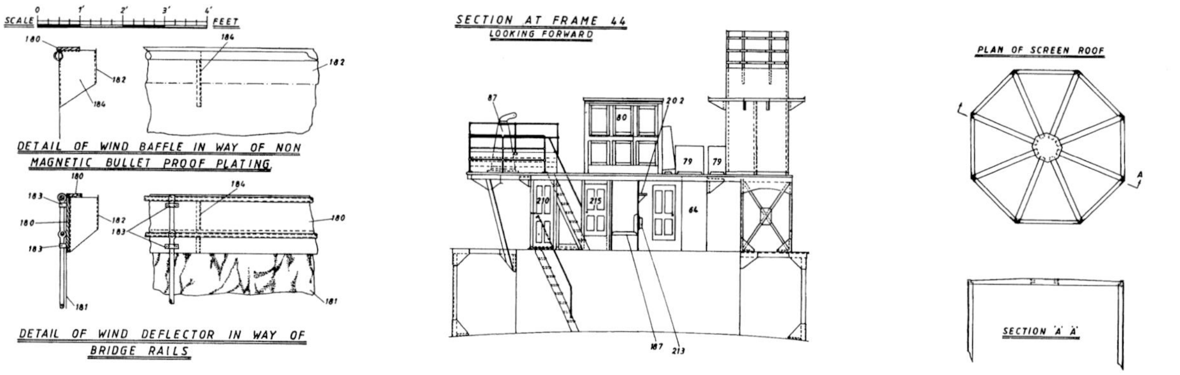

HMS *Potentilla*: construction of bridge and after casing with 2pdr platform
Details for this hybrid ship.

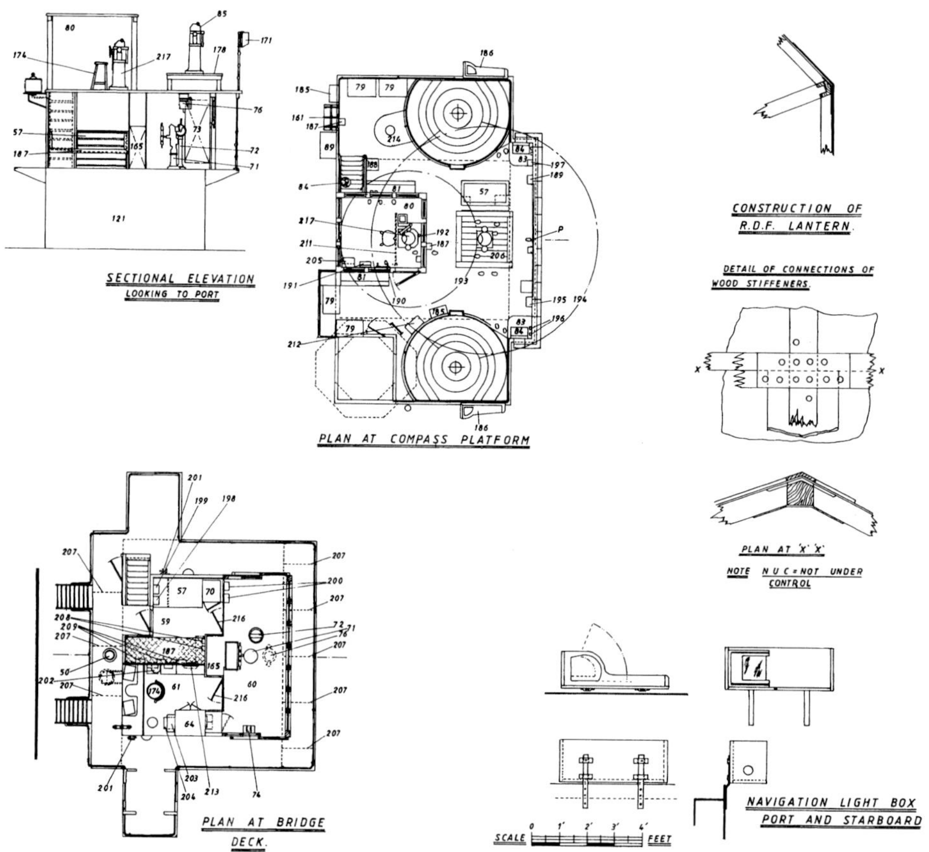

The first part of this key can be found on page 124

180 1" THICK TEAK FACIER BOARD.
181 CANVAS SCREEN OR DOGER.
182 1/8" NAVAL BRASS PLATE.
183 NAVAL BRASS CLIPS.
184 1/8" NAVAL BRASS BRACKET.
185 BOX FOR MASTHEAD FLASHING CIRCUIT AND SIGNALMANS READING LAMP.
186 BOWLIGHT SCREEN.
187 BED SETTEE.
188 BOX FOR SIGNAL PADS.
189 R/T W/T LOUD SPEAKER FITTED IN LIGHT WOODEN SHELTER.
190 TELESCOPE RACK.
191 BINOCULARS.
192 D.G. PILOT LIGHT.
193 6' 0" RADIUS FROM A/S COMPASS.
194 10' 0" MAGNETIC COMPASS RADIUS.
195 A/S LOUD SPEAKER.
196 V.F.C.R. SWITCH AND PUSH.
197 TEAK V/F INDICATOR BOX
198 ECHO SOUND RECORDER
199 ECHO SOUND AMPLIFYER
200 SWITCH PANELS FOR NAVIGATION LIGHTS
201 6" TORPEDO VENTILATOR
202 ELECTRIC FAN BRACKET
203 CHARGING UNIT OVER
204 CHARGING BOARD UNDER
205 BOX FOR SIGNAL BOOKS PATT 1474.
206 WOOD GRATING
207 BRACKET – UNDER
208 2 TEST BOXES
209 SELECTOR SWITCHES AND FUSE BOXES
210 DOOR TO STAIRWAY
211 STORM RAIL
212 SIGNAL FLAG LOCKER TYPE 'C'.
213 ELECTRIC RADIATOR
214 PLATFORM FOR 10" SIGNAL PROJECTOR
215 DOOR TO CHARTROOM
216 NO GLASS PANEL IN THIS DOOR
217 A/S COMPASS

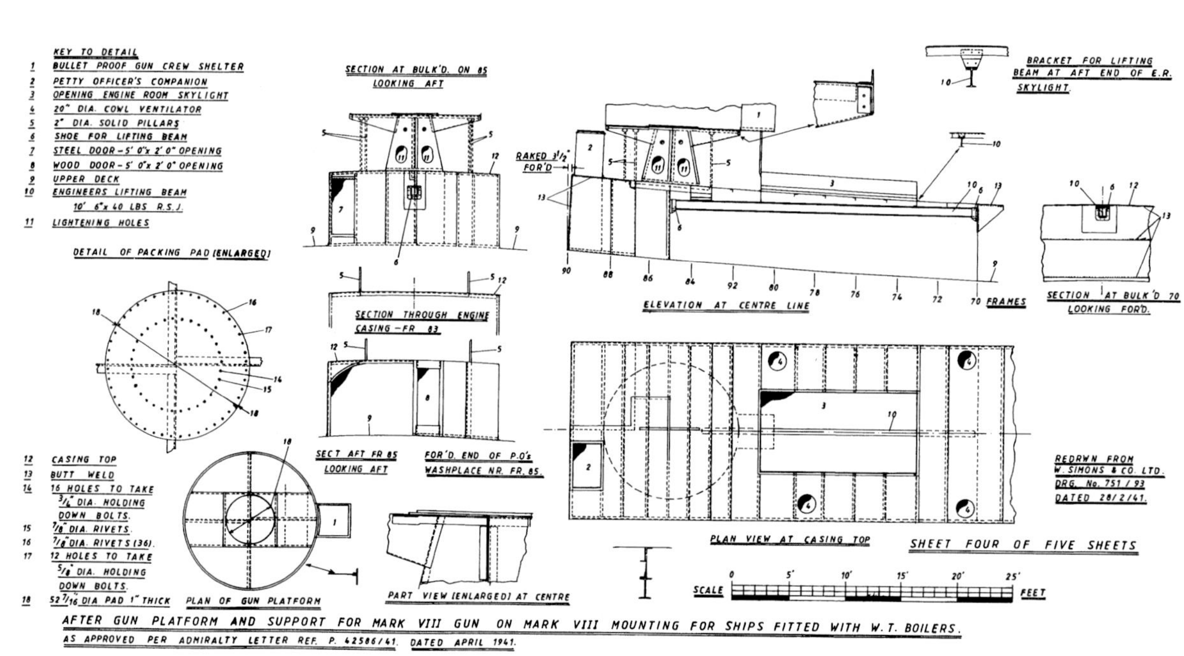

Modifications in deck layout for 'LL' equipped minesweepers; detail of davit
The buoyant but heavy cables were stowed in troughs along the upper deck bulwarks and were originally hauled in by hand, but a large stowage reel (shown on page 110) was soon developed.

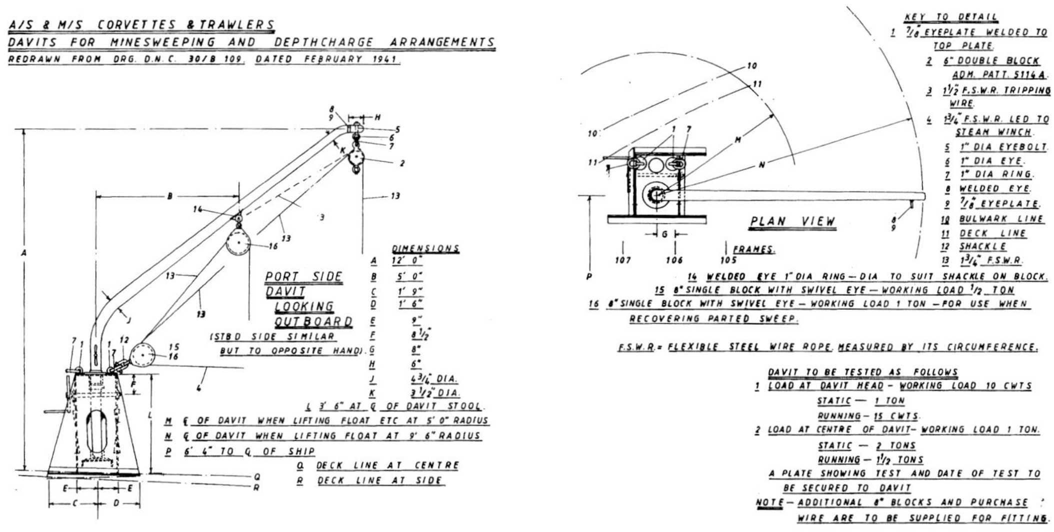

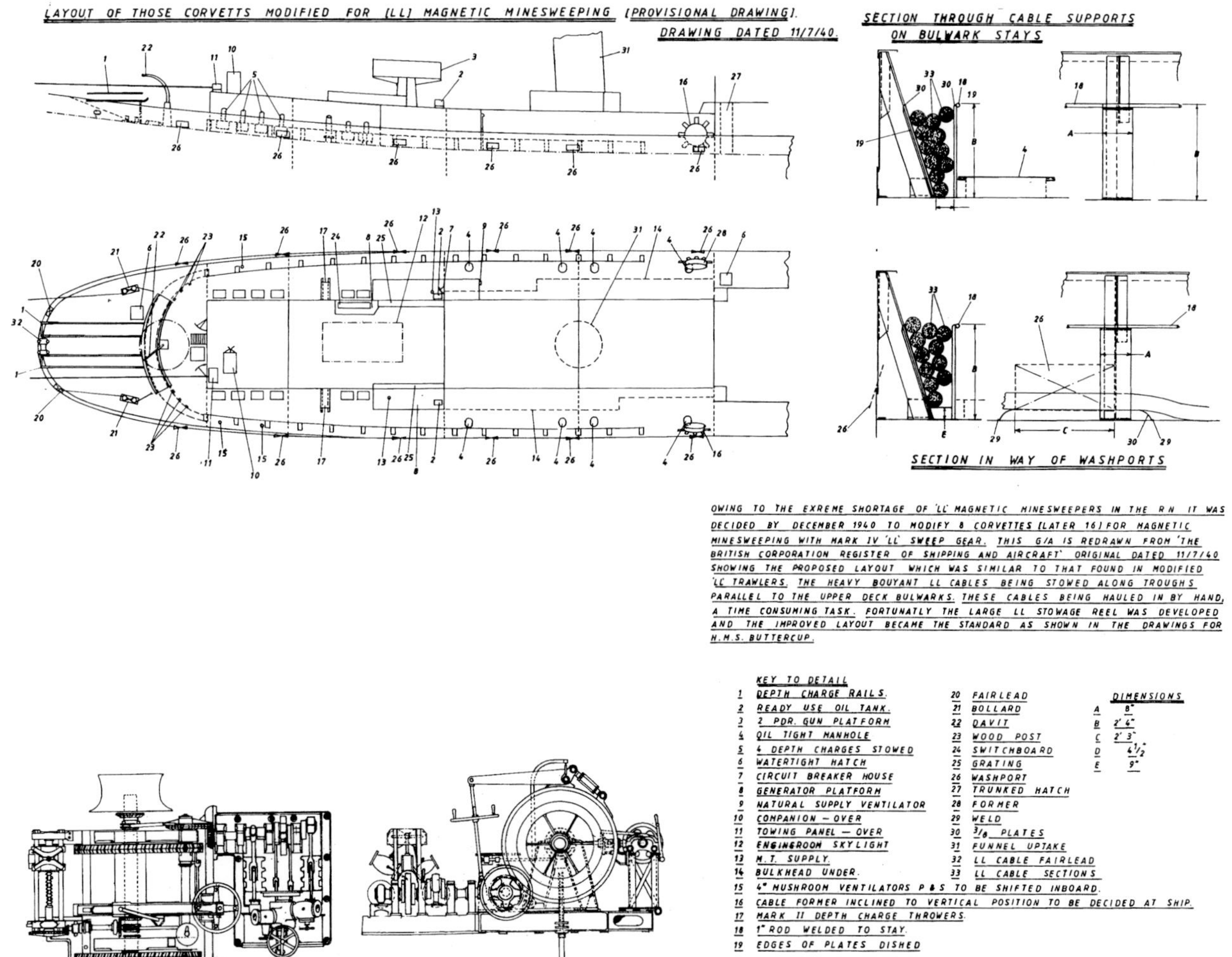

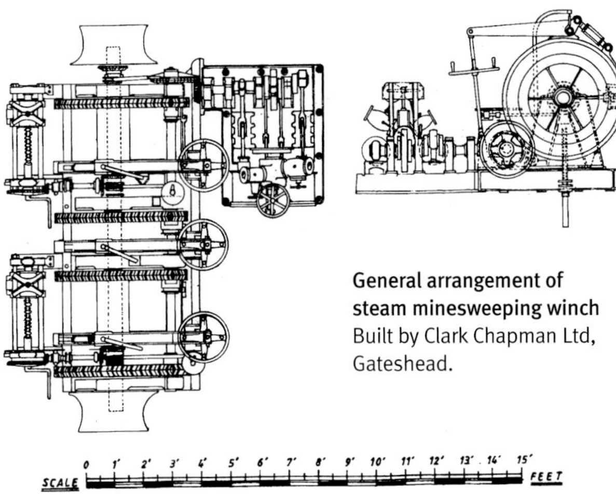

General arrangement of steam minesweeping winch
Built by Clark Chapman Ltd, Gateshead.

Above: Port side of *Vervain* looking aft in July 1942. *(IWM A10626)*

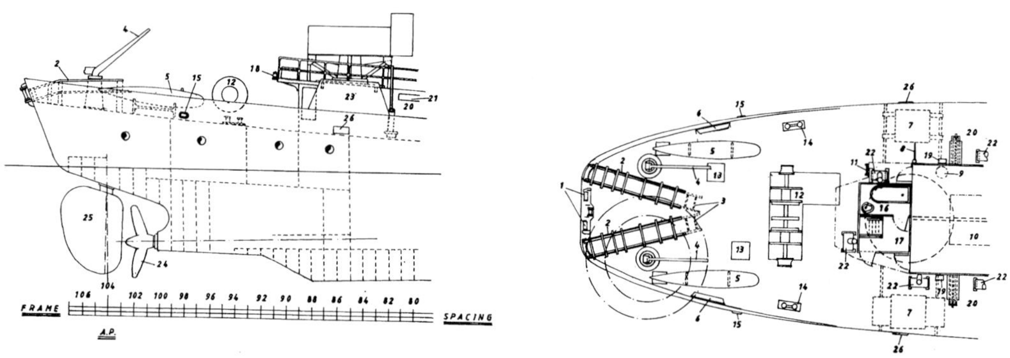

KEY TO DETAIL

1 MINESWEEPING FAIRLEAD
2 FIXED DEPTHCHARGE RAIL
3 PORTABLE SECTION OF RAIL
4 MINESWEEPING DAVIT
5 OROPESA FLOAT
6 MULTIPLANE KITE-OTTER
7 SPARE MULTIPLANE STOWAGE
8 AMMUNITION DAVIT
9 VENTILATOR
10 ENGINE CASING
11 VERTICAL LADDER
12 STEAM MINESWEEPING WINCH
13 WATERTIGHT HATCH
14 MOORING BOLLARDS
15 MOORING PIPE
16 OFFICERS BATHROOM
17 LOBBY
18 OVERTAKING LIGHT
19 DEPTH CHARGE CARTRIDGE BOX
20 DEPTH CHARGE THROWER MARK II
21 NAME BOARD
22 STOWAGE FOR SPARE DEPTH CHARGES
23 SPLINTER SHIELD
24 SINGLE PROPELLER – DIA 10′ 6″ PITCH 10′ 8″ SURFACE AREA – 31 SQ FT THREE BLADES R/H
25 SINGLE RUDDER
26 HINGED WASHPORT

Sweep deck arrangements for Canadian 'Flowers' equipped for wire minesweeping
As in HMCSs *Wetaskiwin*, *Agassiz*, *Chilliwack* and *Trail*.

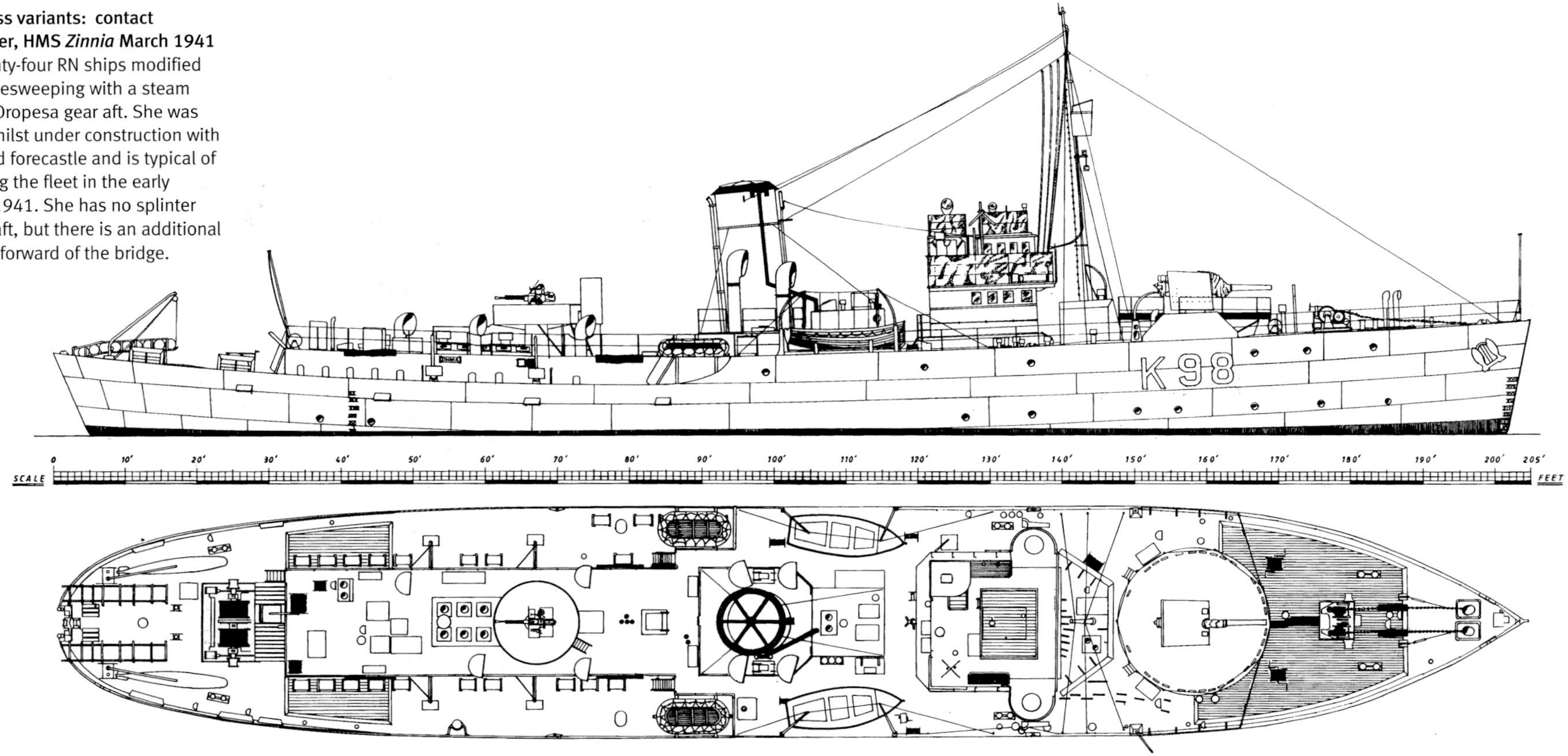

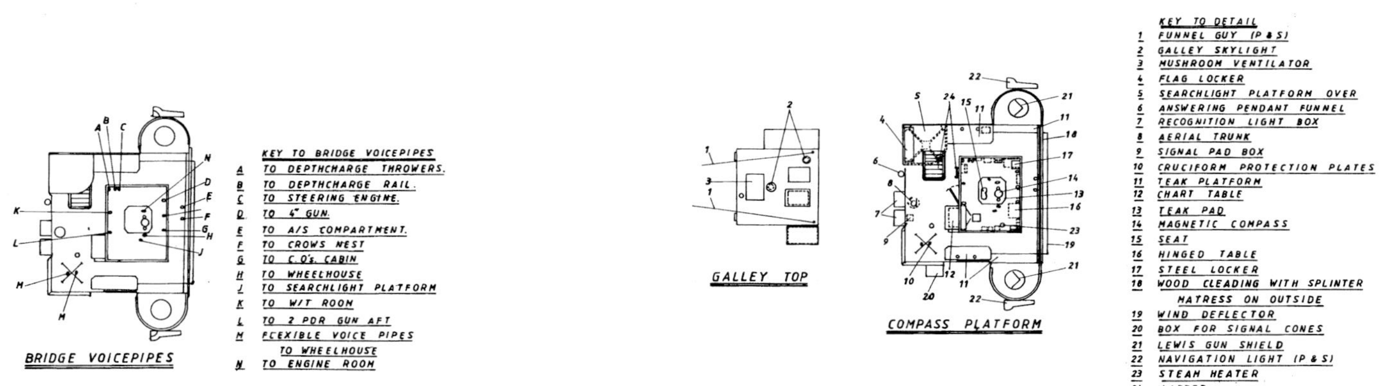

'Flower' class variants: contact minesweeper, HMS *Zinnia* March 1941
One of twenty-four RN ships modified for wire minesweeping with a steam winch and Oropesa gear aft. She was modified whilst under construction with an extended forecastle and is typical of ships joining the fleet in the early months of 1941. She has no splinter protection aft, but there is an additional breakwater forward of the bridge.

'Flower' class variants: fleet minesweeper, HMS *Buttercup* April 1942
The first eight modifications for magnetic sweeping were ordered in December 1940. For this they were fitted with the conspicuous 'LL' Mark V cable reel aft, and required 50 tons of pig iron ballast to compensate for the extra topweight. By February 1941 it was thought prudent to equip them also for dealing with acoustic mines, so they were fitted with SA Type A Mark II gear, with its distinctive A-frame over the bow for the acoustic 'hammer'. They retained the A/S capacity although the number of depth charges stowed was reduced. Ships so fitted eventually included: *Borage, Bryony, Hyderabad* (ex-*Nettle*), *Loosestrife, Oxlip, Pennywort, Poppy, Sunflower, Peony, Erica, Primula, Gloxinia, Delphinium, Salvia, Snapdragon, Dianthus, Lotus* (i) and *Lotus* (ii).

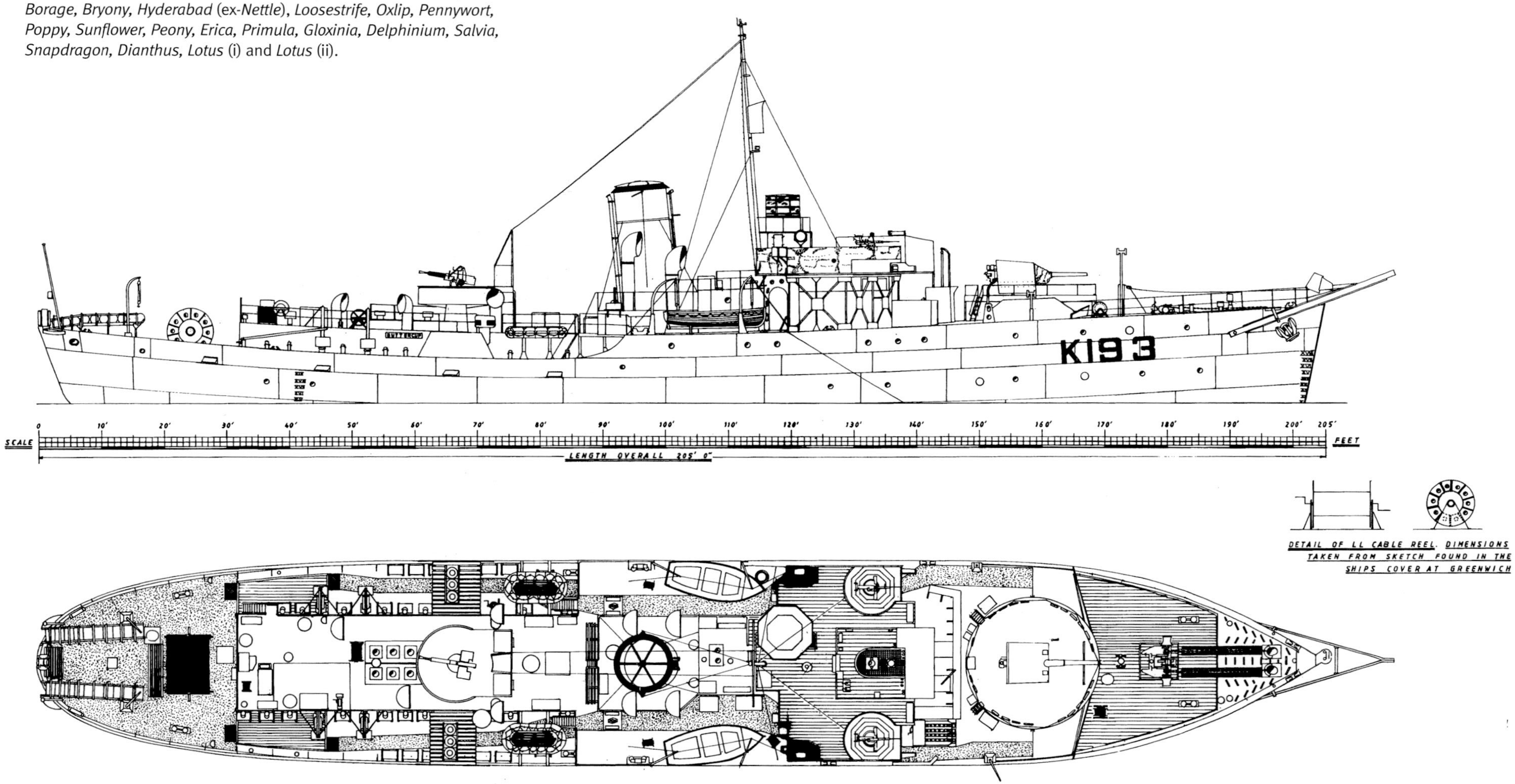

'Flower' class variants: fitted for fleet towage, HMS *Anemone* July 1942
One of the first group ordered, she is shown after a major refit with the extended forecastle, improved bridge, radar and Hedgehog. At the same time she was modified for fleet tug duties – note the two towing safety bars aft. Ships similarly fitted include *Monkshood, Snowflake, Bluebell* and *Narcissus*, but there were others.

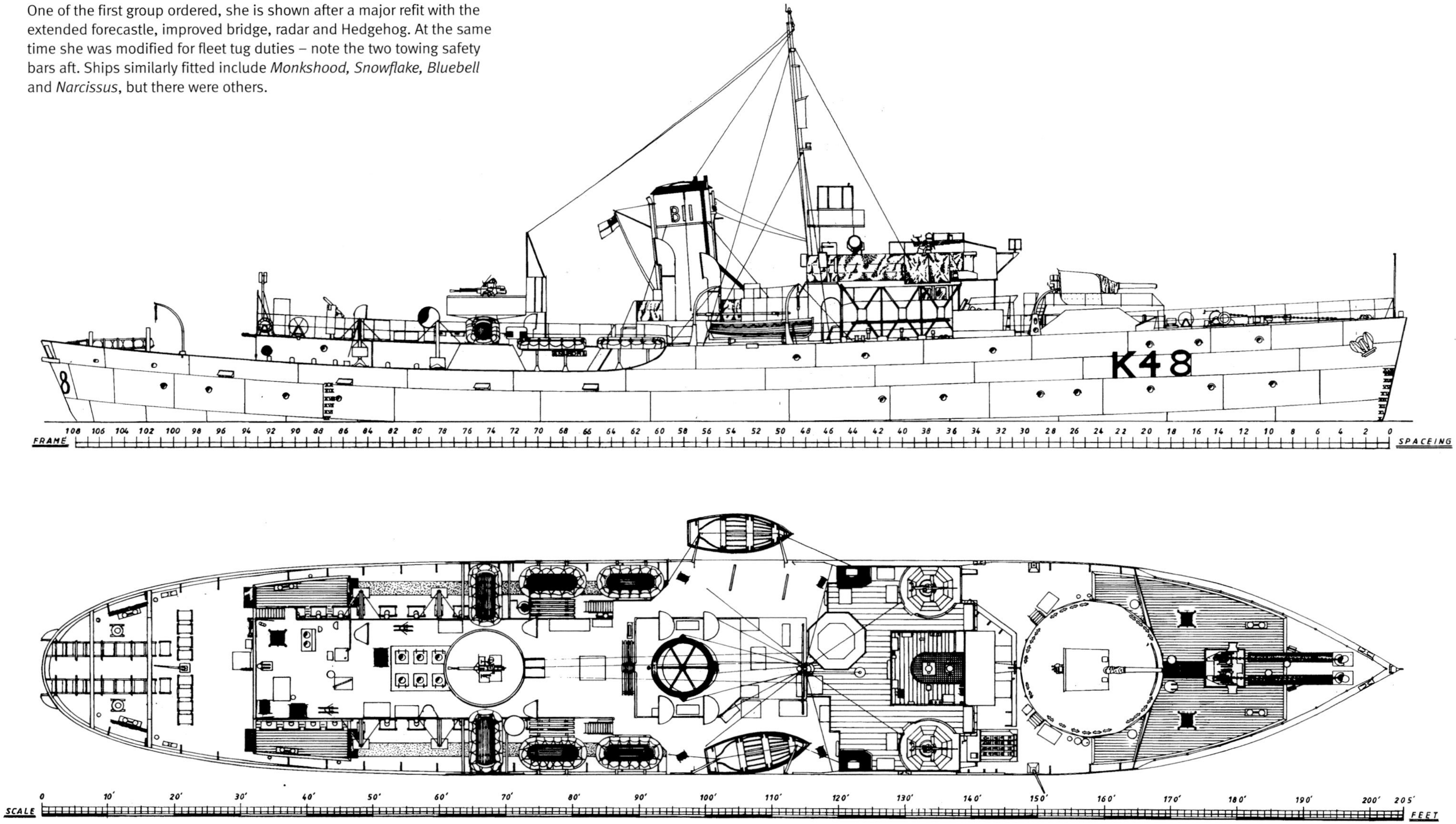

HMS *Alisma* of April 1943
Shown after her first major refit (in 1942) to equip her for Arctic service. Although the short forecastle has been retained, she has a modified bridge (type 'B') with Oerlikons in the wings and Type 271, and a 20in searchlight on a platform above the 2pdr gun crew shelter aft. Fitted for wire minesweeping, she has m/s lights – one on the masthead and one at each yardarm. Less obvious changes are adjustable louvers to the cowl ventilators and additional lifesaving equipment – more carley floats, a wooden life raft (stowed under the port carley floats), and basket stowage racks port and starboard for cork flotation mats.

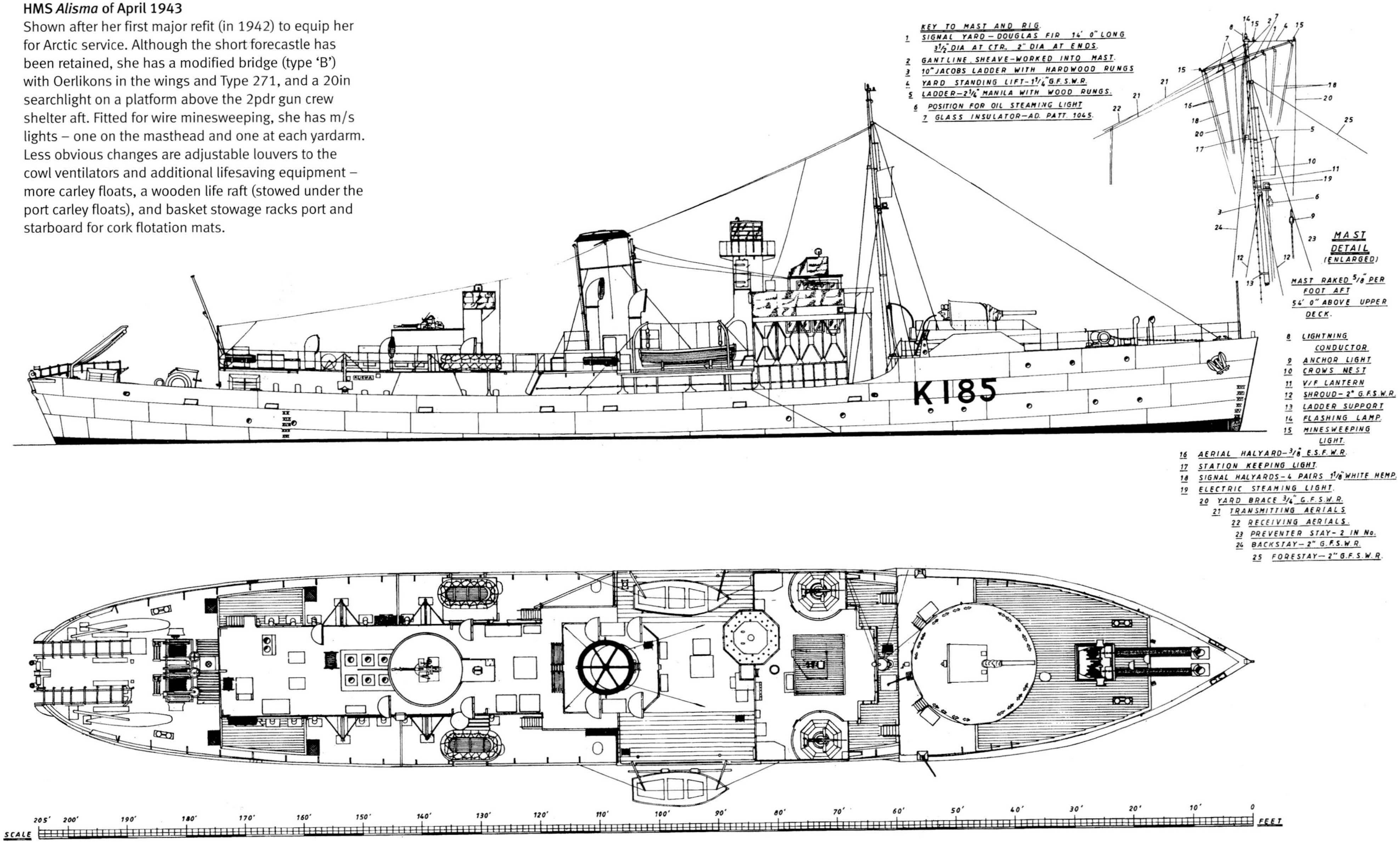

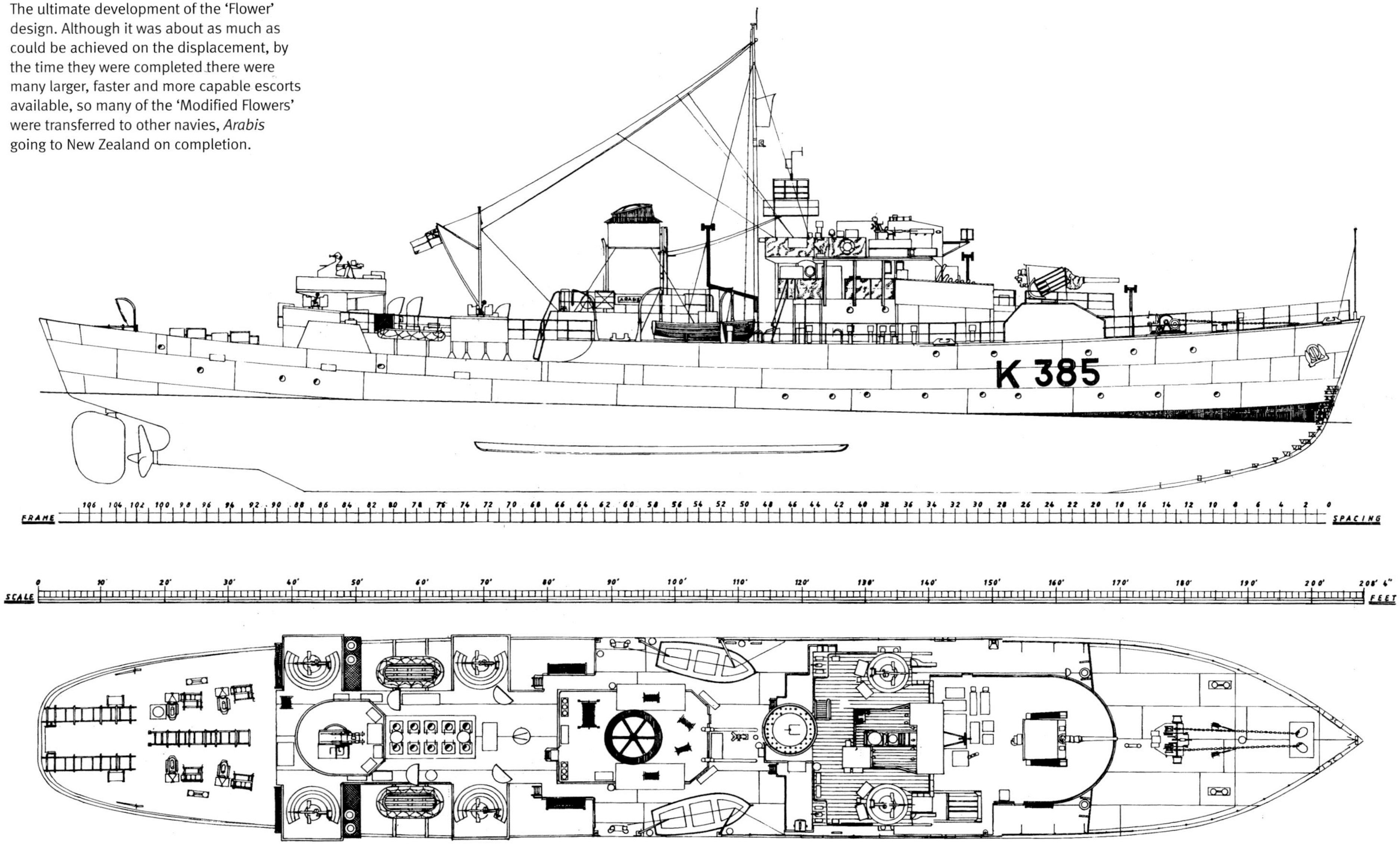

'Modified Flower' class HMNZS *Arabis* as completed March 1944
The ultimate development of the 'Flower' design. Although it was about as much as could be achieved on the displacement, by the time they were completed there were many larger, faster and more capable escorts available, so many of the 'Modified Flowers' were transferred to other navies, *Arabis* going to New Zealand on completion.

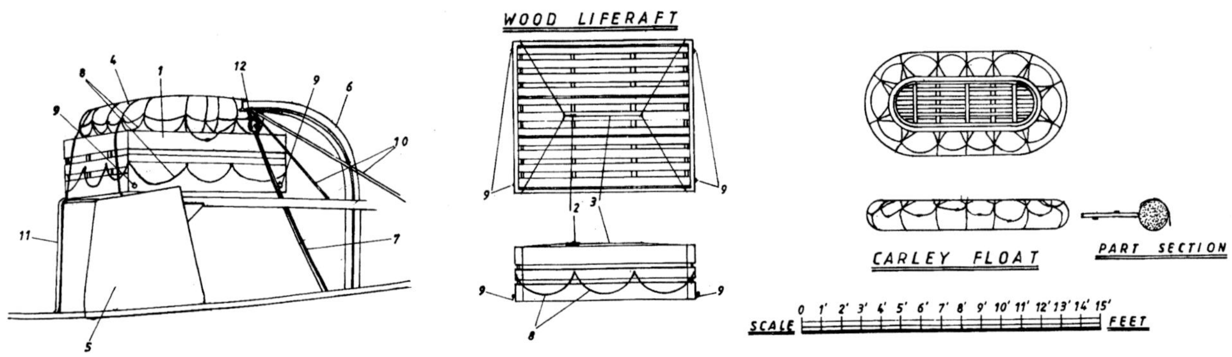

Wooden life raft and carley float details

1. Reversible life raft
2. Slip
3. Lanyard
4. Twenty-man carley float
5. Splinter-proof plating
6. T-bar depth charge davit
7. Depth charge reloading tackle
8. Lifelines
9. Towing/securing ring
10. Steadying stay
11. Supporting stay
12. Block

The 14ft 6in drifter type clinker-built boat

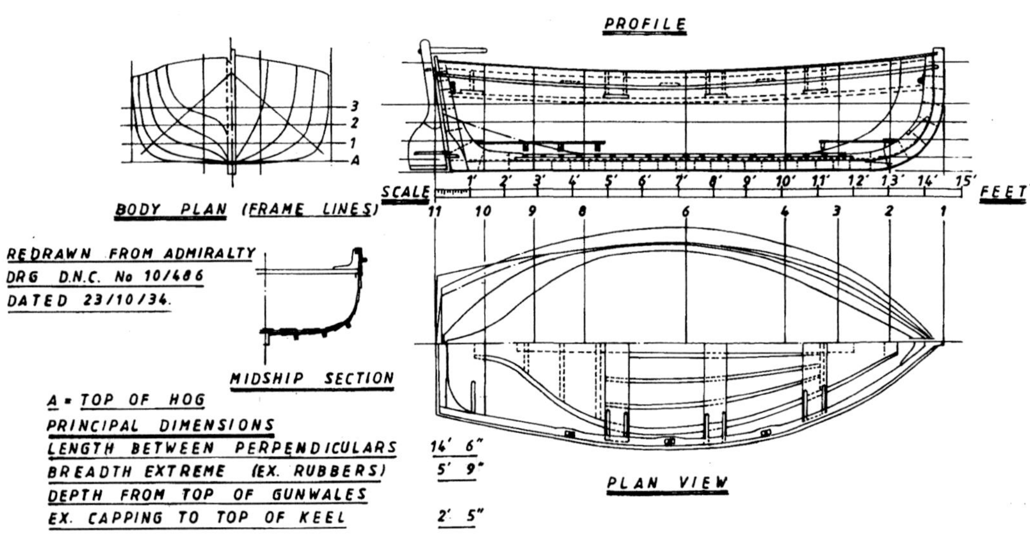

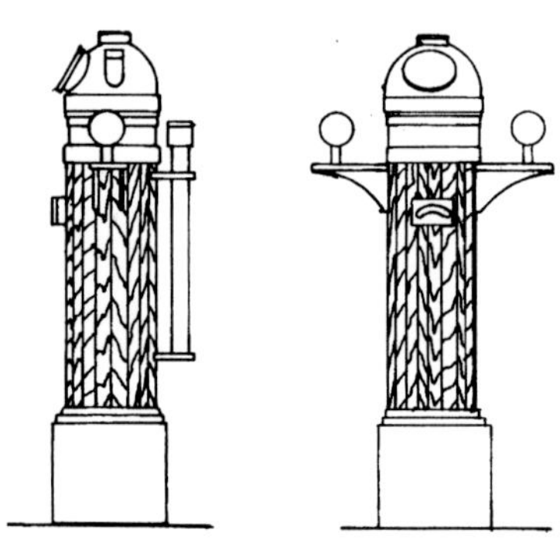

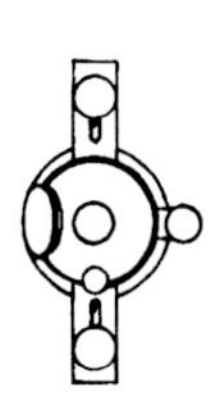

The magnetic compass binnacle

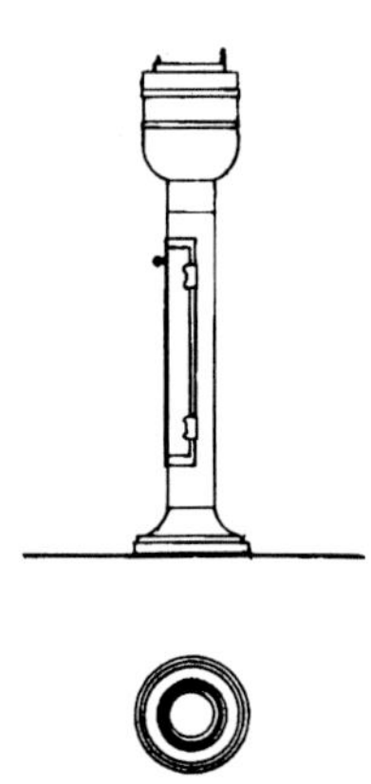

Pelorus

This was a sight from which relative bearings were taken. Usually mounted on the centreline on the compass platform.

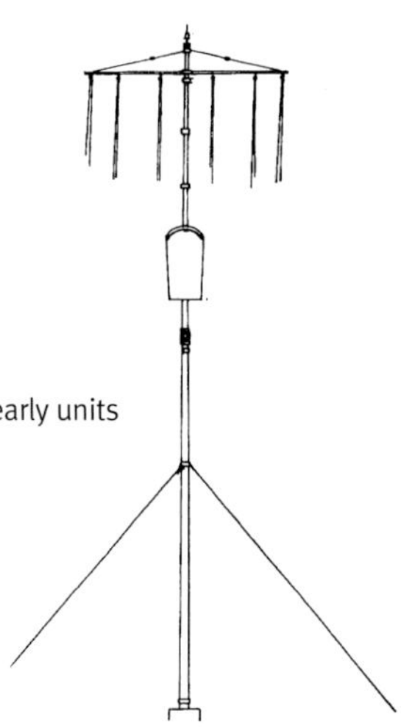

Mast from forward, early units

Midships detail of the Canadian *Athol* at Halifax, NS in January 1944. The Type 271 is uncovered, revealing the framework of the lantern. *(Public Archives of Canada)*

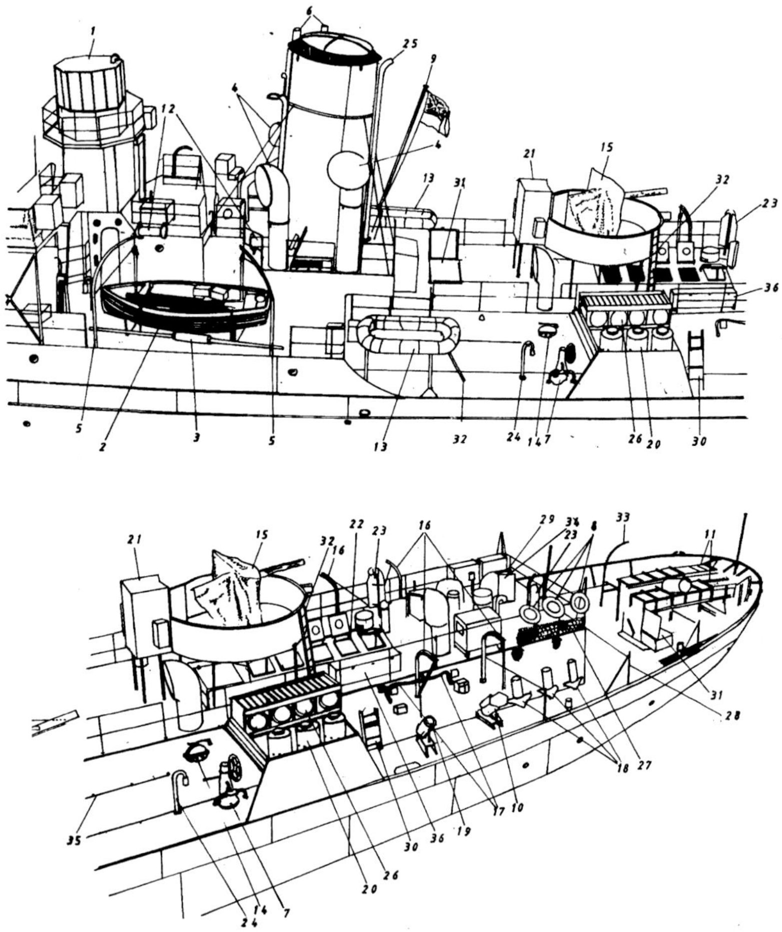

Perspective views of HMCS *Snowberry* as fitted after second refit (at Galverston), 29 January 1942

1. Type 271 radar lantern
2. 16ft 0in trawler dinghy
3. Griping spar
4. Boiler room cowl ventilator
5. Boat davit
6. Galley funnel
7. Downton pump
8. Life belts
9. Ensign staff
10. Mark II depth charge thrower
11. Depth charge rails
12. Rope reel
13. Pattern 20 carley float
14. Hose rack and axe
15. Single 2pdr (under canvas cover)
16. Depth charge thrower reload davit
17. Voice pipe to depth charge thrower
18. Carrier ('arbor') stowed without depth charge
19. Mark II depth charge thrower (without depth charge – the bore is covered)
20. Stowage for smoke floats
21. Shelter for gun crew
22. Engine room skylight
23. Splinter shield for 0.303in Lewis gun (gun stowed away)
24. Gooseneck air pipe
25. Exhaust steam pipe
26. Four-drum survival float
27. Cork flotation net
28. Awning stanchions
29. Companionway
30. Painting punt
31. Hatch (open)
32. Ladder
33. Depth charge davit
34. Open door
35. Grab rail
36. Washdeck locker

HMS *Genista*: rigging details December 1941

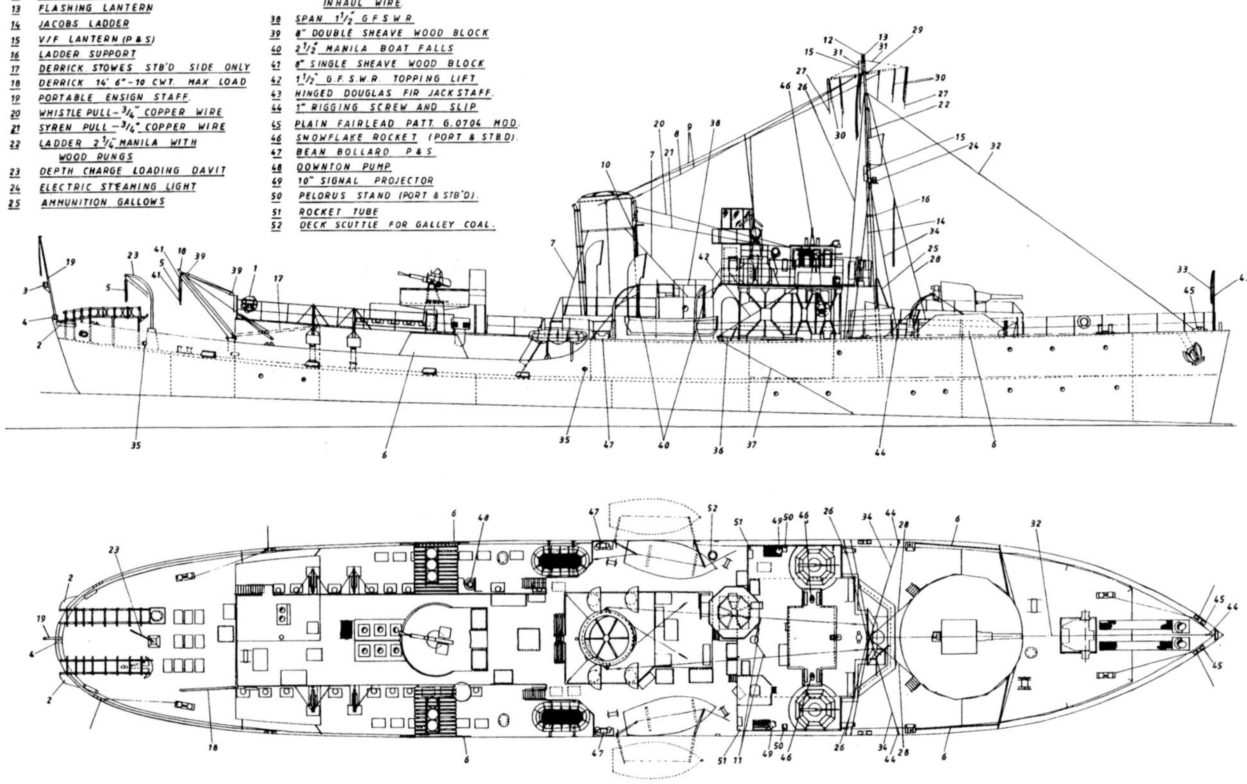

KEY TO DETAIL

1 LIFEBOUY – A.P. 307
2 WOOD CHOCK
3 STERN LIGHT
4 SHADED STERN LIGHT
5 2¼" MANILA
6 SPLINTER PROTECTION
7 FUNNEL GUY 1½" S.W.R.
8 RECEIVING AERIAL
9 TRANSMITTING AERIALS
10 12" IRON LADDER
11 AERIAL FEEDERS
12 LIGHTNING CONDUCTOR
13 FLASHING LANTERN
14 JACOBS LADDER
15 V/F LANTERN (P & S)
16 LADDER SUPPORT
17 DERRICK STOWES STB'D SIDE ONLY
18 DERRICK 14' 6" – 10 CWT. MAX LOAD
19 PORTABLE ENSIGN STAFF.
20 WHISTLE PULL – ¾" COPPER WIRE
21 SYREN PULL – ¾" COPPER WIRE
22 LADDER 2¼" MANILA WITH WOOD RUNGS
23 DEPTH CHARGE LOADING DAVIT
24 ELECTRIC STEAMING LIGHT
25 AMMUNITION GALLOWS
26 BACKSTAY – 2" GSWR
27 YARD BRACE – ¾" GFSWR
28 PREVENTER STAY – 2 OFF
29 DOUGLAS FIR SIGNAL YARD 14' 0"
30 SIGNAL HALYARDS – 4 PAIRS 1⅛" WHITE LINE.
31 1¼" G.P.S.W.R.
32 FORESTAY 2" G S W R
33 FLAG HALYARD – 1⅛ WHITE LINE
34 SHROUD 2" G.S.W.R.
35 9" x 6½" MOORING PIPE
36 DOUGLAS FIR 15' 0" SOUNDING BOOM
37 STOWED POSITION OF ASDIC DOME INHAUL WIRE.
38 SPAN 1½" G F S W R
39 8" DOUBLE SHEAVE WOOD BLOCK
40 2½" MANILA BOAT FALLS
41 8" SINGLE SHEAVE WOOD BLOCK
42 1½" G.F.S.W.R. TOPPING LIFT
43 HINGED DOUGLAS FIR JACKSTAFF.
44 1" RIGGING SCREW AND SLIP
45 PLAIN FAIRLEAD PATT. G.0704 MOD.
46 SNOWFLAKE ROCKET (PORT & STBD).
47 BEAN BOLLARD P & S
48 DOWNTON PUMP
49 10" SIGNAL PROJECTOR
50 PELORUS STAND (PORT & STB'D).
51 ROCKET TUBE
52 DECK SCUTTLE FOR GALLEY COAL.

Habitability

It was often said of the 'Flower' class corvette that it would 'roll on wet grass', and this lively motion had a dominant impact on living conditions. When first conceived, they were intended as a cheap and basic coastal escort vessel, specifically for use in inshore waters. However, due to the acute shortage of long-range convoy escorts, and the fact that after the fall of France Axis submarines were based on the French Atlantic seaboard, corvettes were soon called upon to operate in the Western Approaches and the open Atlantic Ocean, where there was no protection from the prevailing weather conditions. They were small vessels, and of light displacement so, although a seaworthy design, they acted like corks to wave and wind. Life on board was basic indeed, but the crew's mess-decks were right forward, where pitching gave the greatest sense of movement.

A dramatised but realistic portrayal of conditions of service in these ships can be found in the books of Nicholas Monsarrat, *Three Corvettes* and *The Cruel Sea*, especially vivid in the film version of the latter made in 1951. Even though it was soon after the ending of the war, it proved almost impossible to find a corvette to play the part of HMS *Compass Rose*, but fortunately the Greek Navy sent the *Kriezis* (formerly HMS *Coreopsis*) back to the UK for scrapping and she was made available for filming. Modified with an extended forecastle and Type 271 radar, the shots were selective, but she provided a very accurate picture of life on board a corvette with the original equipment. With its rapid motions, the ship was never still, so the crew were always off

HMCS *Owen Sound* demonstrating the lively motions of a 'Flower' in a seaway. This is probably Sea State 5 or 6, only moderate for the North Atlantic. *(National Library of Canada)*

balance, suffering frequent bruising, and worse. The least violent place was amidships, in the machinery spaces, where there was less apparent movement, but even here it was never entirely still. The crew learned to balance against the motion, with all its feelings of seasickness, but it was tiring in the extreme.

The original complement was set at a rather unrealistic 29, but this was soon increased to 47, as they were required in the Western Approaches, with continuous watch-keeping taking its toll. By January 1941 *Asphodel* had a complement of 67 crammed in. But even this was increased as new equipment such as radar was added.

Even though the men messed forward, the ship's galley was right aft, which meant that whatever the weather conditions the trays of hot food had to be carried the length of the upper deck, and up and down ladderways in the early ships. Food was usually cold, and eaten off metal plates with tin mugs. In a method that would have been familiar to Nelson's sailors, the food was prepared by each mess and taken to the galley to be cooked on the coal-fired stoves. Fresh food usually ran out after five days at sea, and there was no fresh bread. Tinned food was the staple diet (herrings-in [tomato sauce], corned beef, tinned sausages, etc), and such dehydrated items as dried peas that had to be soaked for twenty-four hours, all available ingredients often being thrown together to make 'pot mess'. Tea was brewed in a large 'fanny', made with a handful of tea and a tin of evaporated milk. It was usually orange in colour, but wet and warm!

The mess-decks were basic indeed. Seat lockers, wooden benches and wooden tables – but no chairs – all had to be scrubbed daily, with captain's rounds once a week and officer's rounds each evening before pipe down. In another survival from the age of sail, sleeping was in hammocks, all slung alongside each other. Personal kit was stowed in small lockers, with racks on the bulkheads for attaché cases and respirators (gas masks). There was little or no privacy. Officers faired little better, but they did have a wardroom, a steward and wine and spirits, although not normally while at sea. But they did enjoy single or shared cabins.

In violent weather, water frequently

HMCS *Brandon* after an Atlantic crossing. The state of the paintwork forward hints at the conditions the crew have endured. The ship has Type 271 but retains the Canadian SW-1C radar at the masthead. *(IWM A15629)*

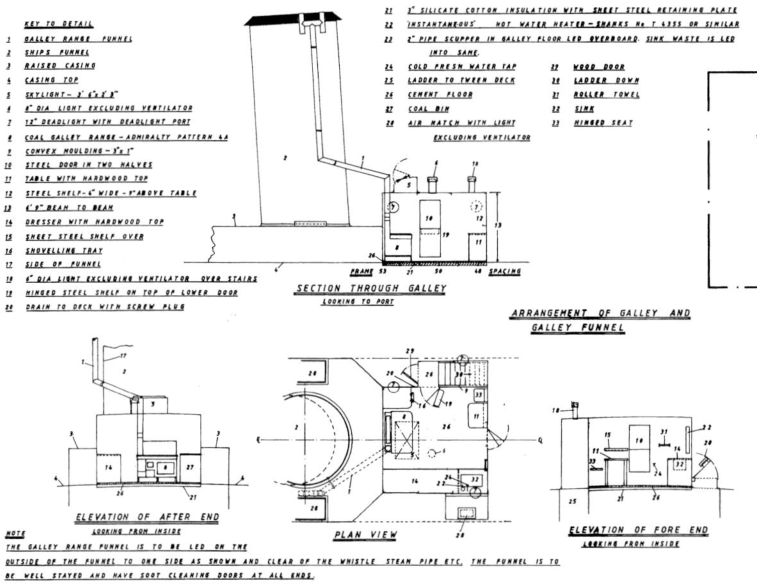

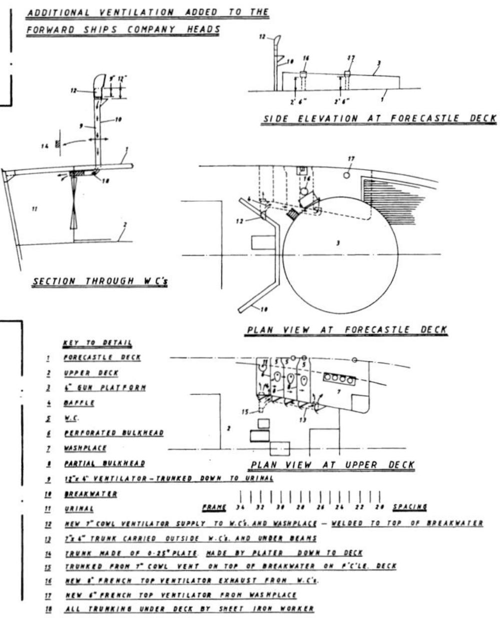

Improvements to crew conditions 1941
Among the first moves to ameliorate poor living conditions in corvettes was to move the galley from aft to forward of the funnel (ordered January 1941), giving the crew a better chance of getting their food uncooled by a long trip along the open deck. Around the same time the ventilation to the ship's company heads and washplace was also improved.

found its way below, washing along the deck in time with the ship's motion. Living conditions were perennially damp, with condensation on the bulkheads. Whilst at sea the side scuttles were clipped shut, with deadlights secure, so there was no natural light. Later as an economy measure, side scuttles were reduced in number to save on building time and money, but it was then found that the poor air quality was prone to induce tuberculosis and so ventilation was improved. In 1942, after analysis of sinkings, escape manholes were added in the mess-deck sides to assist men trapped below.

The first move to tackle these inherent problems was to extend the hull plating aft of the forecastle, which gave greater internal space, and then in 1941 the galley was relocated forward of the funnel. But the problems were never really solved: the ship's company continued to grow in numbers, and internal space was consumed by new equipment added as a result of operational experience.

These changes are best illustrated by comparing the four 'as fitted' drawings reproduced here that represent corvettes at different stages of their development. In the *Honeysuckle*, *Hydrangea* and *Jasmine*, the original short forecastle design that completed in late 1940/early 1941, the crew space directly under the forecastle provided sleeping for 7 men and messing for 37. There were two similar mess-decks below in the forward lower deck, with accommodation for 14 men and 16 men in the after mess. Both had coal-fired stoves. The anchor chain pipes passed through both forward mess-decks. On the port side aft was the wardroom and officer's pantry. To starboard were two officers' cabins.

On the upper deck to port was the crew's bathroom: four hand-basins for the ship's company, with two toilets (heads) and one urinal. Directly under the bridge was the CO's cabin and officers' bathroom with a bath and a toilet to port.

Back aft, to port was the coal-fired galley with its coal bunker forward, to starboard, the petty officers' washplace (two hand-basins), and single head and a lobby aft. On the lower deck was the petty officers' mess (4 men) to port, and two cabins to starboard, one for the coxswain and the other for the engineer. At this time only two depth charge throwers and two DC rails were fitted.

The second example is HMS *Anchusa*, which completed in March 1941. Built by Harland & Wolff, she was one of the early orders with her forecastle extended whilst under construction. The CO's cabin and officers' bathroom were much the same, but the larger galley was moved to the forecastle deck, forward of the funnel.

The hull plating extended aft to the funnel clearly provided more mess-deck area, but also had to accommodate additional crew. The forward upper deck mess was now for 38 seats and 35 hammocks; 18 hammocks were slung in the new area, above the fuel tank manholes. The two mess-decks below contained 16 men (14 bunks and 2 hammocks) and aft again 20 men (16 bunks and 4 hammocks), for a total of 89, plus officers. Aft of these were the wardroom and pantry to port with two cabins to starboard. The petty officers' mess was in the position previously occupied by the galley, with the sleeping area below for 6 plus 2 hammocks. The ship's company bathroom now had an extra hand-basin, but in general conditions were more cramped.

Anchusa had more depth charges and now four Mark II throwers and two rails. There were two twin 0.303in Hotchkiss machine guns on the bridge wings.

The next advance was a major redesign to further improve seaworthiness, resulting in the 'Modified Flower' class. However, the third example, the Norwegian-manned *Potentilla*, was an interim type, built in the period between the advent of the long forecastle and 'Modified Flower' proper. She had the modified hull lines and many of the improvements to be found later – an upright funnel, two Admiralty three-drum boilers (so no large cowl ventilators), a raised 4in gun platform, and two masts. Her 2pdr gun was moved further aft, giving an improved arc of fire. She also had Type 271 surface search radar on her larger bridge, and two single 20mm Oerlikons on the bridge wings. Additional close-range firepower was provided by two twin 0.5in Browning (Colt) machine guns on the US Mark IX mountings supplied under lease-lend.

In terms of her accommodation, there was more space in the bridge. The CO had his cabin and an office, with the officers' bathroom moved to the upper deck, aft of the crew's bathroom, now with six hand-basins and four heads.

The two forward mess-decks provided sleeping for 8 and 12 men, with the two mess-decks below accommodating 14 and 22 men. The petty officers were still aft, with the washplace and head aft on the upper deck and their mess and accommodation on the deck below. The officers' wardroom was now to starboard with its pantry, with the second and third officers' double cabin to port and the first lieutenant forward of them.

The two three-drum Admiralty boilers gave an improved rate of steam production for better acceleration, but no Hedgehog was yet available.

The final stage of development is represented by the 'Modified Flowers' HMS *Burnet*, HMCS *Forest Hill* (ex-*Ceanothus*) and HMS *Charlock*. These had the improved hull lines and were virtually a redesign, updated as a result of operational experience and new equipment coming into service.

Living conditions were still exceedingly cramped, however, and increased fuel meant a longer endurance, although fuelling at sea was still required. By the time they entered service in late 1943/early 1944 the ahead throwing Hedgehog was standard, and the close-range armament had reached seven 20mm Oerlikons – two on the bridge wings, four in sided sponsons, two each side, and one replacing the 2pdr gun aft, thus standardising the ammunition supply. The original 4in gun remained the main armament on its raised bandstand with its two rocket flare launchers. The upper deck appeared less cramped but two depth charge rails were retained with a stowage rail on the centre line and four of the improved Mark IV throwers and stowage racks. The Hedgehog was to starboard, forward of the bridge.

Looking at the internal arrangements, the wheelhouse was under the bridge, with the chart room aft of it and the radio office to starboard. Below these was the CO's cabin to starboard and an officer's cabin to port. The open bridge had the A/S hut forward, and improved unrestricted space suitable for keeping a lookout for air attack, but open to the tiring effects of wind and weather.

Below the wheelhouse was the CO's cabin with the first lieutenant's cabin to port. The forward mess-deck below had sleeping accommodation for 22 men, messing for 36 men and seat lockers for 17 men. In the smaller mess-deck aft there was sleeping accommodation for 14 men, messing accommodation for 20 and seat lockers for 16. On the deck below, forward was sleeping accommodation for 14 men and seat lockers for 16; aft sleeping accommodation for 22 men, messing for 18 and seat lockers for 25. The POs' and ERA's mess aft had 17 men sleeping and 14 men messing, with two wash-basins and a single head on the upper deck above. The ship's company bathroom now had nine wash-basins, and aft four heads and a urinal. The officers still had a bathroom, wardroom and pantry.

Although the design was more efficient, in absolute terms living conditions had not improved much – and they were still small ships subject to whatever the weather produced.

Internal arrangements of early 'Flowers': HM Ships *Honeysuckle*, *Hydrangea* and *Jasmine* of 1940

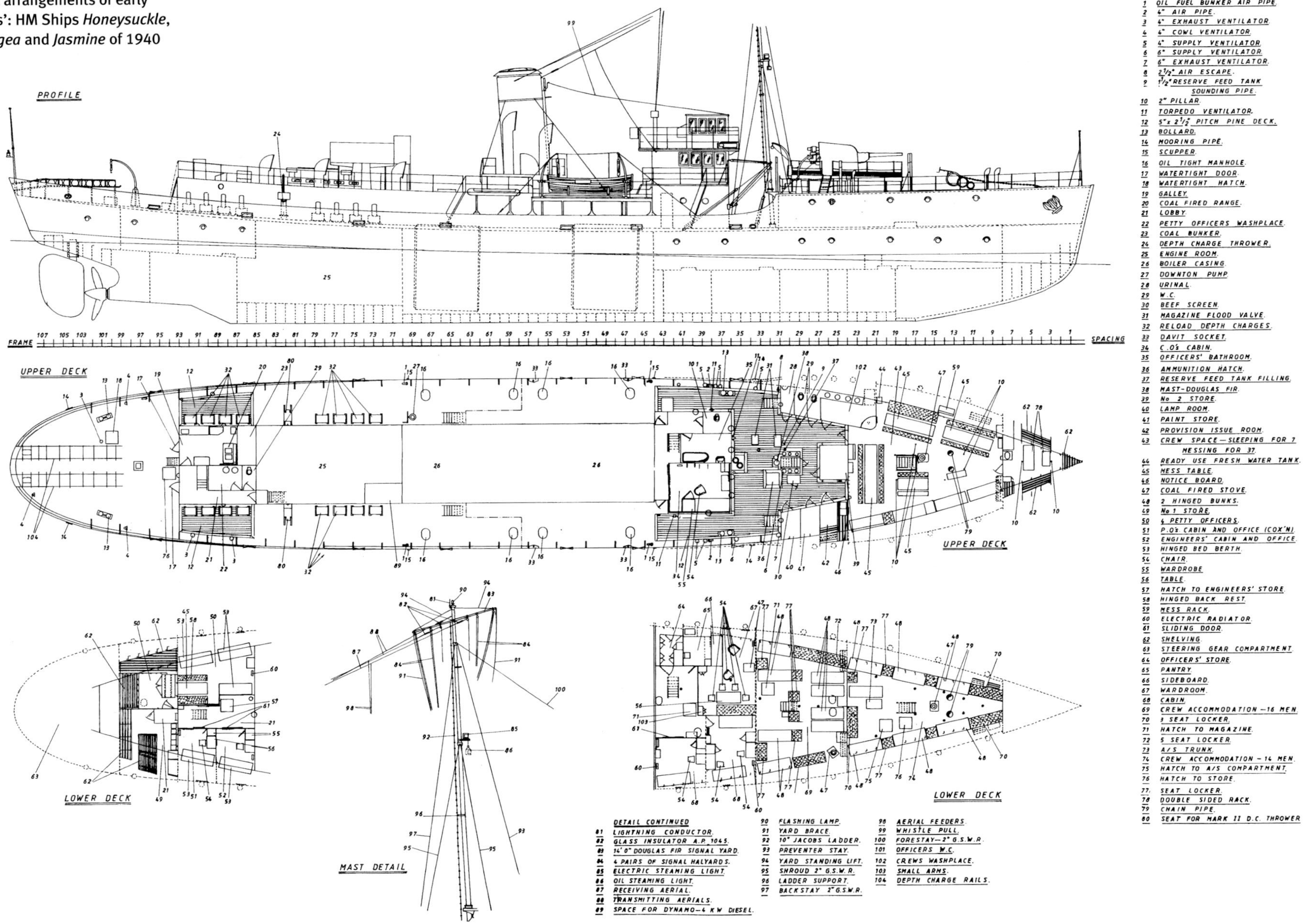

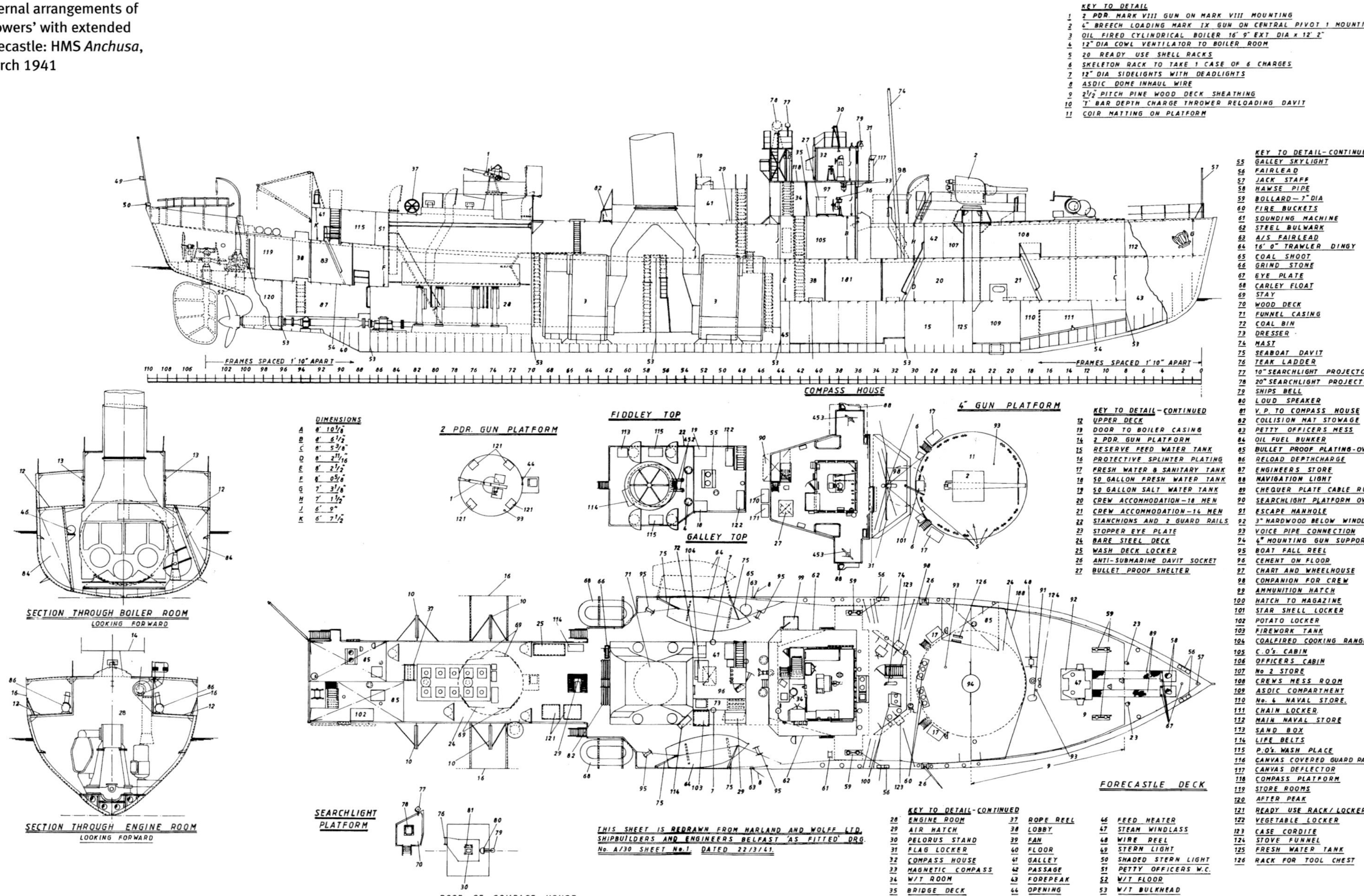

Internal arrangements of 'Flowers' with extended forecastle: HMS *Anchusa*, March 1941

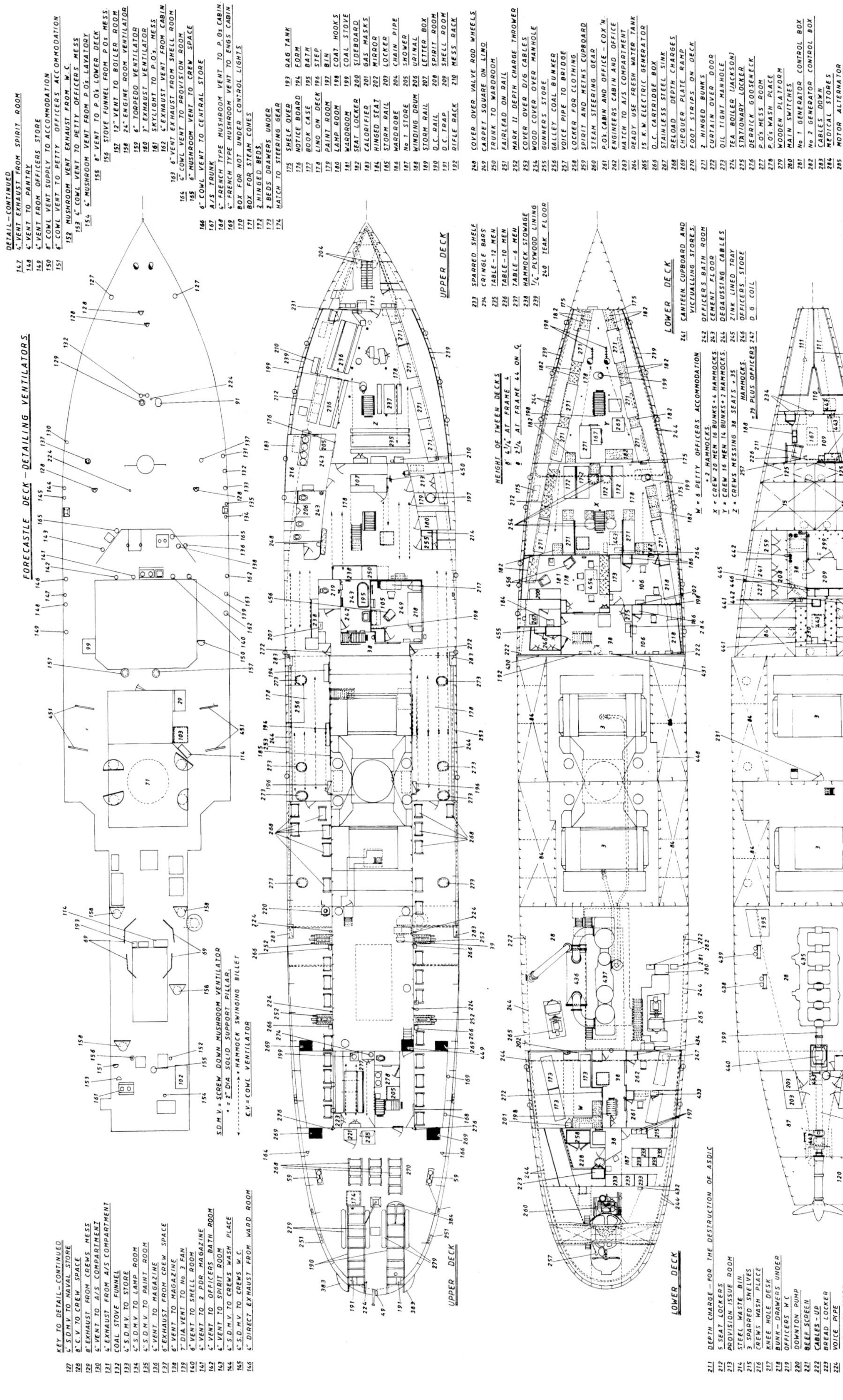
FORECASTLE DECK – DETAILING VENTILATORS
UPPER DECK
LOWER DECK
HOLD
HEIGHT OF TWEEN DECKS
8' 4¼" AT FRAME 4
8' 2¼" AT FRAME 44 ON ℄
FRAME SPACING 1' 10" THROUGHOUT
S.D.M.V = SCREW DOWN MUSHROOM VENTILATOR
• = 2" DIA SOLID SUPPORT PILLAR.
HAMMOCK SWINGING BILLET
C.V = COWL VENTILATOR
W = 6 PETTY OFFICERS ACCOMMODATION + 2 HAMMOCKS.
X = CREW 20 MEN 16 BUNKS + 4 HAMMOCKS
Y = CREW 16 MEN 14 BUNKS + 2 HAMMOCKS.
Z = CREWS MESSING 38 SEATS + 35 HAMMOCKS. + 79 PLUS OFFICERS
KEY TO DETAIL – CONTINUED
127 4" S.D.M.V. TO NAVAL STORE
128 8" C.V. TO CREW SPACE
129 8" EXHAUST FROM CREWS MESS
130 4" VENT TO A/S COMPARTMENT
131 4" EXHAUST FROM A/S COMPARTMENT
132 COAL STOVE FUNNEL
133 4" S.D.M.V. TO STORE
134 4" S.D.M.V. TO LAMP ROOM
135 4" S.D.M.V. TO PAINT ROOM
136 4" VENT TO MAGAZINE
137 6" EXHAUST FROM CREW SPACE
138 6" VENT TO MAGAZINE
139 7" DIA VENT TO No. 3 FAN
140 6" VENT TO SHELL ROOM
141 4" VENT TO 2 PDR. MAGAZINE
142 4" VENT TO OFFICERS BATH ROOM
143 4" VENT TO SPIRIT ROOM
144 4" S.D.M.V. TO CREWS WASH PLACE
145 4" S.D.M.V. TO CREWS W.C.
146 4" DIRECT EXHAUST FROM WARD ROOM
DETAIL – CONTINUED
147 4" VENT EXHAUST FROM SPIRIT ROOM
148 4" VENT TO PANTRY
149 4" VENT FROM OFFICERS STORE
150 8" COWL VENT SUPPLY TO ACCOMMODATION
151 6" COWL VENT TO PETTY OFFICERS ACCOMMODATION
152 MUSHROOM VENT EXHAUST FROM W.C.
153 4" COWL VENT TO PETTY OFFICERS MESS
154 4" MUSHROOM VENT FROM P.O's LAVATORY
155 8" VENT TO P.O's LOWER DECK
156 STOVE FUNNEL FROM P.O's MESS.
157 12" VENT TO BOILER ROOM
158 24" ENGINE ROOM VENTILATOR
159 6" TORPEDO VENTILATOR
160 3" EXHAUST VENTILATOR
161 SKYLIGHT TO P.O's MESS
162 4" EXHAUST VENT FROM CABIN
163 6" VENT EXHAUST FROM SHELL ROOM
164 4" COWL VENT TO PROVISION ROOM
165 6" MUSHROOM VENT TO CREW SPACE
166 6" COWL VENT TO CENTRAL STORE
167 A/S TRUNK
168 4" FRENCH TYPE MUSHROOM VENT TO P.O's CABIN
169 4" FRENCH TYPE MUSHROOM VENT TO ENGS CABIN
170 BOX FOR NOT UNDER CONTROL LIGHTS
171 BOX FOR STEAM CONES
172 2 HINGED BEDS.
173 2 BEDS DRAWERS UNDER
174 HATCH TO STEERING GEAR
175 SHELF OVER
176 NOTICE BOARD
177 BOOK CASE
178 LINO ON DECK
179 PAINT ROOM
180 LAMP ROOM
181 WARDROOM
182 SEAT LOCKER
183 CALORIFIER
184 HINGED SEAT
185 STORM RAIL
186 WARDROBE
187 No 1 STORE
188 WINDING DRUM
189 STORM RAIL
190 D.C. RAIL
191 D.C. TRAP
192 RIFLE RACK
193 RAG TANK
194 FORM
195 BATH
196 STEP
197 BIN
198 COAT HOOKS
199 COAL STOVE
200 SIDEBOARD
201 GAS MASKS
202 MIRROR
203 LOCKER
204 CHAIN PIPE
205 SHOWER
206 URINAL
207 LETTER BOX
208 SPIRIT ROOM
209 SHELL ROOM
210 MESS RACK
211 DEPTH CHARGE – FOR THE DESTRUCTION OF ASDIC
212 5 SEAT LOCKERS
213 PROVISION ISSUE ROOM
214 STEEL WASTE BIN
215 3 SPARRED SHELVES
216 CREWS WASH PLACE
217 KNEE HOLE DESK
218 BUNK – DRAWERS UNDER
219 OFFICERS W.C
220 DOWNTON PUMP
221 BEEF SCREEN
222 CABLES – UP
223 BREAD LOCKER
224 VOICE PIPE
225 HATCH TO STORE
226 HINGED TABLE
227 RUM CUPBOARD
228 PROVISION ROOM
229 4" MAGAZINE
230 2 PDR MAGAZINE
231 HINGED W/T DOOR
232 2" WOOD BULKHEAD
233 SPARRED SHELF
234 CRINGLE BARS
235 TABLE – 12 MEN
236 TABLE – 10 MEN
237 TABLE – 6 MEN
238 HAMMOCK STOWAGE
239 ¼" PLYWOOD LINING
240 TEAK FLOOR
241 CANTEEN CUPBOARD AND VICTUALLING STORES.
242 OFFICERS BATH ROOM
243 CEMENT FLOOR
244 DEGAUSSING CABLES
245 ZINK LINED TRAY
246 OFFICERS STORE
247 D.G. COIL
248 COVER OVER VALVE ROD WHEELS
249 CARPET SQUARE ON LINO
250 TRUNK TO WARDROOM
251 FAIRLEAD ON RAIL
252 MARK II DEPTH CHARGE THROWER
253 COVER OVER D/G CABLES
254 WOOD COVER OVER MANHOLE
255 GUNNERS STORE
256 GALLEY COAL BUNKER
257 VOICE PIPE TO BRIDGE
258 LOCKER FOR CLOTHING
259 SPIRIT AND METHS CUPBOARD
260 STEAM STEERING GEAR
261 P.O's CABIN AND OFFICE – COX'N.
262 ENGINEERS CABIN AND OFFICE
263 HATCH TO A/S COMPARTMENT
264 READY USE FRESH WATER TANK
265 15 K.W. ELECTRIC GENERATOR
266 D.C. CARTRIDGE BOX
267 STAINLESS STEEL SINK
268 RELOAD DEPTH CHARGES
269 CHEQUER PLATE RAMP
270 FOOT STRIPS ON DECK
271 2 HINGED BUNKS
272 CURTAIN OVER DOOR
273 OIL TIGHT MANHOLE
274 TEA BOILER (JACKSON)
275 STATIONARY LOCKER
276 DERRICK GOOSENECK
277 P.O's MESS ROOM
278 P.O's WASH PLACE
279 WOODEN PLATFORM
280 MAIN SWITCHES
281 No 1 GENERATOR CONTROL BOX
282 No 2 GENERATOR CONTROL BOX
283 CABLES DOWN
284 MEDICAL STORES
285 MOTOR ALTERNATOR

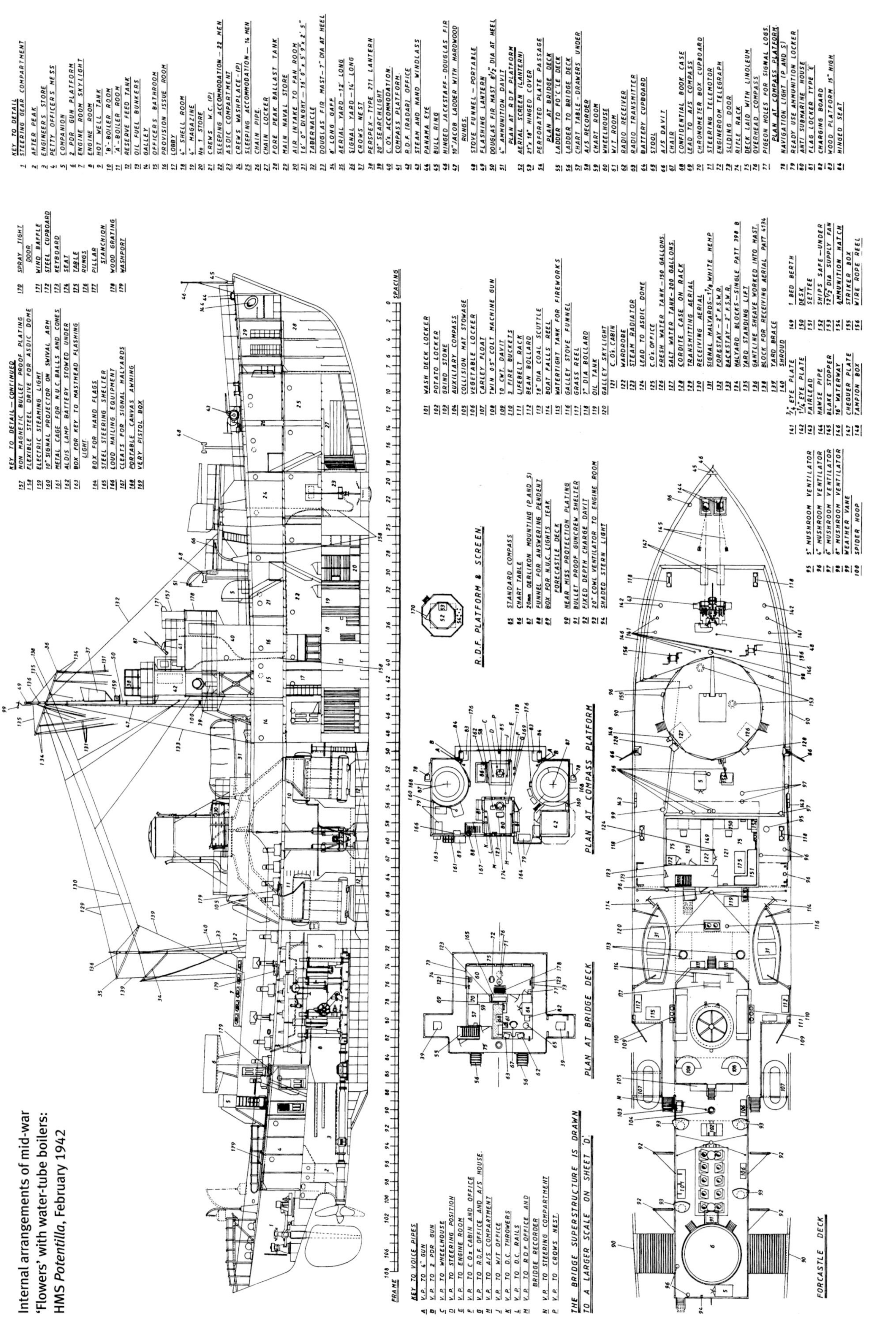

Internal arrangements of mid-war 'Flowers' with water-tube boilers: HMS *Potentilla*, February 1942

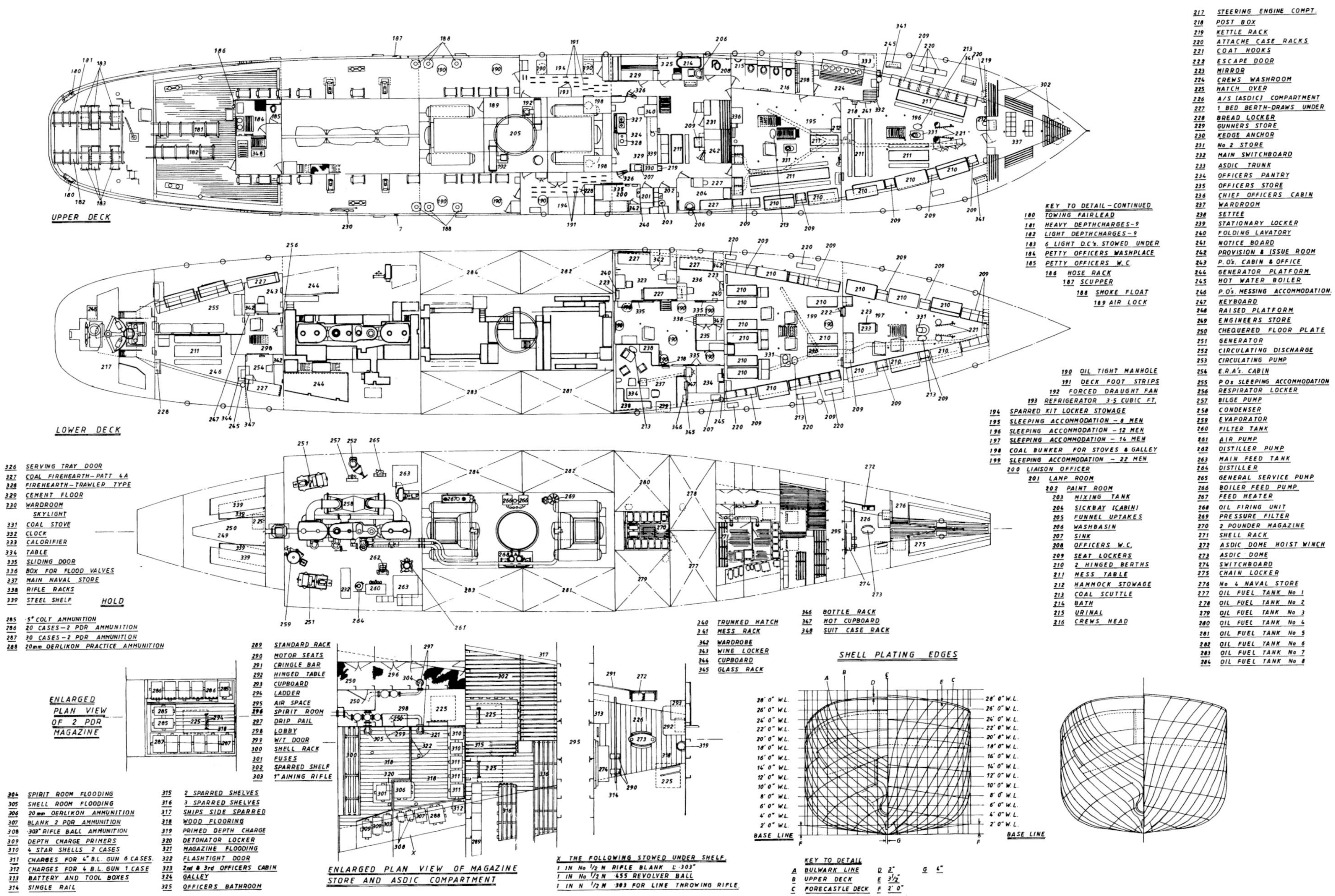
UPPER DECK
LOWER DECK
HOLD
217 STEERING ENGINE COMPT.
218 POST BOX
219 KETTLE RACK
220 ATTACHE CASE RACKS
221 COAT HOOKS
222 ESCAPE DOOR
223 MIRROR
224 CREWS WASHROOM
225 HATCH OVER
226 A/S (ASDIC) COMPARTMENT
227 1 BED BERTH-DRAWS UNDER
228 BREAD LOCKER
229 GUNNERS STORE
230 KEDGE ANCHOR
231 No 2 STORE
232 MAIN SWITCHBOARD
233 ASDIC TRUNK
234 OFFICERS PANTRY
235 OFFICERS STORE
236 CHIEF OFFICERS CABIN
237 WARDROOM
238 SETTEE
239 STATIONARY LOCKER
240 FOLDING LAVATORY
241 NOTICE BOARD
242 PROVISION & ISSUE ROOM
243 P. O's CABIN & OFFICE
244 GENERATOR PLATFORM
245 HOT WATER BOILER
246 P. O's MESSING ACCOMMODATION.
247 KEYBOARD
248 RAISED PLATFORM
249 ENGINEERS STORE
250 CHEQUERED FLOOR PLATE
251 GENERATOR
252 CIRCULATING DISCHARGE
253 CIRCULATING PUMP
254 E.R.A's CABIN
255 P.O's SLEEPING ACCOMMODATION
256 RESPIRATOR LOCKER
257 BILGE PUMP
258 CONDENSER
259 EVAPORATOR
260 FILTER TANK
261 AIR PUMP
262 DISTILLER PUMP
263 MAIN FEED TANK
264 DISTILLER
265 GENERAL SERVICE PUMP
266 BOILER FEED PUMP
267 FEED HEATER
268 OIL FIRING UNIT
269 PRESSURE FILTER
270 2 POUNDER MAGAZINE
271 SHELL RACK
272 ASDIC DOME HOIST WINCH
273 ASDIC DOME
274 SWITCHBOARD
275 CHAIN LOCKER
276 No 4 NAVAL STORE
277 OIL FUEL TANK No 1
278 OIL FUEL TANK No 2
279 OIL FUEL TANK No 3
280 OIL FUEL TANK No 4
281 OIL FUEL TANK No 5
282 OIL FUEL TANK No 6
283 OIL FUEL TANK No 7
284 OIL FUEL TANK No 8
KEY TO DETAIL – CONTINUED
180 TOWING FAIRLEAD
181 HEAVY DEPTHCHARGES-9
182 LIGHT DEPTHCHARGES-9
183 6 LIGHT D.C's STOWED UNDER
184 PETTY OFFICERS WASHPLACE
185 PETTY OFFICERS W.C
186 HOSE RACK
187 SCUPPER
188 SMOKE FLOAT
189 AIR LOCK
190 OIL TIGHT MANHOLE
191 DECK FOOT STRIPS
192 FORCED DRAUGHT FAN
193 REFRIGERATOR 3·5 CUBIC FT.
194 SPARRED KIT LOCKER STOWAGE
195 SLEEPING ACCOMMODATION – 8 MEN
196 SLEEPING ACCOMMODATION – 12 MEN
197 SLEEPING ACCOMMODATION – 14 MEN
198 COAL BUNKER FOR STOVES & GALLEY
199 SLEEPING ACCOMMODATION – 22 MEN
200 LIAISON OFFICER
201 LAMP ROOM
202 PAINT ROOM
203 MIXING TANK
204 SICKBAY (CABIN)
205 FUNNEL UPTAKES
206 WASHBASIN
207 SINK
208 OFFICERS W.C.
209 SEAT LOCKERS
210 2 HINGED BERTHS
211 MESS TABLE
212 HAMMOCK STOWAGE
213 COAL SCUTTLE
214 BATH
215 URINAL
216 CREWS HEAD
326 SERVING TRAY DOOR
327 COAL FIREHEARTH-PATT 4A
328 FIREHEARTH-TRAWLER TYPE
329 CEMENT FLOOR
330 WARDROOM SKYLIGHT
331 COAL STOVE
332 CLOCK
333 CALORIFIER
334 TABLE
335 SLIDING DOOR
336 BOX FOR FLOOD VALVES
337 MAIN NAVAL STORE
338 RIFLE RACKS
339 STEEL SHELF
285 ·5" COLT AMMUNITION
286 20 CASES-2 PDR AMMUNITION
287 30 CASES-2 PDR AMMUNITION
288 20mm OERLIKON PRACTICE AMMUNITION
240 TRUNKED HATCH
341 MESS RACK
342 WARDROBE
343 WINE LOCKER
344 CUPBOARD
345 GLASS RACK
346 BOTTLE RACK
347 HOT CUPBOARD
348 SUIT CASE RACK
289 STANDARD RACK
290 MOTOR SEATS
291 CRINGLE BAR
292 HINGED TABLE
293 CUPBOARD
294 LADDER
295 AIR SPACE
296 SPIRIT ROOM
297 DRIP PAIL
298 LOBBY
299 W/T DOOR
300 SHELL RACK
301 FUSES
302 SPARRED SHELF
303 1" AIMING RIFLE
ENLARGED PLAN VIEW OF 2 PDR MAGAZINE
304 SPIRIT ROOM FLOODING
305 SHELL ROOM FLOODING
306 20mm OERLIKON AMMUNITION
307 BLANK 2 PDR AMMUNITION
308 ·303" RIFLE BALL AMMUNITION
309 DEPTH CHARGE PRIMERS
310 4 STAR SHELLS 2 CASES
311 CHARGES FOR 4" B.L. GUN 6 CASES.
312 CHARGES FOR 4 B.L. GUN 1 CASE
313 BATTERY AND TOOL BOXES
314 SINGLE RAIL
315 2 SPARRED SHELVES
316 3 SPARRED SHELVES
317 SHIPS SIDE SPARRED
318 WOOD FLOORING
319 PRIMED DEPTH CHARGE
320 DETONATOR LOCKER
321 MAGAZINE FLOODING
322 FLASHTIGHT DOOR
323 2nd & 3rd OFFICERS CABIN
324 GALLEY
325 OFFICERS BATHROOM
ENLARGED PLAN VIEW OF MAGAZINE STORE AND ASDIC COMPARTMENT
X THE FOLLOWING STOWED UNDER SHELF.
1 IN No 1/2 N RIFLE BLANK L·303"
1 IN No 1/2 N 455 REVOLVER BALL
1 IN N 1/2 N ·303 FOR LINE THROWING RIFLE
SHELL PLATING EDGES
28' 0" W.L.
26' 0" W.L.
24' 0" W.L.
22' 0" W.L.
20' 0" W.L.
18' 0" W.L.
16' 0" W.L.
14' 0" W.L.
12' 0" W.L.
10' 0" W.L.
8' 0" W.L.
6' 0" W.L.
4' 0" W.L.
2' 0" W.L.
BASE LINE
KEY TO DETAIL
A BULWARK LINE
B UPPER DECK
C FORECASTLE DECK
D 3"
E 3½"
F 2' 0"
G 4"

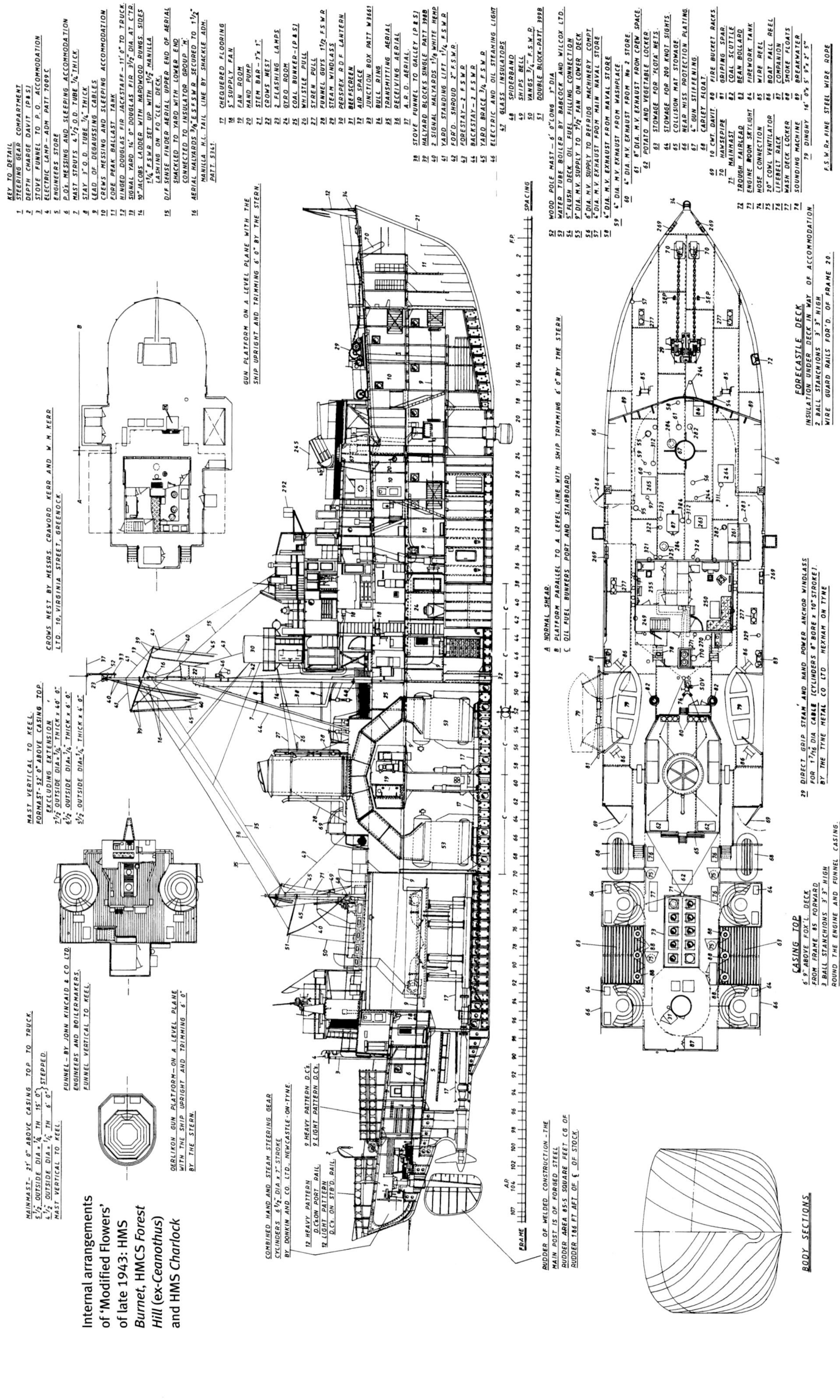

Internal arrangements of 'Modified Flowers' of late 1943: HMS *Burnet*, HMCS *Forest Hill* (ex-*Ceanothus*) and HMS *Charlock*

Selected References

ORIGINAL SOURCES

'The Ships Covers' [selected files on the design]. Held by the National Maritime Museum's outstation at The Brass Foundry, Woolwich Arsenal, London.
No. 611 A-B Flower Class Corvettes.

The Ballast Trust, Monarch Works, 18/20 Walkinshaw Street, Johnstone, PA5 8EU.
Supplied a multitude of original corvette general arrangement and 'Flower' class construction drawings.

The Hampshire Archive Trust, Hampshire Record Office, Sussex Street, Winchester SO23 8TH.
Where the Priddy's Hard Naval Armament Museum, Gosport, gunnery records and BRs (Books of Reference) are now held. The latter include:

BR 258/41 – 2-pounder Mark VIII Gun on Mark VIII* Mounting.
BR 250/41 – 6-pounder Hotchkiss QF Gun on Non Recoil Mounting.
BR 821/43 – 4-inch Mark XIX Gun on CP Mark XXIII Mounting.
BR 971/38 – Quad 0.5-inch Guns on 'M' Mark III Mounting.
BR 267/41 – The Holman Projector Mark II.
BR 1676 – History and Development of the Hedgehog Ahead Throwing Weapon.
BR 197/17 – 4-inch Mark IX BL Gun on CP I Mounting 1917 (original manual).
OU 6336 – 20mm Oerlikon Machine Gun Mark I.
BR 867/42 – Twin 20mm Oerlikon on Mark V (Power Operated) Mounting.
BR 1669 – Handbook of Depth Charges and Equipment.

The Cumbria Record Office, 140 Duke Street, Barrow in Furness, Cumbria LA14 1XW who hold a multitude of original Vickers armament drawings.

HMS *Collingwood* Communications & Radar Museum.
HMS *Collingwood*, Newgate Lane, Fareham, Hampshire, PO14 1AS
'Report and History of Type 271 Surface Search Radar'.

BOOKS

David K Brown, *Atlantic Escorts: Ships, Weapons & Tactics in World War II*, Seaforth Publishing (Barnsley 2007).
A technical history of the Battle of the Atlantic in terms of the relative effectiveness of the ships employed, by a retired warship designer.

Peter Elliott, *Allied Escort Ships of World War II*, Macdonald and Jane's (London 1977).
A general reference book covering all classes.

J A Foster, *Heart of Oak: A Pictorial History of the Royal Canadian Navy*, Methuen (Toronto 1985).
Many photos of 'Flowers' in action.

John Harland, *Catchers and Corvettes: The Steam Whalecatcher in Peace and War*, Jean Boudriot Publications (Rotherfield 1992).
Principally about whalers, but gives the best analysis of the exact relationship between the 'Flowers' and their whale-catcher origins. Well illustrated.

Chris Henry, *Depth Charge: Royal Naval Mines, Depth Charges & Underwater Weapons 1914-1945*, Pen & Sword Books (Barnsley 2005).
The only book on a neglected but important subject.

Chris Howard Bailey, *The Royal Naval Museum Book of The Battle of the Atlantic*, Alan Sutton Publishing (Stroud 1994).
Subtitled 'The Corvettes and their Crews: An Oral History', the book is a series of first-hand accounts of wartime life in the 'Flowers' with many unusual photos.

John Lambert, *Flower Class Corvettes in World War Two* (Warship Perspectives), WR Press Inc (New York 1999).
A modern reworking of the Profile/Ensign/Man o'War type warship monograph, with many photos and drawings.

H T Lenton, *British and Empire Warships of the Second World War*, Greenhill Books (London 1998).
The standard compilation of basic data on British warships of this era; in effect, a much enlarged edition of H T Lenton & J J Colledge, *Warships of World War II*, Ian Allan (Shepperton 1973).

Thomas G Lynch, *Canada's Flowers: History of the Corvettes of Canada 1939-1945*, Nimbus (Halifax, Nova Scotia 1981).
Detailed history of the ships built in Canada and operated by the RCN.

Ken Macpherson & Marc Milner, *Corvettes of the Royal Canadian Navy 1939-1945*, Vanwell Publishing Ltd (St Catherine's, Ontario 1993).
Well illustrated history of the Canadian 'Flower' programme.

John McKay & John Harland, *The Flower Class Corvette Agassiz* (Anatomy of the Ship series), Conway Maritime Press Ltd (London 1993).
This highly regarded series provides a very thorough dissection of the subject, principally in hundreds of detailed drawings.

David Owen, *Anti-Submarine Warfare An Illustrated History*, Seaforth Publishing (Barnsley 2007).
A general overview of ASW technology and tactics.

Alan Raven & Antony Preston, *Flower Class Corvettes* (Ensign 3), Plastow Press Ltd (London 1973).
Short text but many photos and some camouflage schemes in colour.

David Williams, *Naval Camouflage 1914-1945. A complete visual reference*, Chatham Publishing (London 2001).
A large-format general history of visual deception, with many illustrations.

PLANS

All the plans in this book, and others, are available at larger scales from www.lambert-plans.com

MODEL PRODUCTS

NAVIS MODELLBAU, Dr I Kraus, Mozartweg 2, D-82538 Geretsried, Germany www.navis-neptun.de
HP MODELS, Postfach 101151, 46471 Wesel, Germany www.hp-models.com
WHITE ENSIGN MODELS LTD, South Farm, Snitton, Ludlow, Shropshire, SY8 3EZ, United Kingdom www.whiteensignmodels.com
SKYTREX LIMITED, Unit 1, Charnwood Business Park, North Road, Loughborough, LE11 1LE, United Kingdom www.skytrex.com
L'ARSENAL, Boîte Postal No 2, 14790 Verson, France www.larsenal.com
COMMANDER SERIES MODELS, INC, 551 Wegman Road, Rochester, NY 14624, USA www.commanderseries.com
DEANS MARINE, Conquest Drove, Farcet Fen, Peterborough, PE7 3DH, United Kingdom www.deansmmarine.co.uk
REVELL Gmbh & Co. KG, Henschelstraße 20-30, D-32257 Bünde, Germany, www.revell.de
APS MODELS, PO Box 5025, Gwandalan, NSW 2259, Australia
PS SHIPS, PO Box 369, St Helens, Merseyside, WA10 9AU, United Kingdom http://psships.com
METCALF MOULDINGS, 1 Wentworth Cottages, Haultwick, Dane End, Nr Ware, SG11 1JG, United Kingdom http://business.virgin.net/metcalf.mouldings/catalogue.htm
FLEETSCALE, Westward Mouldings Ltd, The New Factory, Greenhill, Delaware Road, Gunnislake, Cornwall, PL18 9AS, United Kingdom www.fleetscale.com
GOLD MEDAL MODELS, PO Box 670, Lopez, WA 98261, USA http://goldmm.com/
TOM'S MODELWORKS, PO Box 304, Santa Rosa, CA 95402, USA www.tomsmodelworks.com
EDUARD MODEL-ACCESSORIES spol. s r.o., Mírová 170, 43521 Obrnice, Czech Republic www.eduard.cz
GREAT LITTLE SHIPS, Trefacwn Fach, Llanrhian, St Davids, Pembrokeshire, SA62 6DP, Wales, United Kingdom http://home.clara.net/djparkins/gls/glsmast.htm

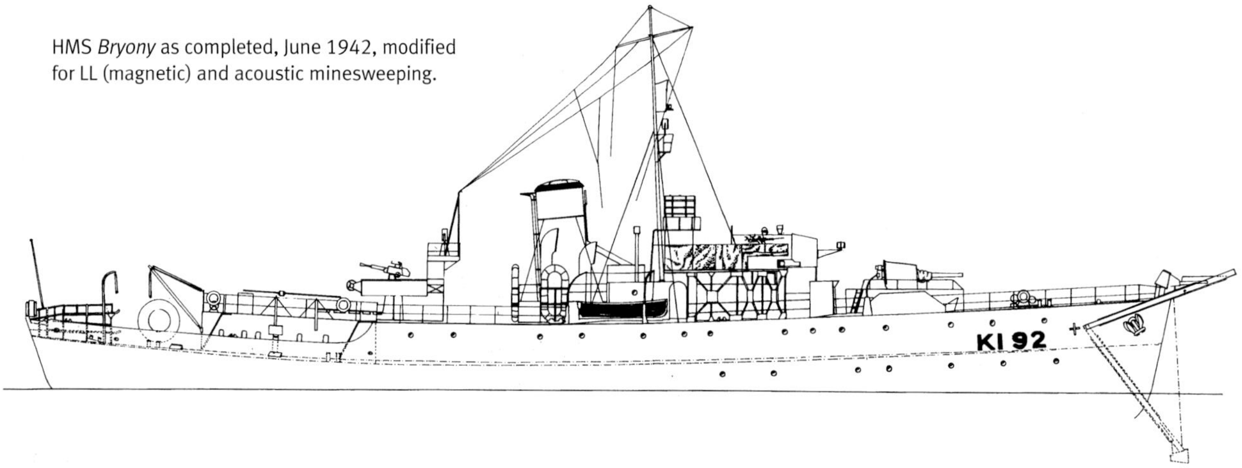

HMS *Bryony* as completed, June 1942, modified for LL (magnetic) and acoustic minesweeping.

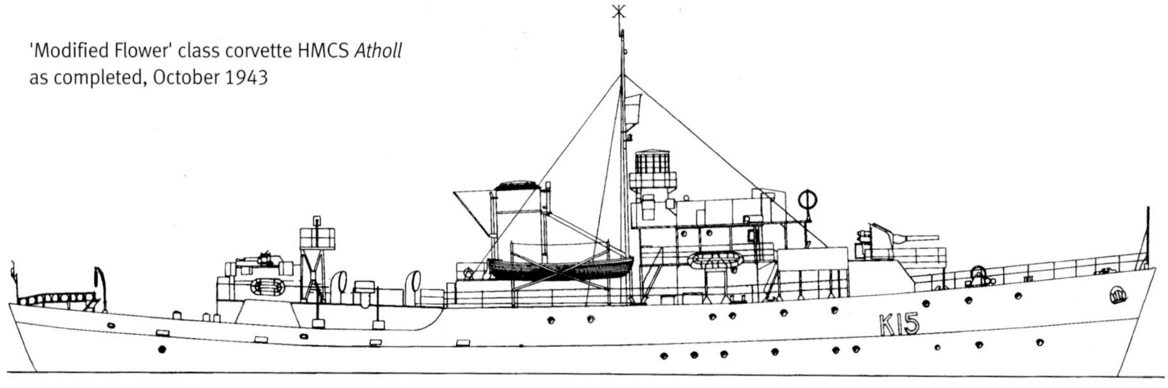

'Modified Flower' class corvette HMCS *Atholl* as completed, October 1943